Preface to 1989 edition

This is a completely rewritten version of the book first published in 1976. I have been greatly helped by the callers under the 'consultation pack', who by their questions have shown what points I had not previously covered, or adequately covered; and I hope that most of the gaps have now been filled.

However, the actual conveyancing *system* has changed hardly at all over the years. Solicitors may have chic offices, equipped with word processors and fax machines, by which they transmit their forms and documents to each other at the touch of a button – but it's still the same old nonsense which they are transmitting. The aims of the system – to confuse, obfuscate and delay – are still the same as they were a century ago. Only the means have varied. Instead of solicitors' clerks sitting on high stools, writing out incomprehensible documents with quill pens, local authority clerks are processing equally futile local search forms, stuffed with equally turgid and irrelevant verbiage. Instead of solicitors being paid by the yard, as they were a hundred years ago, the modern solicitor submits printed forms of enquiries purporting to elicit *fixed* information about the house (does it have mains drainage? is the road maintained by the Council? etc.) *each* time the house changes hands. The overall result is that a conveyancing transaction probably now takes longer than it did in those days when solicitors' clerks *were* scratching away with their quill pens.

Not only have solicitors shown a remarkable ability to withstand any reform: the only effect of those measures which were designed to loosen their stranglehold, and so benefit the public, has been to benefit solicitors at the *expense* of the public. For example, the Land Registry was set up to provide a system whereby people could buy and sell houses as simply and efficiently as they can buy and sell anything else. In the event it is only solicitors who have benefited (in that their work has been cut by half), while the public suffers the same delays and pays even greater costs under the new system than under the old. The only real effect of the Administration of Justice Act 1985, which inaugurated 'licensed conveyancers', and which was popularly believed to have broken the solicitors' conveyancing monopoly, has been to *strengthen* it (see p. 142).

It seems that whatever the well-meaning – and perhaps not so well-meaning – attempts of our legislators, we are stuck with the present system. But this is no reason why you should be stuck with an expensive and inefficient solicitor; and in the following pages I show how you can beat the profession at its own game.

The Conveyancing Fraud

Michael Joseph M.A.

Solicitor of the Supreme Court

Michael Joseph
27 Occupation Lane
Woolwich
London SE18 3JQ

First edition May 1976
Reprinted July 1976
Reprinted September 1977 (with updating notes)
Reprinted November 1978 (with updating notes)
Reprinted April 1980 (with updating notes and preface)
Reprinted August 1981 (with updating notes)
Reprinted January 1983 (with updating notes)
Reprinted March 1984 (with updating notes)
Reprinted September 1985 (with updating notes)
Reprinted July 1987 (with new foreword)

New edition January 1989

FURTHER COPIES OF THIS BOOK ARE OBTAINABLE
FROM THE AUTHOR at 27 OCCUPATION LANE,
WOOLWICH, LONDON SE18 3JQ
Price £4.95 (post free).

Also available are copies of the author's other book, Lawyers
Can Seriously Damage Your Health – Price £3.95 (post free).

ISBN 0 9505023 3 2

Cover design by David Statter

Text set by Jubal Multiwrite Ltd.
66 Loampit Vale, London SE13 7SN.
Printed and bound by Anchor Brendon Ltd.
of Tiptree, Essex

Contents

Introduction

This book is in two parts. The first part examines the traditional system of house purchase and sale *(conveyancing)* as operated by solicitors; and concludes that the service they give is so bad, and so far removed from the claims they make for it, that it amounts to fraud. The second part of the book gives detailed instructions, step by step, to enable the house buyer and seller to do his own conveyancing and so avoid the fraud.

The art of conveyancing, as practised by solicitors, is to do as little work as possible, while relieving the house buyer and seller of as much money as possible. This in itself does not amount to fraud. The fraud lies in the solicitors' claim that they *safeguard* the house buyer in the most important purchase of his life; whereas what they actually *do* is not only useless, it is worse than useless. It is useless because of the methods which solicitors employ to check that the house being bought has no 'quasi-legal' defects. By quasi-legal defects I mean those defects which, while not being exactly legal defects, have a legal *aura* about them – e.g. proposals for new roads or unsightly developments in the offing, mains services not being directly connected, boundary disputes, and so on – and which the house-buyer is led to believe his solicitor will protect him against. In fact this must be the most important part of the solicitor's job, now that the Land Registry has reduced the actual conveyancing *procedures* to little more than a formality, and also has ensured that pure legal defects (e.g. a vendor trying to sell a house he does not own) are virtually non-existent.

Yet the way the solicitor checks that the house has no quasi-legal defects is by sending printed forms of questions to the seller's solicitor and to the local Council, which yield no useful information and are nothing more than a time wasting ritual. Imagine a mechanic checking the condition of a secondhand car, on behalf of a potential purchaser, by sending the seller a list of questions: 'please confirm the clutch is working properly', 'please confirm there is no rust in the bodywork', etc. If this would be an absurd way of checking that a secondhand car you are buying for £950 is 'all right', why should it be any less absurd when employed to check that a house you are buying for £30,000/£100,000 is 'all right'?

As for the solicitor's work being *worse* than useless, this is because the purchaser, having instructed a solicitor, naturally assumes that his solicitor will work his wondrous magic to make sure everything is 'all right'; therefore the purchaser will not *himself* bother to check the common-sense points which should be checked by a brief inspection of the house and by personally asking a few questions at the Council offices. Consequently neither the purchaser *nor* his solicitor checks these things, but they are simply left to chance.

Let me give as examples the three most likely quasi-legal defects to affect a house. Suppose the day after you complete your purchase and move into your new house: (a) you see the secluded woodland beyond the garden fence (which was one of the chief attractions of the place) being bulldozed to make way for a new housing estate; (b) you realise you have a cantankerous neighbour who has had a long-standing feud with your vendor about a boundary fence or whatever, and is all set to continue it with you; (c) a circular lands on your doormat urging you to support the protest against a new trunk road which is proposed to come within a few feet of your front garden. Your solicitor would not have found out about the first two matters and probably would not have found out about the third – (a) because his 'local search' would not pick up planning applications in respect of *adjoining* property; (b) because the only way he purports to find out about neighbour disputes is by sending a printed form of questions to the vendor's solicitor, who traditionally appends stock responses which give away no information. In any case the vendor is hardly likely to disclose this defect if that is the *reason* he is moving, as it could be; (c) because his 'local search' will reveal only such proposals for new roads etc. as have actually been put on the register, and not those which are still at 'committee' stage. On the other hand if, instead of employing a solicitor, you had (a) called at the Council offices and asked the planning department whether it had received any planning applications in respect of the adjoining land; (b) asked the neighbour how he got on with the vendor; (c) asked the road department at the Council offices whether there were any proposals in the offing which might affect the house – you would have found out about these things in a matter of minutes.

These are just three out of *fourteen* possible quasi-legal defects which I list in this book, any one of which could affect the house you are buying, which the solicitor's methods have almost no chance of discovering – but which you will be able to discover in time if you do your own conveyancing following my instructions. They do not involve complex legal points: as in the above examples, they are matters of common sense. Unhappily, common sense has no place in the solicitor's conveyancing ritual, and of course there is a sound economic reason for this. To check the things which should be checked, the solicitor would have to visit each house he is dealing with, and call at each Council office – an impossible task if he has an average work-load of sixty or seventy current conveyancing matters, especially if half the houses are over fifty miles away. On the other hand he can dispatch his printed forms crammed with complicated verbiage without stirring from his desk. In other words, the solicitor is just not equipped to do the job properly; and his mumbo-jumbo and ritual procedures are merely an elaborate smokescreen to conceal this fact both from his clients and himself.

The solicitors' claim that they safeguard the house-buyer against anything 'going wrong' is false. Equally false is their complementary claim that if anything does 'go wrong', a right to compensation automatically follows. Sometimes this is merely insinuated, e.g. 'Solicitors have professional indemnity insurance so that any . . . mistakes or problems should be resolved at no cost to you.' (The Legal Side of Buying a House.*) Sometimes it is brazenly trumpeted, e.g. 'Solicitors

---

* Published by the Consumers' Association (but written by a solicitor).

provide a professional service for which they accept full responsibility. And this means either putting right mistakes which they might make or compensating clients monetarily.' (Law Society's spokesman, Daily Mail 7 July 1976.) The client is led to believe that by paying a solicitor to do his conveyancing he is buying an expensive, but eminently worthwhile, insurance policy to safeguard him in the most important purchase of his life. Yet the solicitor's job is so ill-defined that this notional insurance policy, if it ever has to be referred to, will turn out to be written in invisible ink. For most of the things likely to go wrong the solicitor will have a perfect get-out. The adjoining woodland is being bulldozed to make way for a new housing estate? Well, you should have *told* me that was a particular feature of the house and I would have made a special enquiry about it. There's been a long-standing dispute with the neighbour? Well, this wasn't disclosed in the answers to my preliminary enquiries and it's not my fault if the vendor misrepresents the position. You've heard there is a new trunk road in the offing? Well, it wasn't revealed by my local search – and so on. This is the advantage of encouraging the purchaser to think that the solicitor's job covers the whole spectrum of house ownership (as the Law Society does in its publicity pamphlet), while at the same time being careful never to state what it actually *does* cover.

Even if the solicitor has been clearly negligent, it's not a question – as many people imagine – of writing to the Law Society and getting a fat cheque by return. The Law Society will not be interested, but will merely send out its stereotyped letter (currently being sent out at the rate of 16,000 a year) advising the disgruntled client to find *another* solicitor to advise him on the possibility of suing the first one. And if legal action is decided on, the first thing that other solicitor will do is to ask for a substantial payment on account of costs. Apologists for the system talk so glibly about being able to sue your solicitor if he makes a mistake; but I have known several seemingly open and shut cases against solicitors drag on for year after year to the despair and ruination of their erstwhile clients. A better solution, surely, is to do your own conveyancing and spend a few hours checking and finding out the things which *can* be checked and found out.

Yet I am mindful of the obstacles which prevent this from being an attractive, or with some people even a feasible, course. Any explanation to the layman of a seemingly technical subject is liable to fill him with dread. Those of my readers who cannot face an income tax return without panic, and in whom the thought of handling a bank draft for £35,000 is likely to induce recurrent nightmares, should pass lightly over the 'technical' chapters in Part II. To those who can keep an open mind, I offer the following further points:

(a) The bulk of conveyancing which comes out of solicitors' offices is *not* done by the learned solicitor, but from start to finish by his unqualified and unsupervised clerk (sometimes even his secretary). This is well known by anyone who has worked in a solicitor's office; and in any case the Law Society admits it by frequently publishing solicitors' advertisements in the Law Society's Gazette, for unqualified conveyancing clerks who 'must be able to work with minimum supervision', or 'must be able to work without supervision'. These advertisements alone make nonsense of the Law Society's claim that conveyancing is so complicated that only a solicitor is fit to do it.

(b) If you do your own conveyancing, and you are getting a mortgage, you will *still* be paying a solicitor to check that your seller's title deeds and other documents are in order – namely your *building society's* solicitor. All the work a purchaser's solicitor does after exchange of contracts is duplicated by the purchaser's building society's solicitor. The do-it-yourself conveyancer will merely be paying *one* solicitor to do this work instead of *two*.

(c) Everyone buying a house should realise that there are two different systems of conveyancing operating in this country: the *registered* system, where the house is registered at the Land Registry; and the *unregistered* system, where it is not. The Land Registry was set up at the beginning of this century with the object of simplifying conveyancing to enable people to buy and sell houses as easily as they can buy and sell anything else, i.e. without solicitors. The registered system now covers three-quarters of all houses in England and Wales, and it is continually being extended. Where it applies, the Land Registry issues a comparatively simple land certificate for each registered house to take the place of the previous title deeds, and in appendix 2 (p. 244) I reproduce a typical land certificate. You will see that the name of the current owner is typed in the appropriate space. Moreover, the State guarantees that the person whose name is so typed *is* the owner of the house in question. Thus what was traditionally the most important and mysterious part of the solicitor's job – checking that the seller really owns the house he is purporting to sell – can be safely done by anyone who can read. In addition, enquiries departments were set up attached to each land registry office, where members of the public have access (personally or by phone) to trained land registry staff who will answer their queries and, within reason, give them whatever help they may need in doing their own conveyancing. Unfortunately, although the house purchaser *pays* for these enquiries departments (in the form of high land registry fees which are levied each time a registered house changes hands), he does not *use* them, simply because no-one has ever bothered to tell him they exist. Hence one of the most enlightened reforms of this century has failed for want of publicity.

If on the other hand you are buying an *unregistered* house, your vendor will have paid two highly qualified legal experts (one acting for him and one for his building society) to make sure the house was really his when he bought it. As the Law Society claims that solicitors' work is of such high standard, why should you have to duplicate it?

In conclusion, there are many human activities on which an elaborate superstructure of mumbo-jumbo can be built, to the bewilderment of the layman, and the enrichment of the professional. Which activity happens to be the most susceptible to such treatment depends on the economic structure of the particular society. In those primitive societies where the concept of house ownership is unknown, the magic man is the witchdoctor. In our society, the magic man is the lawyer, whose incantations are as incomprehensible to the educated as they are to the uneducated. And because house ownership is fairly universal, and an average house happens to cost somewhere between £30,000 and £100,000, the lawyer has decided that it is in this field that his services are essential. Someone about to pay or receive £30,000/£100,000 is, after all, the most suitable recipient of a bill for £300/£1,000.

But if as a result of some unlikely economic revolution, the bulk of the average man's resources went not to buying his house but, for instance, to providing his annual holiday, lawyers would abruptly disclaim house transfer work (which would thenceforth be dealt with by post office clerks or similar folk), and instead they would make out an equally convincing case for being employed to deal with the formalities of foreign travel. Only a highly trained expert can deal with the Foreign Office forms and intricate procedures entailed in obtaining a passport, or check whether your existing passport is in order in the light of ever changing Common Market government directions. Only someone well versed in international law is competent to advise you whether you need a visa. Only someone who has been subjected to the rigorous training insisted on by the Law Society is equipped to provide you with all the other travel documents you will need – travellers' cheques, visas, international driving licence, immunisation documents – any one of which could trip you up if you were so rash as to venture abroad without professional assistance. For no extra charge your solicitor will advise on, and arrange, additional insurance to cover you and your dependants in case of accident. In some countries you can be imprisoned if you have a car accident unless you have a bail bond. The law is very complicated on this point. Your solicitor has spent years studying these problems and knows exactly what arrangements to make to protect your interests. Clearly this work is too important and technical to be left to the unskilled, or worse, the charlatan. An Act of Parliament would be hastily passed to protect the public from the unqualified operator, making it illegal for anyone other than a solicitor (or licensed travel agent under the jurisdiction of the Lord Chancellor) to obtain any travel document on behalf of another person. And for the benefit of anyone contemplating getting his travel documents himself, the Law Society would publish a series of advertisements depicting such a person having to pay crippling sums at the frontier because his insurance was inadequate, or languishing in a foreign gaol because his papers were not in order.

Part I

The System

1

Why people go to solicitors for their conveyancing

In times when a good many people find it worth their while to do their own car maintenance, decorating and woodwork, the person who does his own conveyancing is still very much a rarity. I knew a television director who had stripped his car and mounted a new engine in it. He asked my advice on buying his house and I suggested he did the work himself with perhaps a little guidance from me. He was a mercenary gentleman who in normal circumstances would have found the idea of saving a few hundred pounds quite pleasing. Yet he shuddered at my suggestion. 'I want to go to a solicitor,' he said, 'then I'll know it will be done properly.'

It might be as well to begin by looking at the reasons why people instinctively go to solicitors for their conveyancing. Although these will vary according to the individual (some people even think they are legally obliged to employ a solicitor) I think the basic reasons are ignorance of what is involved, and fear which comes from that ignorance. Regarding the first, it is a curious fact that the layman who goes to a solicitor for his conveyancing so that it will be done properly, will have only the vaguest notion of what the aforesaid 'it' comprises, what the solicitor actually does, or is supposed to do, on his behalf – he checks the deeds or something; he makes searches with the local Council; he makes sure I'm paying the money to the right person; *anyhow he makes sure everything is all right.*

This ignorance is not confined to the uneducated man buying his first modest semi, but is found equally in people all the way up the social scale, including those whose business it is to be better informed than the average person on such subjects. For instance an editorial in the *Observer* (16 January 1972) indicates that a solicitor's function is 'checking whether the deeds of the land on which a house stands are in order'; and when I sent a copy of this book, when it was first published in 1976, to the then property correspondent of the *Financial Times*, he telephoned me and said: 'But don't you *have* to employ a solicitor for your house purchase?' Shortly afterwards I was invited to take part in a radio discussion on 'You and Yours' (Radio 4), which the presenter opened by saying: 'But surely, Mr. Joseph, you're not suggesting that people should do their own conveyancing. I mean, I wouldn't know where to begin!'

Twelve years later the situation seems much the same. For example Victoria Wood, in a monologue in one of her recent T.V. shows, complained that whenever she went to a party she found herself 'stuck with one of those awful people who had taken out their own appendix, *or done their own conveyancing*'.

In this consumer-conscious age, when approximately a million houses are bought and sold every year in England and Wales, and when conveyancing has been the subject of innumerable programmes on radio and television, acres of newsprint and a dozen *Which?* reports, why does it remain shrouded by a seemingly impenetrable fog of mystery and ignorance?

The answer, I think, is that conveyancing – unlike car maintenance, decorating and carpentry – is an activity traditionally carried out by *professional* man. And this has one or two far-reaching consequences. Firstly, while we employ certain critical faculties in our dealings with tradesmen and businessmen, we seem to surrender these critical faculties in our dealings with professional man – our respect for him having been instilled since early childhood. Doctor carries a mysterious black bag and makes us well when we are ill. Teacher has unbounded knowledge and holds the golden key to our 'O' level results. Lawyer has spent years studying his subject, and knows off by heart whole legal tomes way beyond our comprehension. These are professional men who have

been to university, who have got *letters* after their names. Who
are we to question their expertise? And having been
conditioned not to question their expertise, it is but a small
step not to question *anything* they tell us.

This situation is compounded by the fact that it is not only
the layman who surrenders his critical faculties in his dealings
with professional man. Those who decide what the layman
hears on radio and television (and reads in books) surrender
their critical faculties as well, believing that professional
matters are so esoteric that only *professionals* are qualified to
comment on them or explain them to the public. While this
view may appear plausible, it has the unfortunate result that –
as regards conveyancing at any rate – the public is fed an
insidious trickle of propaganda masquerading as objective
truths. Some examples:

Architect and author of book on house-buying: 'And of
course you'll have to pay legal fees to your solicitor. In general
they give jolly good value. Of course you *can* do it yourself but
I wouldn't advise it. I've known too many cases of D.I.Y.
purchasers coming unstuck because they found they didn't
own the land they wanted to build that garage on, or grandma
turned out to be a sitting tenant.' ('Woman's Hour', Radio 4,
9 January 1984.)

Barrister commenting on conveyancing: 'I think solicitors
generally are good value.' ('Woman's Hour', 23 September
1987.)

Chartered surveyor answering questions on house-buying:
'I do have a very high regard for the work solicitors do in
conveyancing. If you've got all the time you *can* do your own
conveyancing, but this is a very big transaction you're
involved in and you can't sue yourself for negligence.'
('Tuesday Call', Radio 4, 5 July 1983.)

Solicitor: 'The public really do get a fantastic deal from
solicitors in conveyancing.' ('Lawyers in Action', Radio 4, 6
January 1988.)

Financial expert: 'The vendor must have his own solicitor to
see his interests are protected.' ('Money Box', Radio 4, 25
January 1988.)

Sir Desmond Heap, President of the Law Society, answering a
lady on a radio phone-in who said she had done her own

conveyancing: 'I can only hope for your sake, madam, that you fully investigated all the underground rights of support and footings, cross-covenants and overground rights of aeroplanes. There are some awfully abstruse points involved here, and you were moving in a very dangerous area. I only hope for your sake that you'll be able to sell your house when you come to do so and that you in fact own what you think you own.' ('It's Your Line', Radio 4, 1 May 1973.)

'No, you do not *have* to instruct a solicitor to deal with your sale. You can handle the contract yourself, if you wish. Of course, it is quite legal for you to ignore your doctor and to saw your own leg off. Legal perhaps, but not very wise.' (*Buying or Selling a House* by Llewelyn, Fellow of Royal Institute of Chartered Surveyors.)

Many local radio stations have a regular phone-in programme on legal matters – sometimes a whole programme will be devoted to moving house – where a solicitor (or similar guru) will explain to a grateful programme presenter and respectful public how necessary he, the solicitor, and his time-honoured procedures are. So to a questioner who was buying his own Council house, and wanted to know whether he needed a solicitor, the reply was: 'Just because you've lived in the house for twenty years, don't assume you know everything about it. You still need a *solicitor's* search.' (London Broadcasting Company, 29 January 1988.)

Nothing is permitted to query this 'official' party line. For instance in the last example I rang the programme to make the point that it doesn't have to be a solicitor who makes the 'search', but anyone can do it; and moreover, the layman who actually calls at the Council office will get far more information than is revealed by the standard local search form. 'So you think that *anyone* can do the search?' said the person vetting the calls incredulously; and after a few seconds I was curtly informed that they would not be taking my call. Once when I *did* get through to a B.B.C. phone-in programme on the subject, I was unceremoniously cut off because (as the B.B.C. explained in a letter to a listener who complained that my point had not been adequately dealt with) 'the programme was merely trying to give practical advice, and not engage in *politics*.'

So the lawyers and their co-professionals are given freedom of the air to expound the 'professional' point of view; while anything which *questions* that point of view is regarded as subversive (political), and is therefore suppressed. Similarly with books. Mr. Llewelyn's book – which argues that because you would not amputate your own leg *therefore* you should not attempt your own conveyancing – finds a publisher. My book does not and, as you can see, I had to publish it myself. Mr Llewelyn's book is on sale in every branch of every chain book store. Mine is not.

This incessant propaganda has enormous power – firstly, because virtually nothing is permitted to counter it; secondly, because (unlike party political broadcasts) it does not come wrapped round with the warning: there now follows, or you have just heard, a partial statement on behalf of the solicitors' profession, but it is fed to the public in the guise of objective truths; and thirdly, because it is fed to a public which has *already suspended its critical faculties* with regard to such matters.

So when the lawyers, and their lackeys, either state or imply that conveyancing involves grappling with land laws and procedures of unbelievable complexity, and that the most seemingly commonplace house purchase is fraught with legal implications which the layman couldn't even begin to understand – the public accepts that it must be so. And as those who control the media (having suspended *their* critical faculties as well) allow the profession an ever available platform from which to disseminate this message, you will see why the fog surrounding conveyancing – like that surrounding the Law Courts in *Bleak House* – has little chance of being dispersed.

I was chatting to a teacher who had bought a flat in the same block as my own and she was commenting on the high cost of extras, including legal fees. Although she knew I was a solicitor, she was clearly surprised when I told her I had done my own conveyancing. 'How very clever!' she exclaimed, scarcely able to conceal her wonder and admiration. It was as if I had told her I *had* taken out my own appendix. On another occasion, having to meet a vendor at his house and being pressed for time, I brought my portable typewriter and proceeded to type out a land registry transfer form for him to sign. The form consists of the postal address of the house, the purchase price, and the names and addresses of vendor and purchaser. Yet my audience was obviously impressed by my display of expertise. 'It must be wonderful', the vendor observed, 'to be able to do this sort of work.'

It is a self-perpetuating process. The more respectful the layman is of his solicitor, the more credulous he will be of his solicitor's mystical powers; the more credulous he is, the less likely he is to take any critical interest in the subject himself.

Yet the statements and implications in the profession's propaganda are almost invariably false. The architect/author *doesn't* know of any D.I.Y. purchasers who came unstuck because grandma turned out to be a sitting tenant. To charge £x hundred for a few hours routine and largely useless clerical work is *not* good value. The vendor does *not* have to 'have his own solicitor to see his interests are protected'. The purchaser buying his own Council house *doesn't* need a solicitor to do the 'search'. Amputating your own leg is *not* analogous to doing your own conveyancing, and so on. As for the assertion by the erstwhile President of the Law Society, underground rights of support and footings, and overground rights of aeroplanes, do *not* feature in domestic conveyancing. (A second's thought will reveal that an aeroplane does not fly over any one house; it flies over a whole area. The preliminary enquiries and local search forms, as used by solicitors, refer to many weird and wonderful things such as Ancient Monuments and emergency escape routes, but even these forms have never mentioned underground footings or overhead aeroplanes.) So by implying that because the lady did her own conveyancing and failed to investigate these matters *therefore* her house might be unsaleable, the learned President has, in effect, told a downright falsehood. And he told it to a million people who, presumably, believed him.

And here we may mention a further consequence of conveyancing being an activity carried out by professional man: that whereas the Trade Descriptions Act 1968 makes it a criminal offence for a tradesman or businessman in the course of his trade or business knowingly or recklessly to make false statements about his goods or services, our upright and independent judiciary has conveniently decided that the Law Society – the solicitors' professional body – is *not* engaged in a trade or business, and is therefore outside the provisions of that Act.* Consequently the Law Society can with impunity put óut as much misleading or lying propaganda as it pleases.

Having examined some of the Law Society's (and its lackeys') propaganda put out over the air, let's look at some examples of its writings on the subject, starting with the Law Society's pamphlet *Buying a house? See a Solicitor* – one of a series of pamphlets designed to advertise solicitors' services to potential clients. It opens with the statement: 'Remember a house is not just bricks and mortar. It is very likely the most valuable investment you will ever make. It is also a piece of land with all too often a complicated bundle of legal rights thrown in'; and it goes on to warn the house purchaser of all the frightening things which could happen, and which only a *solicitor* will be able to find out – disputes over boundaries, fences, rights of way, rights of light, road charges, compulsory acquisitions; a dear old lady who turns out to be a sitting tenant; a new fly-over planned to pass within 20 yards of your bedroom window; a sewage farm or a new airport scheduled to be built across the road – 'It is no good leaving these things to chance and then learning the hard way, either by expensive quarrels with neighbours or by having to move out altogether at a thumping great loss. These are just some of the reasons why the *first person* you should go and see as soon as you think of buying a house is a *solicitor*.'

After this warning the pamphlet goes on to list all the *incidental* things your solicitor will do for you, the house purchaser. Not only does a conveyancing solicitor's job apparently include acting as a mortgage broker, tax consultant, insurance broker, money lender, but even when occasion demands as an auxiliary driver of the furniture removal van –

---

*   Re an application by Michael Joseph for Judicial Review, as decided by Lord Justice Stephen Brown and Mr. Justice McCowan, 24 July 1986.

'He may even see that the right furniture van arrives at the right address at the right time with the right furniture in it.' 'Don't forget', the pamphlet urges, 'your solicitor is the only person in the whole business of getting your new home who will throughout be watching your interests. All around there will be people with their own interests to promote. Your solicitor will be promoting yours.' So you will be surrounded by estate agents, mortgage brokers, furniture removers – all in the business for what they can get out of it. Only the solicitor, a moral cut above these people, has entered his profession with the sole object of protecting your interests.

I shall be dealing with this pamphlet in detail later on. For the moment suffice it to say that practically every statement in it is a lie. In fact in an article (printed in the Law Society's Gazette) I suggested that the most blatant lie was the picture, showing a bewildered householder standing outside his house contemplating a conglomeration of road works, fly-overs, high rise flats in course of construction, a railway line and an airport or two, under the caption 'Your Solicitor will warn you if this sort of thing could happen'. After my article appeared the picture remained, but the caption was altered to 'Your Solicitor will always be on your side' – whatever *that* may mean.

Notice how the author of this pamphlet – as well as the spokesmen for the profession I previously quoted – while warning the house purchaser of all the frightening things which could trap him, and which only a solicitor can prevent, are careful never to state *how* the solicitor finds out about these things, nor precisely what conveyancing *does* entail. The witchdoctor doesn't tell his client what is in the medicine: only a lurid account of the bogeys he will encounter should he fail to take it. As we have seen, sometimes these bogeys which only the witchdoctor's magical powers can exorcise, are tangible – grandma who turns out to be a sitting tenant, the new fly-over planned to pass within 20 yards of your bedroom window, etc. Sometimes they are more vague – cross-covenants, under-ground rights of footings, overhead rights of aeroplanes. Sometimes they are even more nebulous, as in the following extract from a pamphlet entitled *Buying a House* by Dudley

Perkins: 'Your solicitor is concerned to find out whether, if you buy that house, you are likely to run into unexpected financial commitments, unexpected interference with your full and free right to occupy the property, and whether the present owner has offended against our multitudinous laws and regulations in some way which might bring trouble to a future owner.' What unexpected financial commitments, or interference with your right to occupy the property, or laws and regulations which the vendor might have offended against, are not specified.

This pamphlet comes with a commendatory foreword by the then President of the Law Society – as does a book entitled *The Services of a Solicitor* by the late H.J.B. Cockshutt, which (according to the foreword) sets out to tell the public something of what solicitors do. Rather surprisingly, as the public has more contact with solicitors in conveyancing than any other field, only a few of its 127 pages are devoted to this topic. This is how Mr. Cockshutt enlightens the public on this vital subject when he does get round to mentioning it on page 30: 'The layman buys a house and asks a solicitor to "look after it". Here, as it happens, quite a lot of strictly legal work is involved, some of it very technical and skilled. Often however his main work concerns other matters, though incidentally all his work in such a case is normally covered by the scale fees.' Mr. Cockshutt is reticent to the point of total silence as to the very technical and skilled legal work involved, but he is more forthcoming about those 'other matters' which the solicitor will obligingly throw in for no extra charge: 'for example he may advise that there should be a check upon the structural condition of the house, drains and electrical wiring and he may arrange at the client's request for this to be done. Quite certainly he will go into the raising of the purchase money for the client in the way best suited to that individual case, to make sure that the client does not take on more than he can manage and that the finance is properly arranged. He will check, of course, matters of Town and Country planning. He will draw attention to the need for temporary fire insurance and if instructed to do so will arrange such insurance. He will go to a lot of trouble to ensure that the actual date of completion fits in best for the client, having regard to the date when he has to leave his old house.' In other words, a solicitor will generally be able to recommend a surveyor if the client does not know of one (and the surveyor in question, also being an estate agent, will no doubt reciprocate such recommendations in appropriate cases). He will not exchange contracts until his client has got a mortgage offer. In the rare case of a purchase without a mortgage, the solicitor will be equally happy to arrange the insurance, thus securing for himself the agency commission. 'Matters of Town and Country planning' involve sending a standard printed form of questions to the vendor's solicitor, who will append standard replies. (I shall be dealing with this in some detail later on.) As for all that trouble to fix a completion date, all a solicitor need – or indeed can – do is to accept the 'usual month' in the purchase contract and insert the same date in the sale contract, and notify his client of such date. 'And after contracts', writes Mr. Cockshutt, 'you get down to the legal work of investigating title.' Mr. Cockshutt knows, but does not mention, that in the case of registered property 'the legal work of investigating title' consists of looking at a copy of the land certificate and seeing the vendor's name in the appropriate space.

The Services of a Solicitor is now out of print, but the Law Society has sponsored a series of books under the general title 'It's Your Law', whose avowed object, according to an advertisement, is 'to eliminate any idea that may be at large that lawyers wish to keep the law to themselves as a mystery'. The first book in the series, by Gerald Sanctuary, bears the rather enigmatic title *Before You See a Solicitor* – and according to its blurb it 'describes what precisely a solicitor does'. Only one chapter, entitled 'Homes', is given to the subject of conveyancing. This chapter runs to twelve pages, of which the first three and the last four and a half consist of a discussion of general principles, leaving a magnificent four and a half pages (p. 47 to 51) to describe what precisely a solicitor does in conveyancing.

In the event, the author's description in these four and a half pages is far from precise. 'Today a host of regulations may affect the purchaser of a house,' he writes, but – like Mr. Perkins – he cannot specify any of them, except for an oblique reference to 'local planning regulations or proposals that may affect the property.' Consider the following passage:

'The first step taken by the buyer's solicitor is to get a clear picture from his client of his intentions. When does he want to move in? Is he buying any carpets, curtains or other fixtures? Does he intend to have the place surveyed? What sort of mortgage arrangements is he making? Does he want the house put in the joint names of himself and his wife? The answers to these questions will involve specialist help and advice from the solicitor, who may also advise on the desirability of a survey. People buying property are often inclined to do without a survey. The solicitor will usually recommend a survey . . . ' and so on, for a further eleven lines on the desirability of having a survey, and whether a mortgage linked to a life assurance policy is better than a straight mortgage of the house alone.

Notice how the author states that the questions: When does the buyer want to move in? Is he buying any furnishings? Does he intend to have a survey? *involve specialist help and advice from the solicitor.* Notice also how, like Cockshutt and the Law Society pamphlet, the author shies away from giving a precise account of what he thinks a conveyancing solicitor's job entails, but instead takes refuge in peripheral matters – what mortgage arrangements is the purchaser making? does he intend to have a survey? etc. – on which the solicitor *may* be, but in fact usually is not, called upon to advise. For example, in the case of a mortgage, this can either be of the house alone or combined with a policy of life assurance. In the former case the monthly repayments comprise both interest and capital; in the latter case they consist of interest only but the borrower has in addition to keep up the premiums on the policy, so that although the capital of the loan does not diminish, it is cleared at the end of the term by the policy maturing. As might be expected, the monthly premiums and interest in the case of a mortgage linked to a life policy come to more than the capital and interest payments under a straight mortgage, because they buy the advantage of life insurance during the term. Now in my twenty years experience as a conveyancing solicitor no purchaser has ever asked me for this nugget of information, presumably because whenever it was relevant someone else – mortgage broker, estate agent, building society clerk, life assurance salesman – had already supplied it by the time he got to me. As for that other faithful old warhorse which invariably comes lumbering into every account of a conveyancing solicitor's work and the value thereof – that the solicitor will advise having a survey – you could just as well argue that the purchaser of a secondhand car needs to employ a solicitor because he will advise having an independent check on the mechanical condition of the vehicle.

The Consumers' Association, which prides itself on being totally independent so 'we can be completely objective and outspoken in our reports', might have been expected to adopt a more detailed and critical approach. But here again we see that that organisation's critical faculties – so keen in its reports on car mechanics, travel agents, baldness treatments etc. – go out of the window when it comes to reporting on *professional* matters. This is how the original and most comprehensive *Which?* report on the subject (March 1970) describes conveyancing: 'When you buy a house you need to find out just what the seller owns and what his rights and duties are. Then you must go through the formalities of having the property transferred to you.' And this is how it describes the role of a conveyancing solicitor: 'When a solicitor acts for you in conveyancing, besides carrying out the investigation and transfer of the property, he is also acting as your legal adviser: this means that you should expect him to explain what your legal position is and what its implications are.' The conclusion of the *Which?* report was: 'You will get the best conveyancing from a good solicitor.' Nowhere, however, does the report state what it considers 'the best conveyancing' entails, nor what a 'good solicitor' is.

Even more surprising is the Consumers' Association's full length book on the subject, entitled *The Legal Side of Buying a House*. This runs to 132 pages of which 85 describe the legal steps which one, Matthew Seaton, takes when he buys his house. Albeit Matthew is himself a solicitor (so we are told), he does not practise as one, and the book sets out to explain in detail how Matthew successfully carried out his own conveyancing, with a view to the intelligent lay reader following his example. Here, if anywhere, we would expect a critical investigation of the solicitor's role in conveyancing, a definitive answer to the question whether he is parish priest or parasite. The question is well put on page 2: 'People do not ask a solicitor to deal with the formalities involved in buying or selling a car or a washing machine. Why then has it always been thought necessary to have a solicitor when buying a house?' The answer, however, is one which the Law Society's publicity agent could not have bettered: 'There are a number of reasons. For one thing you pay a solicitor to take over the responsibility. Also a house cannot legally be transferred as easily as a car or any other chattel. For instance, it is a legal requirement to have a deed ... Furthermore, there are enquiries of a legal nature that should be made about a house to ensure that the buyer will be able to live in it as he intends.'

You pay a solicitor to take over the responsibility. Responsibility for what? We are not told. A house cannot legally be transferred as easily as a car. Perhaps not, but the form or 'deed' which transfers a registered house from vendor to purchaser (and the book is concerned solely with registered property) is probably simpler than the form applying for a road tax licence. And what does that magic phrase 'to ensure that the buyer will be able to live in it as he intends' mean? How many different ways are there of living in a house? Then we find two statements: 'The main function of the buyer's solicitor in the business of buying a house is to enquire into the ownership of the seller'; and 'If this [the land register] shows that the seller is the owner, the buyer does not need to go to any further trouble on the question of ownership.' But because a page separates them, the rather startling implication of these two statements apparently escapes the author.

Matthew Seaton successfully completes his purchase, having meticulously followed the few simple procedures traditionally employed by conveyancing solicitors. That it takes some eighty pages to describe them is partly due to every letter he sends and receives being set out in full. What Matthew and his creator never query is *why* he follows these procedures, and what benefit he thinks he has achieved thereby. For instance, the reader is told 'there are many questions which the buyer's solicitor has to ask the seller's solicitor. This is done mainly on a printed form called "enquiries before contract" '. Matthew was satisfied with the answers he got to these questions from his vendor's solicitor. And what were these answers? Well, apparently they were of the sort that vendors' solicitors traditionally employ: 'Just as there are stock questions so are there stock answers which crop up frequently. Among these answers are "Inspection will show", "Please search", "Other than those apparent on inspection or revealed by the usual searches there are none to the vendor's knowledge", "We cannot say", "There are none of which the vendor is aware but the property is sold subject to any there may be." ' (p. 45/46.) If the book is aimed at the intelligent lay reader, might he not wonder why, if Matthew was satisfied with such answers, he bothered to ask the questions in the first place? Of those questions on the printed form which ask about physical defects of the house, the author says: 'If the answers suggest that the seller's solicitor has not even asked his client about these things, the buyer should press for more information. But an answer which, though non-committal and in general terms, shows that it is based on what the seller has told his solicitor regarding this question, is acceptable.' Again, if a non-committal – i.e. useless – answer is acceptable, whether it emanates from the vendor or the Duchess of York, why ask the question?

But a few of Matthew's questions *do* elicit some information. For instance, he learns that the gas, electricity, drainage 'and other main services' were connected. He could have got this information equally well (or better) by switching on a light, turning on a tap, lighting the gas and inspecting – and perhaps using – the lavatory on one of his visits to the house. (True this would not show that such services came to the house *direct* from the mains, but then neither did the answers that Matthew obtained; in fact no solicitor will ever confirm the services come direct.)

Matthew also gleaned that, according to the vendor, there were no disputes with neighbours. 'Now followed a complicated question dealing with many aspects of planning. It asked "What is the present use of the property?" The answer given was "Private dwellinghouse and premises". This was satisfactory.' Great as Matthew's relief must have been on learning such satisfactory news, it would presumably have been apparent when he first looked over the house that it was being used as a house, and not as a doctor's surgery, or cement factory.

This book, with its uncritical acceptance of traditional conveyancing procedure and its whole-hearted adoption of the conveyancing solicitor's clichés and half truths, could have been written as a Law Society's guide to conveyancing for articled clerks, and in fact most solicitors' offices boast a copy where presumably it is used for just that purpose. I have not heard of any great increase in people doing their own conveyancing with its help, but the publishers will be gratified to know that it is prominently displayed in every lawyers' bookshop.

So assuming that someone had listened to all the broadcasts and had waded through the various publications on the subject, he would find the question, what his solicitor is supposed to do on his behalf, answered only in the vaguest of terms – 'he takes over the responsibility', 'a lot of the work is very technical and skilled', 'there are some awfully abstruse points involved', 'it is no good leaving these things to chance', 'there are enquiries of a legal nature that should be made about a house', 'a host of regulations may affect the purchaser of a house', and so on.

The Law Society's publications concentrate on the incidental things which a solicitor *may* do for the purchaser – he *may* be able to offer bridging finance, he *may* see that the right furniture van arrives, he *may* advise on a structural survey and he *may* arrange for this to be done, if the property is close to a river he *may* ask about previous history of flooding, if there is a woodworm guarantee he *may* want to inspect it. But what are the things he has *got* to do? The Consumers' Association's book spends much time on the 'enquiries of a legal nature' which the purchaser's solicitor makes, but to which of these enquiries has he got to have an *informative answer?* The pundits on B.B.C. Radio tell us that conveyancing solicitors give 'good value' or 'jolly good value' or even 'fantastic value', but what do they actually *do* which represents such good value? In other words, leaving aside the optional extras such as recommending a surveyor, coping with hypothetical and improbable tax matters, and driving the furniture van, what is the purchaser's solicitor's basic job, which if not done properly he will be liable for negligence?

We do not know. We are not told. Nobody seems to know the answer, which perhaps is not surprising as nobody seems ever to have asked the question. You don't question *professional* men about what they are supposed to be doing. Indeed, according to Emmet, the most authoritative textbook on conveyancing, 'How far a solicitor is under an obligation to make the customary searches and enquiries before contract cannot be stated with certainty.' (*Emmet on Title* p. 2.) Apparently there was a case where the point was raised, but no decision was reached by the Court.

Of course, the authors of the various books and pamphlets on conveyancing are not the people who do the actual conveyancing. The late Mr. Cockshutt was a lecturer (and incidentally a brilliant and entertaining one) on a wide variety of legal subjects including contract, tort, and tax. He was president of a successful firm of law tutors which later amalgamated with the Law Society's college. But, so he told me, he never worked as a *conveyancer*. I was myself asked to assist on the *Which?* report on conveyancing (albeit in the event my assistance was minimal), and have first-hand knowledge of how it was produced. The full time solicitor on the Association's staff, who vetted the report, admitted he had not done any conveyancing for the previous eleven years; and the 'project officer' responsible for the report had no previous knowledge of the subject at all. An official of the Law Society has confirmed to me that the Law Society pamphlet was written by its publicity agent who likewise has never done any conveyancing (a fact reasonably apparent from the pamphlet itself); and in an article I wrote in the Law Society's Gazette I listed numerous errors which Mr. Sanctuary made in the chapter which he devotes to the subject. Neither can Sir Desmond Heap, former President of the Law Society – who on the Radio 4 phone-in warned of the dire consequences of failing to investigate underground rights of support and footings and overground rights of aeroplanes – ever have done any house conveyancing.

Another revealing incident was when the Secretary-General of the Law Society wrote a letter in the Law Society's Gazette, refuting a certain Sunday Times article which had implied that the whole business of conveyancing was very simple. 'There are a lot of other points to be looked for in a contract, and many questions to be answered satisfactorily before a buyer can safely commit himself to his proposed purchase,' the Secretary-General wrote. I telephoned the worthy gentleman (by appointment) and asked him what points and what questions he had in mind. He told me he was not expecting such a question: could he perhaps get the Law Society's expert on the subject to ring me back in a couple of hours?

So not only will the people who write the Law Society's publicity material and the *Which?* reports have no inside experience of conveyancing. The top men of the solicitors' profession, who will be its spokesmen and authors, will have no inside experience either. Routine domestic conveyancing, the transfer of The Laurels from Mr. A to Mr. B, will not be handled by the Sir Desmonds and Cockshutts of the profession. It will not even be done to any great extent by partners in solicitors' firms, who I think are not normally willing to do more than a smattering of such routine work. The bulk of house conveyancing is done by assistant solicitors (that is, salaried employees and not principals), and unqualified clerks in solicitors' offices – i.e. the less ambitious members of the profession. Thus the people who actually do most of the conveyancing, and who are content to spend their lives pushing out the palpably nonsensical forms, which such work largely comprises, are unlikely to possess the necessary curiosity to wonder exactly what it is they are supposed to be achieving. The more successful and ambitious members of the profession, who will be its spokesmen, will also lack this curiosity – firstly, because they will be otherwise engaged; secondly, because, being successful and respected members of the community, they instinctively avoid questions honest answers to which might make them uneasy; and thirdly, because they realise that it is in their own interests to keep the conveyancing solicitor's brief as vague as possible.

This is why there is nowhere to be found a precise and authoritative statement of what a solicitor is supposed to do for the house purchaser. An honest account of what a solicitor actually *does* would at once reveal: firstly, that anyone of normal intelligence could carry out the few stereotyped procedures involved; and secondly, that these procedures give the purchaser no protection against the dozen or so quasi-legal defects which might affect the house he is buying. On the other hand, if the solicitor claimed that he *did* find out about and warn the purchaser of those quasi-legal defects, he would be on dangerous ground.

The solicitor's way out of this dilemma is to point to the various traps lying in wait for the uninitiated (grandma who turns out to be a sitting tenant, a new fly-over planned to pass within 20 yards of your bedroom window etc.), with the *implication* that only a solicitor – by means unspecified – can protect the house-buyer from such disasters; and/or to point to a hotchpotch of *peripheral* matters (survey, tax problems, insurance, fixtures and fittings etc.), on which the solicitor claims a special competence to advise.

Then there is the good old stand-by, the solicitor's professional status and qualifications – and how only someone with such qualifications has the necessary expertise to protect the house-buyer in the *biggest financial transaction of his life*. Having looked at some of the first two categories, let's end with a selection of the third:

'You need advice from someone who is *professionally* qualified. Your solicitor has passed Law Examinations of the highest standard and is bound by rules of *professional* conduct made to protect you.' (Buying or Selling Your Home, Questions and Answers about Conveyancing; published by the Law Society.)

'A solicitor is a *professional* person able to take responsibility after having undergone long training and passed stiff qualifying examinations. John Smith knows that he can entrust his life's savings to a solicitor in confidence. There is protection against the consequences of dishonesty, misuse of client's money, and negligence.' (Colin Prestige, Pamphlet.)

'The biggest investment most people are likely to make in their lives is to buy their family home. Despite the large sum of money involved, a few people are prepared to risk using an unqualified conveyancer rather than a solicitor. Unqualified conveyancers do not have the *professional* expertise and knowledge a solicitor has gained through many years of study and practice in the highly complex field of land law of which conveyancing is a part.' (Law Society 'Fact' Sheet.)

'Behind the scenes complex documents need to be prepared, checked, queried, exchanged and checked again . . . It takes a thorough knowledge of the law and many years experience to make sure your conveyance is absolutely foolproof. Only a solicitor has that knowledge and experience.' (Law Society advertisement.)

'Those of us who have had to deal with conveyancing, with the complexities of land law, know the importance of this work to the public. Buying a house is one of the most important transactions entered into by people in this country. They must have the protection which only *our profession* can give them.' (Annual Address by the President of the Law Society, 1980.)

Take an apathetic and gullible public. Using the mystique of the professional, and a propaganda machine which in its subtle way would not disgrace that of a totalitarian state, instil ignorance and fear in roughly equal proportions – complex documents need to be prepared, unexpected interference with your right to occupy the property, multitudinous laws and regulations, highly complex field of land law, etc. Then add the magic ingredient, and the result will be a philosophers' stone in the hands of every established solicitor. And the magic ingredient? The price of the house. The fact that the would-be house owner, who apart from his car has probably never previously made a purchase for more than a thousand pounds, is now buying something which costs anything between £30,000 and £100,000, or even more. This is the most frightening bogey of all, the *coup de grace* which finally sends a man quivering into the comforting arms of a solicitor. Understandably, solicitors make the fullest use of it – 'the biggest investment most people are likely to make in their lives', 'the most important transaction entered into by people in this country', 'John Smith knows that he can entrust his life's savings to a solicitor in confidence'. The implication is that without a solicitor's advice you might pay over your life's savings, might purport to make the biggest investment of your

life, only to find that you had not got a house at all, but
perhaps a chicken run or a coal scuttle; or even if you had
succeeded in buying a house, the highway authority would as
like as not be driving a major road through its sitting room on
the morrow.

And then reassurance: we are the highly trained experts, the
specialists, who know all about these multitudinous laws and
regulations which would trap you, but won't trap us; we know
all about these complex documents with their jargon
incomprehensible to you, but not to us. We'll make sure that
nothing goes wrong; we'll look after you all the way along the
line. Remember, you're spending £30,000/£100,000. Surely
it's sensible to lay out another few hundred employing a
solicitor to protect you?

The layman obligingly agrees. So bemused is he at the prospect of such an astronomical sum passing through his hands,
that it will never occur to him that a transaction involving such
a sum need be no more complicated than getting a passport.
So unquestioning is he of the solicitors' propaganda he has
been fed, that it will never occur to him that buying a house for
all practical purposes probably involves *less* law than buying a
washing machine. And so overawed is he by the professional's
mystique, that it will never occur to him that provided he can
read, and can follow a few simple instructions, he is bound to
make a better job of his conveyancing than the most expensive
solicitor in the land.

2

But who does the conveyancing?

Apart from the activities of a handful of unqualified conveyancing organisations, the even more miniscule band of 'licensed conveyancers', and the odd person who does his own, all conveyancing is done in solicitors' offices. This is partly due to the potency of the profession's propaganda; and it is partly due to an Act of Parliament apparently making it illegal for an unqualified person to set up in business as a conveyancer.

In the last chapter we looked at some examples of the Law Society's propaganda – how the house purchaser 'needs advice from someone who is professionally qualified and has passed law examinations of the highest standard'; how 'only a solicitor has the knowledge and experience to make sure your conveyance is absolutely foolproof'; how the house purchaser 'must have the protection which only our profession can give him', and so on. These are the arguments by which all monopolies, and their enforcement by Act of Parliament, are justified.

The paradox about this monopoly is that although virtually all conveyancing is done in solicitors' offices, the bulk of conveyancing (that is, routine house conveyancing) which comes out of solicitors' offices is *not* done by solicitors at all, but by unqualified clerks *employed* by solicitors. The Law Society attempts to explain away this rather uncomfortable fact by trying to make out that these clerks do only *part* of the work, or that they always work under the *supervision* of a solicitor – e.g. 'It makes sense for an employer to entrust some of the simpler tasks to someone commanding a lower salary. This keeps down the cost to the client.' (Law Society pamphlet on conveyancing); 'Of course a solicitor employs staff to do *some* work for him, which he supervises.' (Law Society's spokesman, Daily Mail, 15 February 1978.)

But unqualified clerks in solicitors' offices do conveyancing from start to finish without *any* supervision, as everyone in the profession knows; and as indeed the Law Society itself must know – if for no other reason than every issue of the Law Society's Gazette carries solicitors' advertisements for unqualified conveyancing clerks, or 'legal executives' (which is merely a grandiose term for the same thing), to deal unsupervised with large quantities of house conveyancing. For example, here are four consecutive advertisements which appeared in a certain issue: 'Solicitors require conveyancer to work with minimum supervision'; 'Solicitors require experienced legal executive to undertake large volume of residential conveyancing'; 'Solicitors require qualified or unqualified conveyancer for heavy residential conveyancing work-load'; 'Solicitors require legal executive to deal with a large volume of conveyancing work'.

Ironically, one of the Law Society's most uneasy moments was when an unqualified conveyancer, a Mr. John Watson, who had himself been prosecuted by the Law Society, retaliated by bringing a private prosecution against a *solicitor's* clerk on the grounds that he had prepared a transfer contrary to Section 22 of the Solicitors Act – the same section which the Law Society invokes to protect its own monopoly. This section lays down that anyone who is not a solicitor and who for a fee or salary prepares a transfer or conveyance (i.e. the actual deed which transfers the house), is guilty of a criminal offence. There are four exceptions – barrister, notary, public officer, and typist who is employed to type out the document – but a solicitor's *clerk* is not one of them. Moreover, by expressly excepting the typist, the Act would seem to leave no room for the implication that a solicitor's clerk is excepted, even though a solicitor was sitting on his shoulders while he prepared the document in question.

If the solicitor's clerk had been found guilty it would mean that unqualified clerks in solicitors' offices would no longer be permitted to do conveyancing from start to finish, thus necessitating a major shake-up in practically every solicitor's office in the country. In view of the importance of the case to the profession *the Law Society itself instructed a Queen's Counsel to defend the clerk*, who argued that in preparing the transfer the clerk was acting as *agent* for his solicitor employer and so was not guilty of infringing the Act – which argument the Bradford-on-Avon magistrates dutifully accepted, and dismissed the case. Sighs of relief all round. Mr. Watson appealed against the magistrates' decision to the Court of Appeal, which could scarcely have upheld such fatuous reasoning. However, before the appeal could be heard the solicitor's clerk conveniently died; and Parliament forestalled any further attempt to embarrass the profession in this way, by slipping in a provision in the Administration of Justice Act 1985 that an unqualified clerk who prepares a transfer or conveyance is not guilty of infringing the Solicitors Act, provided he is *employed* by a solicitor.

There is nothing to stop me, a qualified solicitor, recruiting a dozen clerks from the Jobcentre, and setting them to work morning noon and night on conveyancing matters. Neither need I give them any supervision. In fact for the first 150 years of the Law Society's existence I could have installed each of my dozen clerks in as many branch offices up and down the country, which I need never have even *visited*. As an official of the Law Society wrote in the Law Society's Gazette (19 June 1974): 'There have in recent years been examples of sole principals with no qualified staff conducting their practices from three or four different offices sometimes separated by distances of more than fifty miles, two partners conducting a practice with up to seven separate offices and no qualified staff in their employ, and numerous cases of branch offices at which qualified solicitors rarely, if ever, attend.'

However, in 1975 the Law Society suddenly realised that the existence of numerous solicitors' offices, which were completely uncontaminated by anyone with any sort of legal qualification whatsoever, was scarcely compatible with its claim that only a solicitor has the necessary qualifications to do conveyancing; and as from 1st January 1976 it introduced some rules to curtail my professional activities to a certain extent. Although I can still recruit my dozen clerks from the Jobcentre to do conveyancing, I now have to employ a 'legal executive' of at least ten years standing to be in attendance at every branch office I set up, which I (or a solicitor employed by me) must *visit* every day. For those who wonder why this dramatic flash of knowledge should have occurred to the Law Society in 1975, rather than in 1925 or 2025, the clue is contained in the previously quoted article in the Law Society's Gazette: 'This state of affairs [i.e. the existence of numerous solicitors' offices at which solicitors rarely, if ever, attend] provides a gratuitous bonus to certain unqualified conveyancing organisations who have been able to suggest that their offices are more competently run than the unsupervised offices of certain solicitors to which they have been able to point.' Evidently in the years up to 1975 a number of unqualified conveyancers who were prosecuted by the Law Society *did* use this 'gratuitous bonus' in their defence – to the embarrassment of the Law Society, which consequently felt obliged to disallow a practice which gave those it prosecuted such an obvious handle against it.

Nevertheless these rules make no difference to who actually does the conveyancing; and the aforesaid provision in the Administration of Justice Act 1985, as well as the advertisements in every issue of the Law Society's Gazette, acknowledge the fact (if any acknowledgement is needed) that conveyancing is done, and will continue to be done, by unqualified clerks totally unsupervised by their solicitor employers.

Over the years the Law Society has been diligent in prosecuting unqualified conveyancers for infringing the Solicitors Act, on the grounds that, being unqualified, they are a danger to the public. But as long as those unqualified conveyancers are employed by someone with the magic qualification of 'solicitor', the public is apparently protected in some mysterious way. Indeed the Law Society's utterances on the subject have the consistency of a chameleon. Only a solicitor has the knowledge and experience to make sure your conveyance is foolproof; although of course it makes sense for the solicitor to entrust some of the simpler tasks to his clerk to keep costs down; in fact the clerk can do all the work himself as long as he is *supervised* by a solicitor; or at any rate as long as he works in a solicitor's office; or at any rate as long as he works in an office which is *visited* by a solicitor every day. In fact what the Law Society really says is that conveyancing can be done by any unqualified Joe Soap, as long as the *profits* go to a solicitor.

*

On the other hand, whether a solicitor *is* any better qualified to do conveyancing than an unqualified clerk is a debatable point. To qualify as a solicitor a person has to do two things: be apprenticed or 'articled' to a solicitor for two years, if he holds a degree (five years if he doesn't), and pass the Solicitors' Final examination. During his apprenticeship the 'articled clerk' is supposed to receive appropriate instruction and experience, but whether he gets any of either commodity is very much a matter of chance. Some firms do their best and give their articled clerks reasonable work and instruction; other firms treat them merely as cheap messenger boys; others find them a desk in some odd corner and then ignore them altogether. The Law Society exercises no supervision as to what 'training' the clerk is getting. To pass the Final examination the clerk attends a concentrated six month course of lectures and note-taking, amassing a vast quantity of facts which hopefully he will regurgitate in the examination hall. When I took it, only one *half* out of seven papers was devoted to conveyancing which – as with most exams – was concerned with academic rather than practical matters. Now two papers out of nine are on conveyancing. Thus although a solicitor will have learnt something about the theory of conveyancing, he need not, and often does not, know anything about practical conveyancing. Neither need he ever have done a conveyance. Therefore it would seem that he is no better qualified to do conveyancing than anyone else of average intelligence and education.

Exactly what qualifications *are* needed for the job is difficult to say because (as we saw in the first chapter) no-one seems to know what conveyancing should entail. However, if one accepts that an unqualified solicitor's clerk is likely to possess the same acumen as a bank clerk or post office clerk, then conveyancing as it is actually carried out up and down the country is within the capabilities of the average bank clerk or post office clerk. Michael Zander, I think, puts it quite fairly in his book *Lawyers and the Public Interest*: 'Occasionally a difficult problem poses itself, but the work is well within the capacity of the average school leaver with a couple of 'O' levels, who has undergone a period of training on the job.'

But let my reader judge for himself whether Mr. Zander is doing solicitors' clerks or school leavers an injustice, from the account of what a solicitor or a solicitor's clerk actually does in a conveyancing transaction, which now follows.

3

The steps of
the conveyancing
ritual dance

Although no one, whether spokesman for the profession or outsider, seems able to tell us exactly what a conveyancing solicitor's job is, or what he thinks it is, I can say what a solicitor or his clerk actually *does* in a conveyancing transaction. And as there is not a great deal of difference from the legal point of view between one house and the next, and the same printed forms are in general use up and down the country, I can describe the various processes with some precision. To do so, however, presents a certain difficulty. If I oversimplify the description as some people do ('a purchaser's solicitor sends a form to the local Council and another form to the vendor's solicitor, then he exchanges contracts' etc.), I will rightly be accused of bending the facts to suit my argument. If, on the other hand, I give a reasonably full description of the work, it may appear forbidding to the lay reader, as it will be an unfamiliar subject. And if the overall impression is that conveyancing is a difficult business, one of my main arguments is lost. This can't be helped, but I ask my reader to take this chapter slowly. Remember, in this chapter I am *not* trying to instruct you how do your conveyancing, but merely to outline the processes involved. Remember also that although a description of an unfamiliar process may seem complicated, it does not mean that the process itself is complicated. For instance, a description of wiring a three pin plug would probably seem complicated to someone who had never previously done such a thing.

In order that my reader may be able the better to understand my description, I first offer him a few nuggets of information:

(1) A conveyance is a *deed*, that is a document which is signed by the vendor (with a red disc after his signature), which conveys an unregistered house from vendor to purchaser. The deeds in the case of an unregistered house will consist of a series of such conveyances between previous owners, going back at least fifteen years. In the case of a registered house there are no deeds as such; there is just a single land certificate, and instead of a conveyance the vendor signs a simple land registry form transferring the house to the purchaser.

(2) It is important to grasp the difference between 'registered' and 'unregistered' houses. All houses in England and Wales fall into one or other category. The *unregistered* system is the traditional one whereby the vendor proves his ownership by producing a series of deeds tracing ownership to himself from someone who owned the house many years ago. This system has been superseded in most built-up areas by the *registered* system. Where it applies, the Land Registry, a central government department, issues a land certificate for each house; so that instead of a pile of deeds the vendor has a single land certificate (usually consisting of two or three pages and a plan), which bears his name as the current owner, and a note of any mortgages and restrictive covenants. The registered system now covers about three-quarters of all houses in England and Wales; and where it applies the conveyancer's job – whether professional or D.I.Y. – is much simpler.

(3) A conveyancing transaction is in two stages, the *first* stage being up to exchange of contracts. A contract for this purpose is a written document of which there will be two identical copies. Exchange of contracts is when the vendor's solicitor, having received the purchaser's signed contract, posts to the purchaser's solicitor the vendor's signed contract; so that the purchaser's solicitor holds a contract signed by the vendor, and vice versa. At that moment (the moment of the last posting) vendor and purchaser are contractually bound to each other. Before that moment either is free to call the deal off without giving any reason.

The *second* stage is from exchange of contracts to completion.

Completion is when the purchase price is handed over in exchange for the deeds or land certificate, and the purchaser becomes the legal owner of the house. It generally takes place four weeks after exchange, whether the house is registered or not.

(4) *Freehold* means the owner owns the property absolutely, as distinct from *leasehold* which means that he owns it only for a stated number of years. Houses are usually freehold, whereas flats are always leasehold. For the moment I am not concerned with leaseholds but only with secondhand freehold houses.

Although the term 'solicitor' will be used throughout, remember it will generally be his clerk who is doing the work. For convenience I describe the vendor's and purchaser's mortgagee as a *building society*, although of course it may be a bank or other lender.

So off we go. The parties first instruct their respective solicitors after the initial agreement (usually verbal) has been reached that the vendor will sell his house to the purchaser for a stated sum; and it is the vendor's solicitor who takes the first step, which is preparing the draft contract (the document which the parties will eventually sign and exchange). To do this he needs to see the deeds or, if the house is registered, the land certificate. If there is no mortgage on the house the vendor himself will be holding the deeds (or land certificate), which he will hand to his solicitor. Normally, however, they will be held by the vendor's building society. In such case, if the house is registered, the vendor's solicitor can get an *official copy* of the land certificate by post direct from the Land Registry.* If unregistered, the vendor's building society has either to instruct a local solicitor, to whom it will send the deeds, and to whose office the vendor's solicitor will repair to extract the necessary information; or the vendor's building society will instruct the vendor's solicitor to act for it, and will send him the deeds (against his undertaking not to part with them without remitting the mortgage money outstanding).

Once the vendor's solicitor has a sight of the deeds, or copy of the land certificate, it is but a few minutes work to fill in the

---

* Actually it will be an official copy of the *register*, but for the moment assume that a copy of the register is the same thing as a copy of the land certificate.

blank spaces on a contract form. The contract is usually typed
either on a 'National Conditions' or a 'Law Society Conditions'
form. Each embodies a mass of printed conditions. In fact it is
not necessary to use a form at all, as either set of conditions can
be incorporated in a contract typed on an ordinary sheet of
paper. Whichever form is used, or if no form is used, the
amount of typing will be approximately the same, viz. name
and address of vendor and purchaser; address of house being
sold; price – plus a few standard clauses, the most important
providing for the date of completion (at this stage left blank),
for the purchaser to pay a deposit on exchange of contracts,
and referring to any restrictive covenants appearing in the
deeds or land certificate. A complete contract is set out on
p. 150.

Having had the draft contract typed out, the vendor's
solicitor sends it (with a copy) to the purchaser's solicitor. At
the same time he also sends the copy of the land certificate
(which he will have obtained from the Land Registry) if the
house is registered, or a copy of any restrictive covenants and
the plan taken from the relevant conveyances, if unregistered.

When the purchaser's solicitor receives the draft contract,
he 'peruses' it. As every contract for the sale of a secondhand
freehold house will be in the same form, and contain the same
half dozen or so clauses, there will not be a great deal of
'perusing' to be done. Having 'perused' the draft contract, the
purchaser's solicitor does two things: (1) asks preliminary
enquiries of the vendor's solicitor; (2) makes a 'local search'
with the local Council. He asks his preliminary enquiries by
sending the vendor's solicitor a printed form of questions.
These questions cover such matters as ownership of boundary
fences, whether there have been any disputes with neighbours,
whether water and drainage are directly connected to the
mains, and so on. There is space for any additional enquiries
which the purchaser's solicitor feels are necessary (e.g. he may
ask some additional questions on the particular restrictive
covenants). In Chapter 1 we saw the sort of answers vendors'
solicitors traditionally give to these questions, and questions
and answers are examined in some detail in the next
chapter.

As to the second of the purchaser's solicitor's tasks, the local search is likewise made by sending a printed form – or rather two printed forms – to the appropriate local Council. One of these forms asks for details of any 'land charges' affecting the house. 'Land charges' cover a wide range of matters, but the two most likely to appear will be previous planning permissions and an order prohibiting smoke-producing fuel. The other form consists of a list of questions on such matters as whether the road is maintained by the Council, whether there are any 'notices' (e.g. dangerous structure or public nuisance notices), whether there are any proposals for road widening or compulsory purchase, and the like. These questions are usually answered by the Council attaching a standard printed form of *answers* to the form. Again, I examine the local search questionnaire in more detail in the next chapter.

Some weeks will elapse before the purchaser's solicitor receives the answers to his preliminary enquiry and local search forms. If these answers do not reveal anything untoward, then the purchaser's solicitor – who will previously have got his client to sign one copy of the contract and will have returned the other copy unsigned to the vendor's solicitor – is ready to exchange contracts, subject to two things. Firstly, if the purchaser needs a mortgage he must receive a written mortgage offer before exchange; secondly, if the purchaser is selling his own house simultaneously, his solicitor must be in a position to exchange contracts on the sale before he exchanges on the purchase – that is, he must have in his possession the *sale* contract signed by his client's *purchaser* before he can safely send off his client's signed contract on the purchase. Otherwise the purchaser could find he was committed to his purchase without having secured his sale.

It is the purchaser's solicitor who takes the first step in exchanging contracts, by sending the purchaser's signed contract to the vendor's solicitor. The vendor's solicitor completes the exchange by sending the vendor's signed contract to the purchaser's solicitor. Before doing so the vendor's solicitor will fill in the completion date in both parts of the contract (that is, the part signed by the purchaser which he has received, and the part signed by the vendor which he sends). This date will usually be four weeks from exchange, whether the house is registered or unregistered. Before contracts are exchanged the purchaser has to pay the deposit, usually 10% of the purchase price, either to the estate agents who arranged the sale, or to the vendor's solicitor.

Whereas before exchange of contracts the procedure is largely the same whether the house is registered or unregistered, after exchange it does vary to a certain extent. The public is generally told that the most important part of a purchaser's solicitor's job is to investigate the vendor's title deeds to make sure the vendor really owns the house he is selling. This view is faithfully reproduced by the Consumers' Association, in the passage quoted in Chapter 1 ('The main function of the buyer's solicitor in the business of buying a house is to enquire into the ownership – or title, as lawyers call it – of the seller.') When the house is *registered*, however, there is no investigating to be done. The purchaser's solicitor will have already been sent a copy of the vendor's land certificate, which will show the vendor's name in the appropriate space, and that's that. After exchange of contracts, the purchaser's solicitor merely has to fill in a simple land registry transfer form (address and land registry number of house, price, name and address of vendor and purchaser), and send it to the vendor's solicitor to get it signed by the vendor in readiness for completion. It is this form which, when signed and handed over to the purchaser, legally transfers the house to him.

If the house is *unregistered*, after exchange of contracts the vendor's solicitor sends the purchaser's solicitor copies of the two or three conveyances tracing the ownership of the house from a person who owned it at least fifteen years ago, to the present vendor (or, if the vendor has himself owned the house for fifteen years or more, the single conveyance to the vendor). When the purchaser's solicitor has looked through the copy conveyances, he sends the vendor's solicitor 'requisitions on title', that is, a list of questions on points he thinks need clarifying or on which he wants further information. If the title is straightforward, e.g. there are just a few simple conveyances:

A to B, B to C, C to vendor, the requisitions will consist of unexceptionable statements of the obvious like 'vacant possession must be given on completion', and 'the existing mortgage must be discharged on completion'. There is in fact a printed form containing these and similar 'requisitions'. If the title is more complicated (for instance if there has been a sale off from a larger area of land) some solicitors, as with preliminary enquiries, will ask strings of additional questions, while others will be content merely with those on the printed form. As we shall see in the next chapter, whichever course is adopted will make little difference to the information gained.

At the same time as he sends his 'requisitions', the purchaser's solicitor also sends the draft conveyance (the document which, when signed by the vendor and handed over, legally transfers an unregistered house to the purchaser). It is not a complicated document in the case of a secondhand house, but a much travelled one. It initially goes from purchaser's solicitor who prepares it, to vendor's solicitor; vendor's solicitor 'approves' it and returns it to purchaser's solicitor; purchaser's solicitor has it typed out again on stiffer paper and sends it back to vendor's solicitor; vendor's solicitor sends it to vendor to sign and return in readiness for completion.

If, as is usually the case, the purchaser is getting a mortgage, the purchaser's solicitor has to send the various documents (preliminary enquiry and local search forms with replies, contract, copy land certificate or previous conveyances) to the purchaser's *building society's solicitor* for him to check. This is because the building society does not rely on the purchaser's solicitor, but employs its own solicitor to duplicate the work. In due course the building society's solicitor will send the purchaser's solicitor a printed form of mortgage for the purchaser to sign. Alternatively, the building society may appoint the purchaser's solicitor to act on its behalf. This does not mean that the society is relying on the purchaser's solicitor as such: it is still employing its own solicitor who happens to be the same person as the purchaser's solicitor – who therefore acts in a dual capacity (and receives two lots of fees).

The vendor's solicitor is now holding the land registry transfer form, or fair copy of the conveyance, signed by the vendor; any 'requisitions on title' have been answered by the vendor's solicitor; the purchaser's solicitor has received the mortgage form from the building society's solicitor, which the purchaser has signed. The parties are now ready to complete, subject to the purchaser's solicitor making a pre-completion *search*. If the house is registered, this search is made by sending a form to the Land Registry. Provided this form is returned stamped with the words: 'Since [the date of the copy of the land certificate] no adverse entry has been made thereon', the purchaser's solicitor knows that the official copy of the land certificate which he was initially sent is still up to date, and that the vendor has not entered into any subsequent transaction e.g. a second mortgage. If the house is unregistered, the pre-completion search is made by sending a form to the Land Charges registry. This has nothing to do with the Land Registry, but is a separate register of various interests which someone other than the owner can have in a house – e.g. the vendor's wife might have registered an interest in the house as the matrimonial home, or a finance company might have registered an interest in it as security for a second mortgage. The purchaser's solicitor sends this form to ensure that no-one has registered such an interest. In the rare case of the form being returned showing that someone *had* registered an interest, it would have to be cleared before completion could take place – e.g. a second mortgage would be cleared by paying off the lender out of the purchase price, and getting his receipt.

The procedure on completion is basically the same as for any sale – that is, the purchase price is handed over in exchange for the thing being bought, in this case the house represented by the deeds (i.e. previous conveyances *or* land certificate). It is, however, a little more complicated because whereas in an ordinary sale there is a meeting between vendor and purchaser (or their representatives), in the sale of a house subject to a mortgage, which is being purchased with the aid of another mortgage, two extra bodies are involved: the vendor's building society, whose solicitor will be holding the deeds, which he will release only on being paid all money outstanding under the existing mortgage; and the purchaser's building society, whose solicitor will be contributing part of the purchase price, which he will hand over only on getting the deeds, and the new mortgage signed by the purchaser.

Completion takes place at the office of the vendor's building society's solicitor.* To this office the respective solicitors for vendor, purchaser, and purchaser's building society repair, bearing their respective goodies. Purchaser's building society's solicitor brings bank draft for the mortgage advance; purchaser's solicitor brings further bank draft to make up the total purchase price (having obtained it from the purchaser), and signed mortgage; vendor's solicitor brings signed conveyance or transfer. The purchase price in the hands of the purchaser's and purchaser's building society's solicitors will have been split into a bank draft for the sum required to pay off the vendor's mortgage – notification of which figure will have been previously given – and a separate bank draft for the balance.

After the flurry of documents and bank drafts being exchanged has subsided, vendor's building society's solicitor is left holding a bank draft for the sum needed to pay off the vendor's mortgage; vendor's solicitor is left holding a bank draft for the balance of the sale price; purchaser's building society's solicitor now holds the deeds (relinquished by vendor's building society whose mortgage is paid off), plus conveyance or transfer signed by vendor, and new mortgage signed by purchaser. If the keys are held by estate agents, the vendor's solicitor will authorise their release (by telephone) to the purchaser, and all parties will go away happy. As for the purchaser, so relieved will he be on opening the front door of his new house and finding the door frame does not collapse on his head, that he will probably write his solicitor a fulsome letter of thanks. One thing however will have been left

---

* It is easier to understand the procedure if you regard the vendor's building society's solicitor and the vendor's solicitor as separate people, although in practice the vendor's building society will often instruct the vendor's solicitor to act for it – in which case he acts in a *dual* capacity.

outstanding: the vendor's building society will not have actually sealed the receipt discharging its mortgage. Instead, its solicitor will give the purchaser's solicitor a two-line letter *undertaking* to pay off the mortgage and send this receipt when he receives it from the vendor's building society.

4

What has the solicitor achieved by the ritual dance?

(Part I)

In the last chapter I described the various steps the solicitors for vendor and purchaser take from first to last, in a sale and purchase of a secondhand freehold house. In this chapter I examine what they will have *achieved* by having taken such steps.

They will have attended to the administrative and legal formalities involved – exchanging contracts, getting the house from vendor to purchaser, paying off the vendor's mortgage, getting the balance of the sale price to vendor. This part of the work is simple and easily defined. As we saw, the contract consists of name and address of vendor and purchaser, address of house, price, and half a dozen standard clauses; the land registry transfer form is typed out in a few minutes; if the house is unregistered, the conveyance is not much more complicated; discharging the vendor's mortgage entails getting a two-line undertaking from the building society's solicitor. Attending the completion appointment with the exact amount needed from the various sources (balance of sale price on purchaser's own house, mortgage advance, balance from purchaser) is a little frightening, but that is only because the various bank drafts are in tens of thousands. If someone was selling his car which was subject to a hire purchase agreement, and buying a new one partly with the aid of another H.P. agreement, the arithmetical processes would be the same.

But what *else* will the solicitors have achieved, or rather – as the vendor's solicitor's only task is to get the sale price to his

client – what else will the *purchaser's* solicitor have achieved?
First of all, what else does he *aim* to achieve? As I have
indicated, solicitors are chary of defining their terms of
reference, but we can say that a purchaser's solicitor would see
his work (other than the administrative formalities mentioned
above) as falling into two parts: firstly, up to exchange of
contracts, to check that the property has no quasi-legal defects
(see p. 2 for a definition of this phrase); secondly, after exchange of contracts, to make sure that the vendor has the right
to sell the property, and that it is free from 'encumbrances'.
In Part I of this chapter, I examine the first; in Part II, the
second.

We saw in the last chapter that the purchaser's solicitor
checks that the property has no quasi-legal defects in two
ways: a preliminary enquiries form sent to the vendor's
solicitor, and two local search forms sent to the local
Council.

Preliminary Enquiries

For the last half century or more a printed form of
preliminary enquiries has been used by purchasers' solicitors.
Every now and again the form is revised, a question added
here, a question omitted there. Sometimes the revisions are
more drastic – for instance the form in use up to July 1974 had
twenty-three questions on the subject of 'planning', whereas
the current form has only eight. The pre-July 1974 form had a
section dealing with building defects, which the current form
omits altogether.

Both current and previous forms run to three closely
printed pages – a feat achieved by taking a simple question, and
constructing thereon a superstructure of academic permu-
tations and sub-questions, wrapped up in tortuous verbiage,
so the whole is more redolent of 19th century Chancery
pleadings than requests for straightforward information.

For example, instead of simply asking: 'Is any work which
has been done to the property still covered by a guarantee?'
the question on the form reads: *'Please supply a copy of any of the
following of which the purchaser is to have the benefit: agreement,
covenant, guarantee, warranty, bond, certificate, indemnity and
insurance policy, relating to any of the following matters: the construction*

of the property, or any part of it, or of any building of which it forms part;
any repair or replacement of, or treatment or improvement to the fabric of
the property; the maintenance of any access way; the construction costs of
any road (including lighting, drainage and crossovers) to which the
property fronts, and the charges for adopting any such road as
maintainable at the public expense; a defective title; breach of any
restrictive covenant.'

Similarly, whether there are eight or eighty questions on
planning, there is only one question which a vendor of a
secondhand house can sensibly be asked: Have you or your
predecessor made any additions or alterations requiring
planning permission or building regulations approval? To ask
about a house in a residential area: 'When did the present use
of the property commence?' 'Has this use been continuous
since it commenced?' 'Have any other building, engineering,
mining or other operations been carried out in, on, over, or
under the property?', as the current form does, is little short of
fatuous.

In fact, in the case of a secondhand house being sold with
vacant possession, there are only a dozen or so questions of a
quasi-legal nature which a vendor can answer, and which
therefore a purchaser's solicitor can reasonably ask him: (1) Is
the water supply direct from the mains? (2) Are the boundary
fences firmly in position? (3) Does the position of the
boundary fences coincide with the plan (whether attached to
the deeds or the land certificate)? (4) Is a right of way needed
over a drive or track at the side or rear (usually to get to the
garage)? (5) Does a neighbour or anyone else use a right of way
over the land which goes with the house? (6) What fittings and
other items are included in the sale, and conversely, what
fixtures if any is the vendor going to remove? (7) Is the
drainage direct to the mains sewer? If not, what is the route of
the drain? (8) Are there any drains or pipes which serve any
other house, running under the house or land being sold?
(9) Has the vendor, or his predecessor, made any additions or
alterations requiring planning permission, or building regulations approval? (10) Has the vendor received any Notices, or
had any disputes? (11) Is any work which has been done to the
property still covered by a guarantee; and if the house is less
than ten years old, is there a National House-Building

Council's warranty in force? (12) Are there any periodical outgoings other than rates?

Of these twelve questions, the first six would be conclusively answered by the purchaser's solicitor making a quick inspection of the house itself. An inspection would also be the best way of getting answers to questions (7), (8) and (9), although such answers would *not* be conclusive.

But inspecting the house his client is buying is something the purchaser's solicitor does not reckon to do. It may be that here and there a solicitor has inspected the house being bought, but in my twenty years of being employed by, and working with, conveyancing solicitors, I have never known one actually do so. Two large estate agents in south-east London, from whom I collected keys with a view to carrying out such an inspection, said that they had never heard of a solicitor doing such a thing before. The Law Society's conveyancing expert (whom I asked) confirmed that the Law Society would not expect a solicitor to inspect 'in the ordinary course of things', and indeed the Law Society has expressed its official opinion that 'A personal inspection of the property is not as a rule necessary.' (*Law Society's Digest* Opinion No. 127.) Moreover, the Solicitors' Law Stationery Society, which is the profession's official publisher, has published three books: *Practical Conveyancing*, *Checklists for Solicitors*, and *Practice and Procedure of Conveyancing*, in which the respective authors describe the various steps they consider a purchaser's solicitor should take. In none of them is there any suggestion that a purchaser's solicitor should – or even that he profitably might – inspect the house his client is buying. Any information the purchaser's solicitor may elicit about the house will therefore be contained exclusively in the answers to his preliminary enquiry form and his local search forms.

The astute reader will at once realise the absurdity of the purchaser's solicitor relying on answers to a printed form of questions – even if those questions were relevant and properly drafted – rather than actually checking the points himself. Firstly, if the vendor gives a wrong answer, it will be discovered only after completion, that is after the money will have been paid over. Secondly, the form incorporates a headnote stating that the accuracy of the answers 'is not guaranteed'. Thirdly, the vendor himself may not know, or may not have appreciated, the significance of certain things; e.g. the vendor may never have opened up a manhole and seen that someone else's drain runs under his garden, or having got his neighbour's verbal consent to share a driveway, he may not realise he has no legal right to do so.

This trio of disadvantages would be enough to make the form of preliminary enquiries practically useless, but there is a fourth which ensures that in most cases it is *completely* useless. This is that the vendor's solicitor's chief concern in answering the questions is to do so in such a manner as will give away no information at all. This he does by employing a series of time-honoured rhythmic inanities – 'the deeds are silent, but inspection may reveal', 'we know of none, but the property is sold subject to any there may be', 'please rely on inspection', 'this question is too wide to permit a specific reply', 'please search', 'we believe the usual services are connected but please rely on surveyor's report/inspection for the route of the pipes', and so on. These replies have become so standard that they are universally accepted by purchasers' solicitors – as indeed they were accepted by our friend Matthew Seaton. Occasionally a newly qualified solicitor may try to insist on proper answers to his questions, but he soon gives up, realising it is easier to throw the onus back onto his client than engage in a futile correspondence.

The advantage from the vendor's solicitor's point of view of replying to the questions in this fashion is obvious. He does not have to go to the trouble of consulting with his client over the answers (or if he does so, it need only be in the most cursory manner); still less does he have to look at the house itself. He merely has to spend a few moments dictating the standard answers to his secretary, happy in the knowledge that there will be no comeback either on him or his client.

Moreover, he is encouraged to do so by the fact that even the valid questions on the form are wrapped up in such obscure verbiage that their meaning is not readily apparent, either to questioner or questioned. Consider the following typical example: *'Is the vendor aware of any rights or informal arrangements specifically affecting the property, other than any disclosed*

in the draft contract or immediately apparent on inspection, which are
exercisable by virtue of an easement, grant, wayleave, licence, consent,
agreement relating to an ancient monument or land near it, or otherwise
or which are in the nature of public or common rights?' As an example
of woolly thinking leading to confused drafting, this would be
difficult to surpass. Rather than ask himself what sort of
'rights' there might be affecting a house, the draftsman takes
refuge in vagueness and comprehensiveness. What are
'informal arrangements affecting the property'? Who decides
whether anything is 'immediately apparent on inspection',
and what criteria does he employ to decide it? Do 'rights
affecting the property' mean rights used by the owners of *other*
properties over *this* property, or are they rights used by the
owner of *this* property over *other* properties, or both? What is
the difference between 'grant' 'licence' and 'consent', or
'public' and 'common'? What is a wayleave, and how – and
why – did ancient monuments get into it? The best way of
getting a useless answer is to ask an obscurely worded
question. The vendor's solicitor is unlikely to go to the trouble
of unravelling its meaning and presenting it in paraphrased
form to his client, when he can simply tell his secretary to type
in one of the stock replies, the most popular for this particular
question being: 'No, but the property is sold subject to any
there might be' – which answer, if it means anything, means
'No, but there might be'. If the question was reworded 'Are
there any drains or pipes which serve any other house,
running under the house or land being sold?', and if all the
other questions were similarly reworded, then the vendor's
solicitor could merely send the resulting questionnaire
containing a dozen or so easily understood questions to his
client to fill in the answers. But then, of course, the art of
conveyancing would lose something of its mystery.

Again, because the form is padded out with so many
irrelevant questions, the vendor's solicitor is more likely to
sidestep the valid ones. Thus the question asking whether the
water (and other services) come to the property direct from the
mains is traditionally answered: 'We believe the usual services
are connected but please rely on surveyor's report/inspection
for the route of the pipes', which answer means: 'the property
is connected to a water mains in as much as when you turn on

a tap, water comes out of it; but I do not know, and I am certainly not going to find out, whether it comes direct from the mains, and neither am I going to take the trouble of asking the vendor'. In appendix 3 I reproduce the current preliminary enquiries form, together with typical answers.

Now in the normal course of things it will not matter that the purchaser's solicitor will not have inspected the house, and will have got useless answers to his preliminary enquiries, because in the vast majority of secondhand houses, be they Queen Anne mansions in Hampstead or terraced cottages in Llandudno, there is nothing of any consequence for a solicitor to find out anyway. Most solicitors will of course disagree. What about the hundred and one things a solicitor has to check? What about all those traps lying in wait for the unwary purchaser – all those cross-covenants, agreements relating to ancient monuments, and overhead rights of aeroplanes? Theoretically, it is true, a house *can* be subject to all sorts of complicated rights and covenants; in practice, however, there are seldom more rights connected with a house than with a cigarette lighter. Let's look at it for a moment not from the viewpoint of the frightened purchaser clutching his life's savings in his clammy hands, but of the vendor selling his perfectly ordinary house in which he will have lived without any sort of legal adventure for the past three to eight years. Let my gentle reader perhaps consider for a moment his own house, assuming he is so fortunate as to have one. Your house fronts onto an ordinary suburban road; when you turn on a tap, water comes out of it, and you assume it comes from the mains somewhere under the pavement; when you depress the lever on your W.C. cistern the waste products disappear, you assume, into the main sewer; unlike Miss Betsy Trotwood's, no-one has ever tried to drive donkeys across *your* front lawn. And when you come to *sell* your house, it will not really matter whether your purchaser's solicitor asks your solicitor two or two hundred questions – or indeed whether he asks him any questions at all.

But just once in a way a house *does* have a quasi-legal defect; and here our legal eagle – treating the house, as he does, as an abstract concept on which to pivot his time-honoured procedures, rather than a physical thing to look at – is liable to come unstuck.

Solicitor A acted for a client who bought a country cottage. Shortly after moving in, the client received a curt demand from the neighbouring farmer, across whose land ran the water pipe supplying the cottage, for £100 a year to continue the arrangement instead of the £5 a year he had hitherto levied. A had not found out that the house his client was buying did not have a water supply direct from the mains. Of course he hadn't, since he had merely submitted the standard form of preliminary enquiries and received the standard replies. Even if the question asking whether the water supply came direct from the mains had received an unequivocal affirmative (which it never does), it would not have helped because of the headnote that the accuracy of the replies 'is not guaranteed'. Even if A had obtained a written warranty from the vendor that the water supply came direct from the mains, it *still* would not have helped, because the client (who would discover the defect only after completion) would then merely have a useless* right of action against the vendor.

It is of course exceedingly rare for a house not to have a direct water supply, but I'll warrant that when it *does* occur, the purchaser's solicitor will *not* find it out. I am privileged to live on one of the few unmade roads in London, which has the added distinction of having no water mains under it. This latter detail escaped the notice of solicitor B, who acted for the developer who bought the land on which my house was built; as it has escaped the notice of solicitor C, who acted for a developer who has bought a large area of land adjoining my house. In my case the problem was resolved by a neighbour generously granting a right to lay a pipe under his garden. How it will be resolved by the adjoining developer, who is trying to build six town houses, remains to be seen.

Solicitor D acted for a purchaser who, after moving in, planted some rose bushes against the garden fence. Shortly afterwards they all died from, it transpired, a liberal application of weedkiller dispensed over the fence by the

---

* Why useless? Because the vendor will be careful not to divulge his new address. In any case it is one thing to have a valid action; it is a totally different thing to *enforce* it.

neighbour – an eccentric old lady who claimed it was *her* fence and that therefore any plant touching it was a trespass. In fact there had been a long-standing feud over this and other matters between the neighbour and the vendor, culminating in both parties taking out cross-summonses for assault in the local Magistrates' Court: but of course *D* – who had submitted the standard preliminary enquiry form, and received the standard replies – had not found this out. An unreasonable neighbour is probably the commonest quasi-legal defect of a house. It sometimes happens that someone moves house *because* of his neighbour – in which case he would hardly disclose this fact to his solicitor (even if asked), and so lose the sale.

Solicitor *E* acted for a client who bought a house with a garage built subsequently by the vendor. To drive his car into the garage the vendor had needed to share his neighbour's driveway, for which the neighbour gave verbal consent. The garage is now useless (except as a storeroom), because the neighbour has since sold his house to someone who has withdrawn the consent. A brief inspection of the property would have revealed the need to use part of the neighbour's drive, but of course *E* never inspected it. This is probably the second most common quasi-legal defect of a house. Typically the preliminary enquiry form, while asking about agreements relating to ancient monuments, does not even cover the point.

The above examples are within my personal knowledge. For my last I go to a former President of the Law Society, no less. I previously recounted how on 'It's Your Line' the President warned a lady, who had done her own conveyancing, how unwise she had been to do without a solicitor. The presenter, Robin Day, then asked him to give an example of what *could* have gone wrong. The example Sir Desmond Heap gave was of a *solicitor* (Mr. *F*) who had failed to find out that the property his client was buying had a neighbour's drain running under it; so the client, who subsequently discovered this drain on trying to clear a site for a new garage, found he could not build the garage after all – as cogent an argument for using a solicitor for one's conveyancing as anyone could hope for.

The significant point is that solicitors *A B C D E* and *F* had *not* been negligent. They had duly followed the traditional practice of sending out a standard form of preliminary enquiries containing forty or fifty questions, and receiving standard replies. This procedure 'works' quite satisfactorily in the vast majority of cases, but does not 'work' in the exceptional case – that is to say, as long as there is no quasi-legal defect to find out about a house, nothing will go wrong; but in the exceptional case where there is, the chances are that it will.

Local search

The second tool whereby the purchaser's solicitor checks the house his client is buying, is the 'local search' form* which he sends to the local Council. The purchaser may think – as indeed he is led to think – that his solicitor will find out and warn him of all the things that 'they' might intend doing to ruin his new house, but in fact the local search is pretty well as useless as the preliminary enquiry rigmarole. First of all, practically all the questions on the local search form relate to the actual house being bought. Therefore it will not reveal any planning application which may have been made in respect of neighbouring or nearby property. Thus suppose one of the most attractive features about the house you are buying is that it adjoins an area of secluded woodland, which (unbeknown to you) has been acquired by a developer who has got planning permission to put up a housing estate in its place; or suppose a developer has bought the house next door and has put in an application to demolish it and erect a monstrous block of flats. The local search would not reveal either of these things.

Even if the local search was made more comprehensive to cover adjoining property, it would be of only limited use, as there would be nothing to prevent our developer putting in an application for such a development the day after the search, or the day after the purchaser moved in. This is an inevitable defect of owing a house anywhere, when you come to think of

---

* Actually (as mentioned on p. 39) there are *two* forms, but for convenience I refer to it here as a single form.

it. It's just that I suspect many people (including the Law Society's publicity agent) have not come to think of it.

Another defect of the local search is that it will reveal only such matters as have been *actually put on the register*, and not those which are still in 'committee' stage.

'Out of Court' (B.B.C.2, 21 January 1987) gave a good illustration of what can easily happen. A purchaser had bought his dream-house set in an extensive garden in Sussex – only to find, shortly after moving in, that a new major road was going to run through the garden. His solicitor had not warned him of this, because at the time he submitted his local search it was only a 'proposal' *and therefore was not noted on the Council's register*. The Times (21 June 1986) reported a similar case where a couple bought a house in Norfolk for £150,000. Two weeks after moving in they discovered that it was under threat of demolition, being in the path of a proposed new bypass. Again, no inkling of this had been revealed by their solicitor's local search. Said the Council's spokesman: 'we sympathise with the purchasers, but we are asked very specific questions on these forms which require specific answers, and there can't be any maybe's about it.'*

I have known of a purchaser who, on the first morning in his new house, found a circular on his doormat urging him to support the protest movement against a proposed trunk road which would disastrously affect his – and the neighbouring – properties. I have also known of cases where a proposal for a new road, and a proposal for a redevelopment scheme, were sufficiently advanced to be a blight on a whole area for several years, yet were *not* sufficiently advanced to be noted on the Council's register and so revealed by a solicitor's local search. In such cases, rather ironically, everyone will know about the blight *except* the purchaser and his solicitor, neither of whom will visit the Council offices.

When the local search forms are returned, the solicitor has to interpret the replies. Usually such replies are a simple

---

* Significantly, the burden of both the Times article, and the 'Out of Court' television item, was whether the local Councils in question had a *moral* duty to disclose what they knew about the proposed roads in their answers to the purchasers' solicitors' search form; not how much better off the respective purchasers would have been doing their own conveyancing and *personally calling* at the Council offices.

negative or affirmative (see appendix 4), and are therefore even more standard than those given to the preliminary enquiries. In fact most Councils give their replies by attaching a printed sheet of *answers* to the form, so the purchaser's solicitor merely has to run his eye down this sheet of answers; and if he sees no writing among the print, he will know the answers are 'standard' and his local search is 'clear'.

Of course, occasionally a question *does* receive an other than standard reply, but in that event all the solicitor can do is simply relay the information on to his client and leave him to decide whether he wants to proceed with his purchase in the knowledge, for example, that the Council is considering a comprehensive redevelopment at some distant date, or whatever the entry happens to be. Thus despite the fact that the local search form contains liberal references to obscure sounding Acts of Parliament, the layman is as capable as a solicitor of sending it to the Council offices and interpreting the replies – that is, provided he can read.

Therefore as regards the first of the purchaser's solicitor's tasks – checking that the property has no quasi-legal defects before his client is contractually bound to the purchase – the purchaser's solicitor's tools (preliminary enquiry and local search forms) are virtually useless; and in the exceptional case where the property *does* have a quasi-legal defect, the purchaser is far more likely to discover it by spending half an hour inspecting the property *himself*, and calling at the Council offices *himself*. The few things he should look for, and ask about, are set out more fully in Chapter 12.

4

What has the solicitor achieved by the ritual dance?

(Part II)

But, the solicitor might argue, finding out about such things as purport to be covered by preliminary enquiries and local searches is really an optional extra on our part; our main task is investigating the vendor's title, making sure he really owns the house, and that the purchaser is therefore paying his money to the right person. This, of course, is the advantage of keeping the solicitor's brief as ill-defined as possible. When, for example, solicitor A's client comes storming into the office to complain that his house has no water supply, A can always say that finding out about such matters as water mains is the *surveyor's* responsibility. As we have seen, there is even some doubt whether a purchaser's solicitor is *obliged* to make 'the customary searches and enquiries before contract.' (Emmet on Title, 15th ed. p. 2.)

Yet if a solicitor argues that his main task is investigating the vendor's title, he is on shaky ground, which is becoming ever more shaky as the areas covered by the alternative system of land registration are continually being extended. Three-quarters of all houses in England and Wales are now registered and, as previously mentioned, when the house is registered there is no investigation of the vendor's title to be done. By tradition, solicitors' charges are for 'investigating title and preparing and completing conveyance, including perusal and completion of contract.' Yet the occasions when a solicitor actually has to investigate the vendor's title, and prepare and complete the conveyance, are becoming fewer; whereas the occasions when he merely has to glance at the copy of the vendor's land certificate to check that the vendor's name is typed thereon, are forever increasing. Nevertheless, we can still profitably take a look at what solicitors claim is their most important and complicated task.

Investigating Title

If the house is unregistered, the vendor will have a set of deeds going back at least fifteen years. The way the purchaser's solicitor investigates the vendor's title is by inspecting copies of these deeds (which the vendor's solicitor sends him after exchange of contracts), and sending the vendor's solicitor a list of questions on any points on which he is not satisfied or on which he wants further information. This is the 'very technical and skilled' work referred to by Mr. Cockshutt in his book *The Services of a Solicitor*. It is this aspect which is 'extremely complex and demands a detailed knowledge of the law relating to the title to land' (Sanctuary, *Before you see a Solicitor*). Yet what the purchaser's solicitor does under this heading is an academic nonsense. I explain.

The purchaser's solicitor, especially if he is newly qualified, can convince himself he is doing a thorough job by asking a string of questions on the vendor's deeds, e.g. 'Who now holds the original of the 1963 conveyance?' 'Was a memorandum of the 1979 conveyance endorsed on the 1963 conveyance?' 'Please explain why the ordnance survey divisions of the later conveyance plan do not coincide with the earlier conveyance plan', and so on; but the only answers he will get will be variations of *I don't know*. This is partly because the vendor's solicitor will probably have no special knowledge of the vendor's title deeds, having seen them for the first time shortly after the vendor asked him to act on the sale. He will therefore be in no better position to answer any questions thereon than the purchaser's solicitor, and will have to improvise by giving what he hopes are intelligent and plausible replies. But it is chiefly because the unregistered conveyancing system, so far from being precise and scientific, is in fact exceedingly imprecise and haphazard. For example:

A. Houses are always conveyed by reference to a plan. This plan may be drawn on a conveyance fifty years old or more. It is almost invariably described in the conveyance as being 'for identification purposes only' – the exact significance of which phrase is obscure, but presumably means that the plan is not accurate – and in any case it is usually drawn so roughly, and on such a small scale, as to be useless in determining where the boundaries should be. Whereas this may not matter so much with town and suburban properties whose gardens are fenced (or if not the boundary line will usually be obvious), it is often a major source of dispute in the case of country properties, especially those having a large area of land, where the physical boundaries will often be marked by hedges, strands of rusty wire, or nothing at all. I have known of several neighbourly quarrels over such matters. In one case there was nothing on the land to show where the boundary should be, or even where it had been. Each party nailed up a length of wire where he thought the boundary should be, which the other promptly removed. A lawsuit was started but abandoned because of the impossibility of either party proving anything either way (two acres of land being represented on the conveyance plan by a rectangle some two inches by three inches). There must be thousands of similar cases. The initial reaction of someone threatened with a boundary dispute would be to look at his deeds, thinking not unnaturally that somewhere amongst them will be a carefully prepared plan showing who owns what. He would be wrong. Accurate plans showing the position of the boundaries of the land going with a house have no part in the conveyancing system, whether unregistered or registered.

B. As long as the house is at least fifteen years old there will be a series of original conveyances going back over this period, all exclusively relating to the house, and all to be handed over on completion. On the other hand, where a developer has built several houses on the same estate, the individual purchasers will *not* get the prior title deeds for the obvious reason that the developer will have only *one* set of deeds relating to his land, which he will need to keep until he has sold the last plot on the estate. In such cases the purchaser will merely get a conveyance to himself, and a typed summary or copy of the previous deeds on which some solicitor's clerk will have written 'examined with original at office of Messrs. Bloggs & Co. of such and such address, signed Moggs & Co. of such and such address'. When the purchaser comes to sell a few years later, this is all he will be able to give *his* purchaser. With what contempt would a solicitor refuse a vendor's title consisting of one original conveyance to the vendor, say five years old, and a typed summary of the previous deeds. Yet as long as this typed summary bears some scarcely legible formula scrawled by some anonymous clerk representing a possibly defunct firm of solicitors, the vendor's title has in some magical way been made completely acceptable.

C. The object of the houseowner holding a set of original title deeds going back over many years is to prove he owns the house, because only he (or his building society) will have possession of such deeds. However, if the deeds are retained by the vendor for the above reason, the only thing preventing the vendor either negligently or fraudulently selling the same house – or part of the garden – over again is a note of the sale, which the purchaser's solicitor will ask the vendor's solicitor to write on the conveyance to the vendor which the vendor retains. Thus if the vendor attempted to sell the same house – or land – over again, the second purchaser would be warned of the prior sale. At least, that is the theory. In practice this note is often stapled or pinned, so a purchaser's title may well depend on a scrap of paper attached by a staple or pin to a conveyance, as to whose whereabouts he has no control or even knowledge.

D. When an individual plot or house is sold off from a larger area, there will often be nothing on the plan of the individual plot to show that it is part of the larger area owned by the developer. For instance, the developer may have originally bought a large field, and the plan on the conveyance to him will consequently show just a field and not the various roads and houses subsequently built on it. In these cases it is the practice for the purchaser's solicitor to ask the vendor's solicitor to mark on the copy of such plan the position of the smaller plot being sold off, which the vendor's solicitor will do with a pencil cross.

Thus so far from being 'very technical and skilled', investigating the vendor's title turns on such things as a pencil cross, a scrap of paper attached by a pin which may or may not be still attached a year later, a few words scrawled by an anonymous clerk. And as to how much land goes with a house, or where the boundaries should be, the system does not claim to provide an answer, but in the event of dispute leaves the parties to fight it out as best they can.

The purchaser's solicitor can investigate the vendor's title till he's black in the face. He can ask as many precise questions or 'requisitions' as he likes. But he will not get any precise information, simply because there is no precise information to be had. 'Was a memorandum of the 1979 conveyance endorsed on the 1963 conveyance?' We assume it must have been. 'Who now holds the original of the 1963 conveyance?' We cannot say. 'Please confirm that the plot of land conveyed by the 1979 conveyance is wholly within the land conveyed by the 1963 conveyance.' We presume this to be the case; and so on. A good many solicitors come to realise the fatuity of asking such questions, and leave the tedious process entirely to the *building society's* solicitor to whom they will send the 'abstract' of the vendor's title without even looking at it themselves.

In fact Parliament itself has acknowledged the fatuity of the procedure, in that by the Law of Property Act 1969 it cut the period of thirty years, over which the vendor had to produce his previous title deeds, to fifteen years. Before this Act was passed the vendor traditionally had to show, and the purchaser's solicitor had to inspect, title deeds going back at least thirty years. Since the Act, the vendor's title starts with a conveyance at least fifteen years old. The purchaser's solicitor's task of investigating title has therefore been cut by half (without, curiously enough, any corresponding reduction of fees). Instead of having to inspect deeds going back at least thirty years, he now has to inspect deeds going back only fifteen years. Yet no one seems any the worse for this drastic measure. I have yet to hear of any purchaser suffering from any 'flaw' in his vendor's title as a result of his solicitor examining the title deeds covering only half the previously stipulated period. So what is the magic in the period of fifteen years? If the period can be satisfactorily cut from thirty years to fifteen years, why not cut it still further to ten or five? Or simply require the vendor to produce the actual conveyance to himself, possession being nine tenths of ownership, with such conveyance making up the remaining tenth?

I can imagine the shudder of horror which most solicitors would give at the prospect of their clients paying their life savings, without any show of investigating the vendor's title. Yet when it comes to the purchase of flats, solicitors appear to have no qualms in advising their clients to pay several hundred thousand pounds for a lease, without any investigation of the title of the person who *granted* that lease. Flats cannot be held for ever and ever (freehold) but only for a stated number of years (leasehold), albeit that number might be ninety-nine. The very expensive flats will normally be in the larger towns and will therefore be registered at the Land Registry. But whereas in the case of a freehold house the land certificate will bear a note *title absolute*, which means the Land Registry examined the title deeds before it issued the land certificate and guarantees that whoever is specified as the owner *is* the owner, the land certificates of most leasehold flats bear a note *good leasehold title*. This signifies that the Land Registry has *not* inspected the title deeds of the person who granted the lease, and does *not* guarantee that he had the right to grant such lease. Yet purchasers' solicitors and building societies' solicitors normally consider *good leasehold title* perfectly acceptable. Thus if you bought a leaky country cottage for £20,000 your solicitor would throw up his hands in dismay if you told him not to bother to investigate the vendor's title. That, he would insist, is the most important part of the job. If, on the other hand, you bought the lease of a flat in the fashionable part of town for £250,000, he would be quite happy for you to proceed, even though no-one has ever investigated or proposes to investigate the ownership of the person who granted that lease.

I think the procedure the purchaser's solicitor carries out (or pretends to carry out) of investigating the vendor's title is a nonsense. However, the building societies could put the question beyond peradventure. Building societies grant approximately three-quarters of a million mortgages a year, and each time a mortgage is granted on an unregistered house, the building society's solicitor investigates the vendor's title. How often has a building society refused to proceed with a mortgage on an unregistered house because its solicitor found a 'flaw' in the vendor's title? I put this simple question to three of the major building societies. The spokesman for Abbey National said they did not keep such statistics. Neither did the Woolwich Equitable. And although the Nationwide Building Society apparently specialises in fact-finding surveys and records, this particular question was one on which, for some reason, it had no records either.

When it comes to registered houses, although there is no such thing as investigating the vendor's title, purchasers' solicitors still solemnly submit, and vendors' solicitors still respectfully answer, the printed form of 'requisitions on title', a form which has strained to the limit its draftsman's capacity to think up unnecessary questions. However, submitting 'requisitions' is the most important part of a purchaser's solicitor's job, so 'requisitions' he submits.

While the purchaser's solicitor is meticulously carrying out this 'very technical and skilled work' which demands 'a detailed knowledge of the law relating to the title to land', his attitude to such mundane matters as getting the vendor's building society's receipt for the paid off mortgage, and checking that the house has been vacated, is more cavalier.

It is obvious that on completion the purchaser's solicitor, having paid over to the vendor's building society's solicitor the amount needed to discharge the vendor's mortgage, should get the receipt discharging this mortgage. Yet the purchaser's solicitor does not get this receipt. All he gets is a letter from the vendor's building society's solicitor *undertaking* to pay the building society the amount required to discharge the vendor's mortgage *and to send the receipt when he receives it from the building society.* Apparently it is beyond a building society's capabilities to seal the receipt and send it to its solicitor before completion, so it can be handed over in exchange for the outstanding mortgage money. The building society's solicitor has first to get the money, and only then will he submit the receipt to the building society to be sealed – which slovenly

practice is encouraged by the Law Society which recommends
that purchasers' solicitors accept it.* Whether there have been
any cases where the vendor's building society *hasn't* eventually
handed over the receipt for any reason (e.g. if its computer
coughed up the wrong redemption figure), and what would
happen in such a case, I don't know. What I do know is that
after completion, in the case of a *registered* house, the
purchaser's solicitor (or rather the purchaser's building
society's solicitor) will usually wait for the receipt *before* he
sends the documents to the Land Registry for the purchaser's
name to be put on the register. Meanwhile the protection of
the land registry search is often lost, since it expires thirty days
from the date it is issued. In fact according to a survey (see
p. 132) in over *half* the cases this protection is lost. In these
cases the purchaser could find himself bound by a second
mortgage fraudulently obtained by the vendor some weeks
after completion, because the register would still show the
vendor as the owner. (I explain this point in greater detail on
p. 200.)

As inconvenient as a concealed second mortgage would be
a concealed tenancy. 'Just suppose', hints the Law Society's
pamphlet darkly, 'the dear old lady knitting upstairs when you
looked over the place was not the owner's mother but a sitting
tenant . . . Your solicitor will be on the look out for problems
such as these.' But will he? It is true that the contract will
contain a clause providing for vacant possession to be given
(which is implied in any case), and it is true that the purchaser
would have a legal action against the vendor when he
discovered the knitting tenant. But as he would discover her
only *after* completion – when the money will have been paid
over – such an action would be valueless. The astute reader
will realise that the best way of safeguarding against such a
disaster is for completion to take place *at the house itself*, so the

---

* Law Society's Gazette, 22 October, 1986. Presumably the reason the Law Society
encourages this practice is: (a) it makes conveyancing just a little bit more
complicated than it need be; and (b) the vendor can be made to believe he *has to
have* a solicitor because only a *solicitor*'s undertaking to send this receipt will be
acceptable to the purchaser's solicitor. Indeed this was one of the reasons the
Royal Commission gave for retaining the solicitors' conveyancing monopoly –
that it was possible to pay over purchase money against a *solicitor's undertaking to
discharge a mortgage* (para. 21.25).

purchaser's solicitor can see for himself that the place is empty before handing over the money. But this is never done: completion takes place either at the vendor's building society solicitor's office, or else at the vendor's solicitor's office – either of which might be twenty or two hundred miles from the house. As completion does not take place at the house, the only other way for the solicitor to ensure the house is empty is for someone from his office to inspect it just before completion. But this is never done either, as the solicitor will certainly not send out *two* members of his staff – one to completion, the other to the house itself.

In the first part of this chapter we examined the first of the purchaser's solicitor's tasks – checking that the house has no quasi-legal defects before exchange of contracts. And we saw that because the solicitor neither inspects the house nor calls at the Council offices, but instead engages in a ritual exchange of printed forms, he finds out virtually nothing about the house; and that the few things which should be checked he leaves to chance. After exchange of contracts the solicitor carries out his second task – making sure the vendor sells the house free from 'encumbrances'. And here again we see that his academic rigmarole affords the purchaser no protection against the few hazards that might, exceptionally, arise. And here again we see that the purchaser is better equipped to do the job properly himself.

5 The solicitor leaves everything to chance

In the last chapter I touched on a few things which the purchaser's solicitor, despite an impeccable performance of the ritual dance, will have left to chance: whether the house has a direct mains water supply; whether its owner needs, but does not have, a right of way to the garage; whether there is a current dispute with a neighbour; whether there is an inconvenient sewage pipe from another house under the garden; whether planning permission has been granted for an unsightly development on the neighbouring land; whether there is a proposed new trunk road in the offing which is still in 'committee' stage, and therefore not on the Council's register; whether there is a concealed second mortgage; whether there is a concealed tenancy. But these are not the only things which our solicitor will leave to chance.

'The land your house is built on', according to the Law Society's pamphlet, Buying a House? See a Solicitor, 'can involve you in disputes over boundaries, fences, rights of way, rights of light, road charges or compulsory acquisitions . . . The price you pay and the amount you borrow are daunting enough. But suppose that the previous owner needed, but didn't bother to get, planning permission to build that nice new garage. The dear old lady, knitting upstairs when you looked over the place, was not the owner's mother but a sitting tenant. A new fly-over has been planned to pass within twenty yards of your front bedroom window. Those fields across the road are scheduled to become a sewage farm or part of a new airport . . . It is no good leaving these things to chance and then learning the hard way, either by expensive quarrels with neighbours or by *having to move out altogether at a thumping great loss. These are just some of the reasons why the FIRST PERSON you should go and see as soon as you think of buying a house is a solicitor.'* A powerful argument for using a solicitor, except that the pamphlet omits the rather relevant fact that leaving 'these things' – and several other equally important things – to chance is exactly what a *solicitor* will do. Let's take them one by one.

Boundaries

As we have seen, if the house is unregistered the boundaries will be shown by a plan almost invariably described as being 'for identification purposes only', attached to a possibly ancient conveyance. Accurate surveyor's plans (or even plans with clear measurements) have never been insisted upon; instead solicitors use rough sketch plans. If registered, the position is little better: the plan will be an extract of the ordnance survey map drawn on a scale of 1 to 1250, and will be subject to the proviso printed on every land certificate: 'the exact line of the boundary will be left undetermined'. Neither will be any use in resolving a boundary dispute. If such a dispute does arise, the parties will have to fight it out as best they can.

Fences

There is usually nothing in the deeds to show, and there is nothing a solicitor can do to find out, who owns what fence. Neither is there any obligation on the part of a houseowner to fence his land. Although sometimes there is a covenant to keep a certain fence in good repair, this cannot be enforced by the neighbouring owner. The preliminary enquiry form does include a question asking who owns the boundary fences, which is traditionally answered: 'the deeds are silent but inspection may reveal.'

Rights of way

After boundary disputes, the most common dispute is between neighbours having mutual rights of way over a single drive. Land Registry plans (being on such small scale) and conveyance plans (for identification purposes only) do not define such rights of way precisely; and again the solicitor does, and can do, nothing to prevent such a dispute arising. As he does not inspect the property, he does not even ascertain whether the houseowner *needs* any right of way over anyone else's land, or whether anyone else exercises a right of way over *his* land.

Rights of light

The right of a houseowner to a reasonable amount of light through his windows is not an automatic right; it has to be acquired, either by specific grant by the neighbouring landowner, or else by the light having been enjoyed for over twenty years. A specific grant is very unusual. Therefore if a house is less than twenty years old, a neighbour can erect an edifice on his own land to any height – even if it diminishes or completely cuts out light to the adjoining windows. The neighbour would have to get planning permission, which the local Council *might* refuse because of the resulting loss of light to an adjoining house; on the other hand, it might not. In any event *no* planning permission is needed for a wall or fence up to *two metres* high. Anyone owning a house less than twenty years old with windows overlooking his neighbour's land can rely only on the hope that the neighbour will not want to build so as to obstruct his light – or if the neighbour (who of course might be a property developer) does, that the Council will not let him. The purchaser's solicitor can do nothing to ensure that the supply of light to such a house will continue. All he can do is warn the purchaser of the danger; but as he never inspects the house (and is probably not aware of the point anyway), he does not even do that.

Road charges

It is true that the local search submitted by a purchaser's solicitor will show whether the road abutting the property is or is not maintained by the Council – as would a few seconds telephone call. Only if a road or track is *not* maintained by the Council will any question of road charges arise, and it will arise only if and when the Council decides to take over the road: that is, if the Council converts an unmade road or track into a standard road, it will charge the frontagers proportionately. The vast majority of roads fronting houses are, of course, standard roads already maintained by the Council, whereas most pathways at the rear or side will not be maintained by the Council. The question of road charges is usually relevant only when a new estate with new roads is being developed. But in the rare case of a secondhand house abutting a road which is *not* maintained by the Council, there is nothing a solicitor or anyone else can do to find out when the Council will take it over, or what road charges would be payable if the Council does take it over.

That nice new garage which needed but failed to get planning permission

This particular bogey is a favourite with solicitors. For instance, in a booklet by I.M. Wright, which runs to twelve and a half pages including copious illustrations, and is appropriately titled *The Compleat Conveyancer*, 'that nice new garage' has turned into 'that charming south wing' which you, the purchaser, are ordered to demolish because planning permission had not been obtained for its erection. Yet all a purchaser's solicitor does to prevent such a calamity is to ask the vendor's solicitor (by means of his preliminary enquiry form) whether during the past four years any buildings have been erected on the land being sold, or have been added to. A false answer to this question will be discovered only after completion, and probably would not even give the purchaser a right of action – which in any case would be useless. The local search will show whether there are any proceedings actually afoot in respect of a contravention of the Planning Acts; it will not show whether the vendor has done anything which might give rise to such proceedings in the future. Nor is there any way of getting the local Council officially to 'clear' a property.

In fact whether the house itself needed, but did not get, planning permission is something which the purchaser's solicitor leaves to chance – at any rate when a reasonably large estate of houses is built. When an estate of houses is built, the planning permission will read something like this (to quote from an actual permission): 'TAKE NOTICE that the XY Borough Council ... HAS GRANTED PERMISSION for development of land between River View Park and Imperial

Drive being residential development for AB Development Co.
Ltd. referred to in your application for permission dated —
reference —, subject to conditions specified hereunder.' All a
solicitor knows from this document is that some time ago
planning permission for some houses in the vicinity of the two
roads mentioned was given. Unless he takes the trouble to call
at the Council offices and look at the plan lodged with the
planning application (which of course he does not), he will not
know whether the house his client is buying is covered by that
permission or not.

Planning permissions are invariably subject to conditions,
but there is no follow-up by the planning authority to ensure
those conditions have been observed. The District Surveyor
will come crawling round to ensure the 'building regulations'
have been observed, but no-one from the planning department will.*

*The dear old lady knitting upstairs who turns out to be a sitting
tenant*
We've already seen how a purchaser's solicitor, unable to
have completion at the house, and unable or unwilling to
inspect the house just before completion, does nothing to
guard against this apparition. The house could be full of dear
old ladies for all the solicitor knows.

*The new fly-over planned to pass within 20 yards of your bedroom
window, on the other side of which is the proposed site for a sewage farm
or part of a new airport*
Almost half the Law Society's pamphlet is devoted to a trick
picture (rather cleverly done, incidentally) which, when half
opened, shows a man standing by his house surveying a
peaceful rural landscape. When fully opened, man and house
are unaltered, but the rustic scene has changed into a vast
urban complex featuring what seem to be several airports, a
fly-over in course of construction, a multi-storey car park, a

---

* Thus after I built my house I was plagued by the District Surveyor insisting (in the
middle of winter) that I had to have a vent cut in an outside door; otherwise an
adjoining lavatory would be next to 'unventilated living space'. But no-one from
the *planning department* ever came near to see whether the house had been built in
accordance with the plan.

power station, a railway line, and numerous high rise blocks. The caption of this ambitious tableau is 'your solicitor will warn you if this sort of thing could happen' – modified in later editions to 'your solicitor will always be on your side'. The caption over the original unspoilt landscape (in both editions) is 'your solicitor will safeguard your interests'. The message of the Law Society's pamphlet, both text and picture, is that employing a solicitor will ensure that one does not find oneself in the unenviable position of the gentleman in the picture.

In fact this is probably one of the most popular misconceptions of a solicitor's powers – that he will in some mysterious way protect a purchaser from major roads, fly-overs, airports, and all the nasty things that 'they' can do to ruin your environment. We have already seen that he does no such thing. Any information a solicitor may pick up about these matters will be contained in the replies to his search forms, and the value of these replies is negligible: firstly, because most of the questions relate to the property itself and *not* to the adjoining land; and secondly, because the search will *not* pick up proposals which haven't progressed sufficiently to be noted on the Council's registers. A third defect of the local search is that even when it *does* pick up a certain proposal, there will often be no means of knowing when it will be implemented; or if implemented, whether it will actually affect the house in question. The cumbersome processes by which local Councils exercise their powers is both helpful and unhelpful. It is helpful in that the houseowner generally has some five years grace or more from the time an idea for a new road or whatever is first mooted, to when the bulldozers actually start crashing in. It is unhelpful in that there are so many stages such a resolution has to go through, and so many uncertainties as to what will ultimately be carried out, that a whole area can be blighted for five to ten years – with no-one knowing, and no-one (whether solicitor or sausage manufacturer) being able to find out, exactly what will come, where it will come, if it will come, and when it will come.

Expensive quarrels with neighbours
The commonest cause of such a quarrel is a boundary dispute which, as we have seen, the conveyancing system does

nothing to ameliorate and everything to exacerbate. Neither will the purchaser's solicitor even find out whether there *is* a current dispute, since although the preliminary enquiry form does include a question on the point, a false answer will be discovered only after completion.

'Your solicitor will be acting for you alone' continues the Law Society's pamphlet *'when he explains which fixtures and fittings are included in the purchase price . . . '*

Just as the position of boundaries, and shared rights of way, are the most likely subjects of dispute between neighbours, the question of fixtures and fittings is the most likely subject of dispute between vendor and purchaser. Ideally there should be a comprehensive list of the fixtures and fittings which are included in the sale attached to the contract; and, ideally, completion should take place at the house itself, with the purchaser present to check the list before the money is handed over. The latter is never done; and as to the former, there is a list only if the vendor is including some particular and moderately expensive items. If the bargain struck between the parties contains no mention of fixtures and fittings, the written contract will probably be equally silent on the point, and the matter will be left to chance. In fact, there is no satisfactory definition of a *fixture*, which the vendor is obliged to leave as part of the house; and a *fitting* which, being a separate chattel, he may remove. The classic legal rulings – something is a fixture if it cannot be removed without damaging the fabric of the house, or if it is fixed in such a way as to indicate permanence – do not really help. In most houses there will be such things as bathroom cupboards, pelmets, light fittings, shelving, to which the parties may not have given much thought. However, the purchaser may get a nasty shock on moving in to find that every single item has been scrupulously removed. In such a case he would do well not to incur any further expense by telephoning his solicitor.

Even if the purchaser or his solicitor has been more businesslike and has insisted on a list of items being attached to the contract, it will merely give the purchaser a useless right of action if the vendor dishonestly removes some or all of them, as this will be discovered only *after* completion.

. . . and 'when he advises how insurance can best be handled'

He doesn't, of course. It is the purchaser's *building society* which always arranges insurance (thereby securing for itself agency commission), and collects the premium in monthly instalments added on to the monthly mortgage repayments. What the purchaser's solicitor should do, however, is to notify the building society or its solicitor the moment that contracts have been exchanged, for it is from that moment that the purchaser is at risk. In other words, if the house is burnt down after exchange of contracts but before completion, the purchaser still has to pay the full purchase price and cannot – in the absence of specific agreement – recover anything under the *vendor's* insurance. Most solicitors, I think, do *not* make sure that the purchaser's risk is covered by the building society from exchange of contracts, and most building societies do *not* automatically give insurance cover from acceptance of the mortgage offer but only from completion of the mortgage. If I am right, most purchasers are at risk without insurance for the month between exchange of contracts and completion.

'His own charge is in fact for making sure your home is truly yours when you move in'

The way a solicitor makes sure your home will be truly yours, if unregistered, is by examining the vendor's title deeds. Yet if I see an empty house and care to type out a fictitious conveyance to myself, backdate it fifteen years (making sure the price mentioned does not attract stamp duty) and sign the name of a fictitious vendor at the bottom, I will have perfect proof that I am the owner of that house, which a purchaser's solicitor is bound to accept. A solicitor does not check the genuineness of a previous vendor's signature. In any case, there is nothing to check it with. In fact, once one found someone who wanted to buy it, an empty house is easier to steal and resell than a typewriter; because whereas if I tried to sell a stolen typewriter a cagey purchaser might ask to see the receipt given when I bought it, and would be able to tell the difference between a shop receipt and a home made one, his solicitor would *not* be able to tell the difference between a genuine conveyance and one I typed out the day before completion. (Empty registered houses, incidentally, are even easier to steal and resell than unregistered ones.)

'He will help to make sure that you, the people moving into your old house, and the people moving out of your new house and so on, can all move at the appropriate time'

Obviously it is vital for both vendor and purchaser to know the date the transaction will be completed: the vendor has to know the exact day he will get the purchase price for his old house, and be able to buy and move into his new house, just as the purchaser has to know the exact day to load up his removal van and take possession of *his* new house. It is true that there will always be a date for completion in the contract which the parties will have agreed upon; but when that day arrives, either vendor or purchaser may calmly inform the other that for whatever reason, or for no reason, he is not able to complete that day, and moreover does not know when he *will* be able to. If this happens (and it sometimes does), the only thing the other party's solicitor can do, apart from spluttering over the telephone, is to serve a 'notice to complete' which gives the defaulting party a further *three weeks* to complete – and in the event of continuing default after that period, certain legal rights accrue to the party serving the notice. Indeed there is considerable learned legal argument as to whether the party anxious to complete can serve his notice immediately the day fixed for completion has passed, or whether he has to wait a 'reasonable time' before doing so. In fact a solicitor will always wait at least a week before serving a 'notice to complete', so the defaulting party has at least four weeks grace beyond the date in the contract before he has to complete.

So much for the Law Society's pamphlet, and all the things it is no good leaving to chance. But let's continue our list without its help.

The state of the property on completion

This is another frequent source of disaffection between purchaser and vendor, which again is the result of completion not taking place at the house, and the purchaser not being allowed possession until after the money is paid over. And once again the law governing the question is not much practical use: the vendor is not liable for accidental damage occurring between exchange of contracts and completion, unless such damage was caused by his negligence or recklessness. So if on taking possession the purchaser finds that the vendor has dumped ten years accumulated rubbish in the back garden, he should save the cost of a telephone call to his solicitor and put it towards hiring a refuse skip.

Drainage of the house

If the drain of a house does not lead directly into the mains sewer, but is a common drain going under neighbouring gardens, how is the purchaser to know what route it follows, and where it does join the mains? In particular, how is the purchaser to know that the necessary right to use this common drain was granted? The answer to the first question is that the local search will *not* show the route of a common drain nor where it joins the mains sewer, but will merely state 'drainage by combined operation'. The answer to the second question is that if the house is over twenty years old, its occupiers will presumably have been using the common drain the while, and will probably have acquired a legal right to do so. If the house is less than twenty years old, and was built as part of an estate, the owner will have been granted rights of drainage under the *developer's* adjoining land – but without such adjoining land, or the route of the drain, or where it joins the mains sewer, being specified.

Restrictive covenants

The origin of these, the most popular of the profession's bogeys, and how they are used to frighten the layman and send him scampering into a solicitor's office, is examined in a subsequent chapter. A restrictive covenant is a condition written into a conveyance or transfer when someone sells land and retains other adjoining land, whereby he controls the use of, or the buildings on, the land he *sells* for the benefit of the land or property he *retains*. Sometimes the conditions are short and simple (e.g. to use any building on the land only as a dwellinghouse and not for any business). Sometimes they drool on for several pages, with elaborate stipulations about building lines, permitted height, number of houses to the acre, and so on. The point about restrictive covenants is that once imposed, they are enforceable not only by and against the original vendor and purchaser, but by and against their successors; and they are still enforceable (provided certain conditions are fulfilled) even if the areas of land originally intended to take the benefit of, and be bound by, the covenants have been further split up. At least that is the theory. The land on which most houses are built is subject to restrictive covenants of some sort, imposed at some time or other. However, whether the covenants were imposed a year ago, or a hundred years ago, there will generally be no way of finding out *who* is entitled to enforce them, whether there is *anyone* still interested in enforcing them, and whether (if there is such a person) he *could* enforce them. Often there is even no means of finding out whether the covenants have been broken.

The confusion and vagueness arises from the fact that although the wording of the covenants will be slavishly copied out onto every land certificate, or referred to in every subsequent conveyance, the property which was intended to *benefit* from the covenants is rarely defined. Thus, O reader, if you look at your land certificate or title deeds, you may find that the land on which your house is built is subject to the common covenant not to erect any building without the consent of Bill Bloggins (who sold the land fifty years ago) or his successor in title. But as there is probably no way of ascertaining who or where Mr. Bloggins or his successor may be, you will not know – and when you come to sell your house your purchaser will not know – whether the covenant has been broken or not. Or you may find that the land on which your house is built is subject to a covenant not to build more than x number of houses to the acre, imposed when a large area of land, including yours, was sold fifty years ago. But as there will probably be nothing to show the original area of land on which this covenant was imposed, again there will be no means of ascertaining whether or not it has been broken.

Rights of drainage of other houses

Just as a house is often subject to covenants not to do this that or the other without the consent of Bill Bloggins or his successor, with no way of finding out who or where Bill Bloggins or his successor may be, so there is sometimes a note in a conveyance, or land certificate, that the land on which the house is built is subject to rights of drainage in favour of adjoining property. Once again, the adjoining property is rarely specified. Thus the householder knows that someone somewhere may have the right to run a drain under his land, but he will not be able to find out who. Neither will his solicitor.

Alternatively there may be a drain which serves some other house, already running under the garden of the house being bought – although no right to do so is noted in the deeds. This can be important if the purchaser is contemplating further building. Yet his solicitor will not find it out, as he does not inspect the property (in any case an inspection would not necessarily reveal it), and the existence of such a drain will not be revealed by the local search.

So there we are. All these things the purchaser's solicitor leaves to chance. In fact under the conveyancing system, as traditionally operated, practically *everything* of importance about a house, and its transfer from vendor to purchaser, is left to chance. The order I set out the various items followed the presumably fortuitous order in which they are mentioned in the Law Society's pamphlet, but they can be re-grouped under the following headings:

Things a purchaser's solicitor leaves to chance because he does not inspect the house before contracts are exchanged
1. Whether the house has a water supply direct from the mains.
2. Whether the boundary fences are firmly in position.
3. Whether such position coincides (roughly) with the plan on the deeds or land certificate.
4. Whether the owner of the house needs, but does not have, a right of way over anyone else's land – usually to get to his garage.
5. Whether a neighbour (or anyone else) uses a right of way over the land which goes with the house, there being no note thereof in the deeds or land certificate.

6. What fixtures, fittings and other items, if any, are included in the purchase price (although this point is sometimes covered by one of the parties making a list).
7. Whether the house drains directly into the mains sewer.*
8. Whether there is a drain which serves another house, running under the land.*
9. Whether the vendor has made any additions or alterations requiring planning permission or building regulations approval.*
10. Whether there are any disputes with neighbours.†

Things a purchaser's solicitor leaves to chance because he does not inspect the house before completion

1. Whether there is an undisclosed tenancy, or anyone is still living in the house.
2. Whether the vendor has removed any fixture, fitting or other item which he has contracted – either expressly or impliedly – to leave.
3. Whether the vendor has negligently damaged the property; or left piles of rubbish.

Things a purchaser's solicitor leaves to chance because the law governing such matters is such that he cannot do otherwise

1. Whether the house, if less than twenty years old, will continue to have its light unobstructed.
2. Whether the vendor will actually give possession on the completion date in the contract.
3. If the house is unregistered, whether the deeds are forgeries.

Things a purchaser's solicitor leaves to chance because of the system which has evolved (both unregistered and registered) as a result of the profession's slovenly practices over the years

1. Where the boundaries of the land should be, particularly

---

* These matters will not *necessarily* be revealed by inspection; nevertheless, under the present system an inspection is the best way of *trying* to find them out.

† This is best ascertained by *asking* the neighbours.

in the case of country properties, and the extent of any rights of way.

2. Whether any restrictive covenants are still enforceable, and if so, who is entitled to enforce them; and whether certain restrictive covenants have been broken.
3. If the house uses a common drain under adjoining property, the route of such common drain, and whether a right to use it was granted.
4. Whether the vendor's building society will send the receipt discharging the vendor's mortgage, after completion.
5. If the house is registered, whether the purchaser's building society's solicitor will delay sending the documents to the Land Registry (because he is waiting for this receipt), with the result that the purchaser runs the risk of being bound by a second mortgage fraudulently obtained by the vendor after completion.

Things a purchaser's solicitor leaves to chance because of the limitations of the local search – or because the records kept by the local Council are defective

1. Whether there are any planning applications, or planning permissions which have not yet been implemented, in respect of adjoining property.
2. Whether there are any proposals in the offing – usually for a new road – affecting the house, which are still in 'committee' stage and so not yet on the register.
3. If there *is* an actual proposal on the register, when it will be carried out, and whether it will affect the house if it is carried out.
4. Whether the house (or garage) was erected without planning permission, or building regulations approval; alternatively, whether the conditions of the planning permission were observed.
5. Whether there is a drain which serves some other house, running under the land.
6. In many cases, whether the house drains directly into the mains sewer. In every case where it does not, the route of the drain, and where it *does* join the mains sewer.
7. In many cases, whether there is a public right of way over the property.

Owning a house anywhere carries a certain risk whatever the system. No-one can guarantee that in two or twenty-two years time Orbital Ringway III will not decide to go within five yards of your front garden, or that a developer will not see your neighbour's garden as the perfect site for a block of flats. But these inevitable hazards are exacerbated by the conveyancing system, which has three basic defects: first, the profession's slovenly practices which have evolved over the years; second, the few bits of quasi-legal information about a house are either imperfectly recorded in one of several different places – the plan, the deeds, the Council registers – or else they are not recorded anywhere at all; third, the purchaser's solicitor neither inspects the house he is dealing with, nor calls at the Council offices. An individual solicitor cannot do anything about the first two defects; and even if he wanted to, he will not usually be in a position to do anything about the third.

Nearly all house conveyancing is done by assistant solicitors or clerks, i.e. solicitors' employees; and the emphasis in solicitors' offices not unnaturally is on each employee carrying as large a work-load, and thereby earning for his firm as much money, as possible. To inspect every house before contracts are exchanged and again before completion, and to call at the Council offices, would entail a vast amount of extra time and travelling. Alternatively, if the house was far away, someone from a local firm would have to be instructed and paid to do it. What commercial firm is going to do – or allow its employees to do – three times the usual amount of work *when the usual amount of work seems to be perfectly adequate in ninety-nine cases out of a hundred?*

What the solicitor *will* do however (at any rate if he is prudent and knowledgeable) is to spare five minutes dictating a comprehensive letter to the purchaser, explaining all the things which he has *not* been able to find out, and which he does *not* guarantee – a sort of Law Society's pamphlet in reverse: 'Although I asked the usual questions whether the drainage and water supply were directly connected to the mains, I could not get any conclusive replies, so you should ask your surveyor to check these points. My local search was clear, but you will appreciate that it does not cover any planning application which may be made for any neighbouring development. I enclose a plan of the property, but you should be aware that this indicates general boundaries only, and therefore will not be much use in the case of a subsequent boundary dispute', and so on. If a month or five years later a letter lands in the firm's letter-box, commencing with the ominous words: 'You acted for me on my purchase of this house and I have just been notified . . . ', the solicitor will be able to hunt out the letter he wrote to the purchaser before contracts were exchanged. Sighs of relief all round.

*

On the other hand, how often anything actually *does* go wrong is impossible to tell. Such incidents as do occur do not usually come to Court, or get reported. Presumably there is a greater possibility of a vendor being uncouth than fraudulent, so that a purchaser on taking possession is more likely to find a gas fire ripped out than a hitherto concealed tenant. Boundary disputes are not uncommon, especially in country properties. Occasionally a purchaser will be dismayed to see a neighbouring development starting up shortly after he moved in; and as we have seen, if the property is in the path of a proposed new road or in a proposed redevelopment area – which proposal is still in committee stage and not yet on the Council's register – the solicitor's methods have no chance of revealing it. Most solicitors will, I think, have been caught out by one or other of the items I have listed at least once.

By and large, however, the vast majority of purchasers seem to get by without mishap, despite the haphazard system and their solicitors' slovenly methods. After all, in ninety-nine cases out of a hundred there *won't* be a new bypass in the offing; the neighbour *won't* be a property development company concerned to erect a block of flats, but Mrs. Muggletrop concerned only to peg out her washing; the house *will* have a direct water supply whether the solicitor checks it or not; the vendor *won't* have fraudulently obtained a second mortgage, nor concealed a tenancy; neither will he have built that charming south wing without getting planning permission (the nice new garage, incidentally, doesn't need planning permission in any case); a common drain *won't* be cut off; a neighbour's drain running under the garden *won't* cause any trouble; a porch erected in breach of restrictive covenant *won't* matter, and so on.

Another thing that mitigates the defects of the system is the average householder's reluctance to quarrel with his neighbours, so despite the opportunities for disputes, most people seem to manage without them. Another is that legal defects (unlike other defects) tend to *lessen* with time, until they eventually disappear altogether. Thus if someone did some building in breach of a restrictive covenant, then provided no-one objected at the time, he would have less cause to worry as each month passed. If there has been a breach of the planning laws, the local authority is generally estopped from taking proceedings after four years. If a house has precariously enjoyed light for ten years, in another ten it will have an indefeasible right to do so. If fifteen years ago a builder ran a drain under someone else's garden without being granted a right to do so, in another five the precarious right is likewise converted into an indefeasible one. If six years ago a householder erected a fence wrongly appropriating some of his neighbour's garden, and no action is taken meanwhile, then in another six that neighbour's land will become *his* land, and the fence will then be in the *right* position.

That things rarely seem to go positively wrong in conveyancing matters is one of the reasons why the system is accepted without query by solicitors and their clients alike. Moreover, I suspect that most solicitors are not even *aware* of its defects, and regard the fact that things hardly ever go wrong (if fact it be) as evidence of the value of their conveyancing work. To quote the conclusion of Mr. Wright's booklet on the subject (*The Compleat Conveyancer*): that you very rarely, if ever, hear of anything going drastically wrong in conveyancing 'is perhaps some evidence that our work and the system which we have inherited and help to maintain are not wholly without value.'

In helping to sustain this view, the conveyancing procedures we examined in the previous chapter, useless in themselves, yet perform a valuable function: they enable the solicitor to believe he is doing something precise and scientific, thereby concealing both from him and his client the fact that practically everything of importance connected with a house and its transfer is left to chance. Printed forms, ritual procedures, verbal formulas – these are the lawyers' drugs by which they protect themselves from uncomfortable thought processes.

Let me give one or two examples. I'm fairly sure that most solicitors do not realise that under the conveyancing system boundaries are left vague and that the deeds will generally be useless to resolve a boundary dispute, because the realisation might bring in its wake a disturbing thought that what they do for such large sums of money may not be much use to their clients. They therefore protect themselves from this knowledge by a verbal formula. In a conveyance, instead of describing the house by its postal address, our solicitor will describe it: 'All that piece or parcel of land together with the messuage or dwellinghouse erected thereon or on some part thereof situate at and known as number 12 Mustard Street in the parish of Thing in the town of Thong in the County of York.' He sees that his description runs to over forty words and has a reassuring legalistic ring about it. He is therefore satisfied that he has somehow described the property more precisely, or at any rate more *legally*, than if he had simply written '12 Mustard Street, Thong, Yorkshire'. The point is neatly illustrated by an entry in the Solicitors' Journal (29 November 1974). An English solicitor had been investigating an American title insurance scheme and 'had been appalled at the number of boundary disputes, which was hardly surprising as the description of the house was limited to the property's postal address'. Exactly how the traditional conveyancing description of a house lessens the chance of a boundary dispute was not explained.

It is not only solicitors who have to be drugged by verbiage. Government departments also occasionally need to be shielded from uncomfortable truths. Consider the following formula printed on every land certificate: 'The exact line of the boundary will be left undetermined . . . to ascertain the exact boundaries . . . the land should therefore be inspected and such enquiries as to and perambulation of boundaries made as may be necessary' – a conglomeration of polysyllables meaning nothing more than: 'our system will not show you where the boundaries should be. If you can get any information by looking at the place or asking the neighbours you're welcome to try'.

We saw that the Law Society's pamphlet states that one of the reasons for using a solicitor is that a purchaser might otherwise find himself involved in expensive boundary disputes; and when I wrote an article in the Solicitors' Journal on how useless the preliminary enquiry form was, they printed a letter from the draftsman defending his form, in which he stated: 'a purchaser does not want to find he has a dispute about the boundaries'. The author of the pamphlet, and the draftsman of the form, evidently think that by sending a printed form containing the question: 'Is the vendor aware of any disputes regarding boundaries?', the purchaser's solicitor has in some magical way done something to prevent such a dispute arising. In fact I suspect that the thinking processes of the gentlemen in question have not advanced beyond a hazy notion that because the purchaser's solicitor has asked a question on boundaries, boundaries are therefore one of the things he has checked are 'all right'.

A less than brilliant student feels that as long as he has written at length on an examination question, he must have answered it. A solicitor feels that as he has used fifty words to describe the property his client is buying, he must have described it more precisely than if he had used only five; that as he has sent a form containing some forty complicated questions to the vendor's solicitor, and another form containing another forty complicated questions to the local Council, he must have done something to check that the house is 'all right'; that as he has sent the vendor's solicitor a further sheet of questions on the title deeds, he must have done something to safeguard his client in the largest financial transaction of his life.

And that therefore the work he has done justifies his bill of – well, let's see.

6

The sting

Before we do, however, what have we learned so far? That the Law Society in its publicity material, and solicitors (and their lackeys) in the media, put out the message that only a solicitor is competent to do conveyancing and thus protect the house-buyer in the most important commercial transaction of his life. This message is reinforced by Act of Parliament which apparently makes it illegal for an unqualified person to set up in business as a conveyancer. Yet the bulk of the actual conveyancing which comes out of a solicitor's office is not done by a solicitor at all, but by an unqualified and unsupervised clerk *employed* by a solicitor. In any case, whether done by learned solicitor or unqualified clerk, it consists of little more than obtaining meaningless answers to printed forms of largely irrelevant questions, and so affords the house-buyer virtually *no* protection in the most important commercial transaction of his life. In a word, conveyancing as traditionally carried out in solicitors' offices is a fraud; and the Law Society has escaped prosecution under the Trade Descriptions Act only through the good offices of our noble and impartial judiciary, which has conveniently decided that the Law Society is not engaged in a trade or business and so is outside the ambit of that Act (see p. 15).

Even more convenient for the Law Society is the fact that although conveyancing solicitors do occasionally come in for some criticism in the press and in Parliament, such criticism is invariably confined to peripheral matters such as costs, and whether the solicitors' monopoly should be retained. The basic issues are never touched on. There is no newspaper journalist, editor, radio or television journalist, producer, consumer affairs watchdog, representative of the Consumers'

Association, Member of Parliament – who has ever betrayed the slightest interest in exposing the idiocies of the *system*. Neither have any of these luminaries shown any interest in the fact that the house-buyer is more likely to discover any quasi-legal defect in the house he is buying by using his common sense, and inspecting the property *himself* and calling at the Council offices *himself*, than by employing a solicitor. Thus the fraud continues, as it will so long as the public remain so docile and the journalists so complaisant.

But have the pickings been reduced, as some commentators would have us believe?

From 1883 to 1st January 1973 solicitors charged for their conveyancing work in accordance with a scale. Under this scale their fee depended on the price of the house, not the amount of work they actually did. The fee was the same for the vendor's and the purchaser's solicitor; but unregistered and registered houses were differentiated, the fee for the latter being significantly less than for the former.

Under this scale, if an unregistered house changed hands for the (?) average price in 1972 of £20,000, the vendor's solicitor's fee would have been £155 plus perhaps £10 for 'incidentals'. The purchaser's solicitor's basic fee would have been the same, but he would charge an additional fee for the mortgage – about £35 if the building society had a separate solicitor; or £70 if the building society did not have a separate solicitor but appointed the purchaser's solicitor to act on its behalf. So for an unregistered house changing hands in 1972 for £20,000, the vendor's solicitor's fee would have been £165, and the purchaser's solicitor's fee would have been £200/£235. Someone who was both buying and selling such a house (who would have to pay his solicitor for *each* transaction) could therefore have expected a solicitor's bill in the region of £360/£400 if both houses were unregistered. As mentioned, the scale fees for *registered* houses were considerably less – e.g. the basic fee of £155, for buying or selling an unregistered house for £20,000, would drop to £90 if the house was registered.

Therefore the scales were generous only as long as a substantial proportion of the houses which a solicitor dealt

with were unregistered, which would be the case for most of
the time they were in operation. However with the sudden
increase in land registration in the late 1960s, solicitors found
that the scale fees – hitherto their statutory franchise to an
apparently inexhaustible gold mine – were beginning to work
to their *disadvantage*. Accordingly, as from 1st January 1973
they were scrapped, leaving solicitors to charge a 'fair and
reasonable amount' for the work they did.

At the time the abolition of the scales was announced, the
usually meagre correspondence columns of the legal journals
swelled and resounded to wails of protest from solicitors with
country practices (who would still be dealing mainly with
unregistered property), who viewed the change with the alarm
of someone seeing one of the roof supports of his gold mine
beginning to crack. Their fears proved groundless. The
abolition of the scale fees did not lead to any decrease in
charges. In fact the reverse. For the next few years solicitors
still largely kept to the previous scale for unregistered houses;
but they increased their charges for *registered* houses – so that
over the ensuing years the gap between the charges for
unregistered and registered houses diminished, until it
eventually disappeared.

During the late 1970s and early 1980s, with the tremendous
leap in house prices, the scales were finally forgotten (as was
the differential between registered and unregistered houses);
and solicitors charged a straight percentage of the price of the
house – usually about 1%-1¼% on the cheaper houses, and
about ¾% on the more expensive ones. This seems to be borne
out by a survey, described by the Law Society's Gazette (2
September 1987) as 'the first major independent study of
conveyancing charges', which was based on information given
by 800 people who moved house in the South-east. The results
of this survey are as follows:

	1983	1985	1986
Average sale price of the survey sample	£36,700	£44,300	£50,380
Average solicitor's fee	£290.60	£287.50	£313.90
Average purchase price of the survey sample	£44,400	£55,400	£55,560
Average solicitor's fee	£367.20	£345.30	£330.00

According to this survey* the average 1983 solicitor's fees represent about 0.8% of the house price, both for the sale and purchase; and whether the house was registered or unregistered made no difference. By 1986 the average solicitor's fees dropped to about 0.6% of the house price, both for sale and purchase, although due to the increase in house prices the actual fees were much the same. So according to this survey, for an 'average' purchase and sale in 1983, the 'average' solicitor's combined fee was £658; and in 1986 it was £644.

These fees, however, are just for the sale and purchase. They do not include the purchaser's solicitor's additional charge for the *mortgage*. When a purchaser buys a house with the aid of a mortgage (as of course the vast majority do) the building society, or other lender, does not rely on the purchaser's solicitor but appoints its own solicitor. Although the building society usually appoints the purchaser's solicitor, this does not mean it is relying on the purchaser's solicitor as such: the building society is still instructing its own solicitor, who for greater convenience happens to be the same person as the purchaser's solicitor. The purchaser's solicitor therefore acts in a dual capacity and picks up *two* fees, one for the purchase and one for the mortgage, both of which are payable by the purchaser. This mortgage fee is still determined in accordance with a scale (or 'guidelines') agreed between the Law Society and the Building Societies Association: £52.50 for a mortgage of £10,000, £67.50 for a mortgage of £20,000, and £72.50 for a mortgage of £25,000, (excluding 'incidentals'). So to the average purchaser's solicitor's fees in the survey add, say, £70 for the additional mortgage fee.† This brings the 1983 average overall purchase and sale fee to £728; and the 1986 average overall purchase and sale fee to £714.

These fees do not include stamp duty or land registry

---

*   *Competition in Conveyancing: an analysis of solicitors' charges* by Simon Domberger and Avrom Sherr. Incidentally the 1986 findings were contained in a subsequent paper by the same authors.

†   I asked one of the joint authors of the survey why he had not included this additional mortgage fee in the results. He replied that as it was laid down by a scale it was unnecessary to include it in the survey: if a solicitor's bill did not differentiate between the purchase and the mortgage fee, but merely gave an *overall* total, that bill was not used for the survey.

charges – which are, of course, nothing to do with solicitors' fees. In fact the final tweak to the purchaser's nose comes from the Land Registry. For typing the purchaser's name in place of the vendor's name on the register (and on the land certificate, which is a copy of the register), the Land Registry will charge according to a scale, again based on the price of the house. For our 'average' house costing £40,000/£60,000 the land registry fee is currently £60/£80.

Incidentally, since the abolition of the old scale fees a client can contest his solicitor's bill by appealing to the Law Society, which has power to reduce it. Very few people avail themselves of this right, presumably because very few people know about it. The Law Society's pamphlet, while stating that the solicitor's bill 'must by law be fair and reasonable', is careful not to tell the reader what he can do if he considers it is not, and neither need the solicitor tell his client of this right. But in any case, only if a bill was way in excess of the above averages would the Law Society be likely to intervene.

*

Now a fee in itself cannot be cheap or expensive: it can be one or the other only in relation to the amount of work it pays for, or – in the case of relatively unskilled work such as this – the amount of *time* it takes.

When a *registered* freehold house is bought and sold (and about three-quarters of all houses in England and Wales are now registered), the procedures and documents involved do not vary from one house to the next. The actual time the solicitor is engaged can therefore be estimated reasonably precisely:

Vendor's solicitor:
1. Filling in form to send to Land Registry to get a copy of the register *(5 minutes)*.
2. On receipt of copy register, writing out contract for typist to type *(5 minutes)*.
3. Dictating answers to purchaser's solicitor's preliminary enquiries *(5/10 minutes)*.
4. Sending contract to vendor for him to sign; when returned, sending vendor's signed contract to purchaser's

solicitor to effect exchange of contracts *(5 minutes)*.

5. Writing to vendor's building society for details of amount required to pay off vendor's mortgage, and relaying this figure to purchaser's solicitor *(5 minutes)*.
6. Answering purchaser's solicitor's form of 'requisitions' *(3 minutes)*.
7. Sending transfer form, received from purchaser's solicitor, to vendor to sign *(3 minutes)*.
8. Attending completion appointment *(10 minutes –* although if vendor's building society does not appoint vendor's solicitor, then completion takes place at the building society's solicitor's office, and some travelling time will be involved).

Basic total *45 minutes*.

Of course some further letters and telephone calls will be necessary e.g. chasing up purchaser's solicitor, fixing completion appointment, and so on. Allow a further 35 minutes for these.

Add on 10 minutes for nose-picking and drinking coffee.
Actual total: approximately 1½ hours.

Purchaser's solicitor (who is also acting for purchaser's building society):

1. Reading draft contract and copy register, and sending printed form of preliminary enquiries, plus any additional enquiries, to vendor's solicitor *(5/15 minutes)*.
2. Sending off local search forms – typist's time only.
3. Checking answers to preliminary enquiries and local search forms *(5 minutes)*.
4. Sending contract to purchaser for him to sign, with report of 'findings' *(5/10 minutes)*.
5. Sending signed contract to vendor's solicitor *(3 minutes)*.
6. Sending 'requisitions' form and transfer form to vendor's solicitor *(5 minutes)*.
7. Filling in printed mortgage form, received from building society, and sending it to purchaser to sign *(5 minutes)*.
8. Writing to building society for amount of mortgage advance, and writing to purchaser for any balance

needed *(5/10 minutes)*.
 9. Sending search form to Land Registry *(3 minutes)*.
10. Attending completion *(10 minutes,* plus travelling).
11. Sending documents to Land Registry *(5 minutes)*.
Basic total (excluding travelling to completion) *70 minutes*.
Add on 45 minutes for further letters and telephone calls, as before.
Add on 5 minutes for nose-picking and drinking coffee.
Actual total: approximately 2 hours.

It may be thought that putting a time to these various processes, although plausible, and although I have added over 50% margin in both cases, cannot be done with any accuracy in practice. After all, whenever we do a job around the house or on the car it always seems to take double or treble the time we estimated. But whereas sparking plugs and screws can prove unaccountably intractable, the conveyancing forms and procedures are the *same* with every registered house. There is just no way in which a solicitor, however erudite, can embellish a building society mortgage or a land registry transfer; there is just no way in which he can spend more than a few moments writing out a contract. In fact so stereotyped are these documents that the solicitor need not spend *any* time writing them out: a reasonably intelligent secretary can type them out on her own, with a model to work from.

Moreover a busy solicitor will probably be dealing with sixty or seventy current conveyancing matters – and an applicant for such a position would be ill-advised to admit he could not handle this sort of work-load. Anyone dealing with sixty or seventy conveyancing matters just would not have the time to exceed my allotted times. Indeed with some items I have probably been over-generous in the time I have allotted; for instance a busy solicitor would probably *not* spend quarter of an hour reading each copy register and sending out each set of preliminary enquiries, but would more likely deal with half a dozen such matters in a single dictating session, spending but a few moments on each.

The above estimates of the time involved in the conveyancing processes apply to registered houses. When it comes to unregistered houses, if the vendor's title is simple – consisting of one or two standard conveyances – then the time taken both by the vendor's and purchaser's solicitor will be much the same as when dealing with a registered house. If the vendor's title is more complicated the purchaser's solicitor, if conscientious, will spend some time going through the deeds and asking 'requisitions on title', which the vendor's solicitor will have to answer. But as about three-quarters of all houses in England and Wales are now registered, and the majority of those which are unregistered will nevertheless have straightforward titles, any complicated titles will presumably feature but rarely in the solicitor's work-load.

Let's go back to the survey whose overall findings I previously quoted, viz. that in 1986, for acting on the sale and purchase of an average house the solicitor charges in the region of £644 – plus an additional fee of about £70 for the mortgage. So for approximately three and a half hours 'solicitor's' work (plus a couple of hours typist's work, and an hour or so travelling by a junior clerk to and from the completion appointment) the solicitor charges £714 – *which represents a rate of about £200 an hour*. This, then, is the much vaunted reduction in solicitors' conveyancing fees supposedly brought about by the advent of 'licensed conveyancers', and hailed by the Consumers' Association as 'a great leap forward for consumers' (*Which?* July 1985).

I mentioned that the building society usually appoints the purchaser's solicitor to act for it on the mortgage. However, sometimes the building society does appoint a separate solicitor. In that case his job is merely to check the documents which the purchaser's solicitor – or D.I.Y. conveyancer – sends him after exchange of contracts (preliminary enquiry and local search forms, copy register, draft transfer), and send the purchaser's solicitor a print of the standard mortgage form and a standard form of 'requisitions'. If the house is registered there is really no way the building society's solicitor can spend more than *half an hour* on the job. Moreover he has even less responsibility than the purchaser's solicitor, because even if there is a quasi-legal defect (an imminent development next door, a boundary dispute etc.) that is generally of no concern to the building society, whose interest in the house is solely that it will fetch the amount of the loan then outstanding if it has to be sold.

When the building society appoints a separate solicitor, his fee is that laid down by the 'guidelines', plus 50%. So for an average mortgage of £22,000, the guidelines stipulate a fee of £70 where the building society appoints the purchaser's solicitor. However, if the building society appoints a *separate* solicitor, that solicitor's fee will be £70 plus 50%, i.e. £105 – which again is a rate of about £200 an hour.

*

Now the senior partners of some 'top' City firms currently admit to charging at the rate of £100 an hour, sometimes even £150 an hour. But how does the rank and file solicitor get away with charging *£200 an hour* for routine conveyancing work – which for the most part is not done by a solicitor at all, but by an unqualified clerk or even a moderately bright typist?

By two devices.

First, the old trick of charging a percentage of the value or price of the thing on which work has been done, rather than charging for the actual work itself. The solicitor's fee is therefore not related to the work he does, but to the price of the house which is being bought or sold.* The price of a house depends on its size, position and general desirability, none of which factors affects how much work a solicitor does in transferring it. Buying or selling a house for £100,000 (for which a solicitor would charge £500/£600) entails no more work than buying or selling a house for £30,000 (for which a solicitor would charge £250).

The second device is to drag out the conveyancing processes over three months or so, so the customer will not know how much time the solicitor has actually spent, and thus will be kept ignorant of his solicitor's (and building society's solicitor's) true rate of remuneration. The first device needs no further explanation. Let's spend a little time on the second.

---

*   This method of charging was once challenged by a client; but it was upheld by the Court, which ruled that the time spent by a solicitor was *not* a basic factor in assessing a fair charge, but the value of any property involved was the weightiest single factor – Property and Reversionary Corporation v. Department of the Environment, 1975.

As we have seen, a conveyancing transaction is in two stages: (1) from verbal agreement to exchange of contracts; and (2) from exchange of contracts to completion. The second stage takes a month, and the completion date inserted in the contract will almost invariably be 'the usual month' from the date contracts are exchanged. This period traditionally was to allow the purchaser's solicitor time to investigate the vendor's title, and the building society's solicitor time to prepare the mortgage deed. But even though mortgage deeds are now always standard printed forms, and in the case of registered houses there is no question of investigating title – so the solicitor's work after exchange can consequently be reckoned in minutes – it still takes a month from exchange of contracts to completion.

The time scale of the first stage, from verbal agreement to exchange of contracts, is more variable. It might take a month if there is no hold-up on the part of the purchaser's or vendor's solicitor, building society, or local Council, and neither party is simultaneously buying or selling *another* house. But this period would be exceptional. The norm is two or three months. During this first stage the purchaser's solicitor makes his preliminary enquiries of the vendor's solicitor, and his local search with the local Council, and the purchaser gets his mortgage offer. Let's examine these three items, and particularly the time element involved, a little more closely.

1. Preliminary Enquiries

The time it takes for the purchaser's solicitor to send a printed form of enquiries to the vendor's solicitor, and get the replies, is generally two or three weeks. The actual *information* contained in such replies could be obtained direct by the purchaser from his vendor inside three minutes. Indeed, such information as is usually given is so nebulous that it is hardly worth having at all, and in 99% of all cases it amounts to no more than: the vendor has not had any disputes or received any 'notices', has not made any additions to the house, and may or may not be leaving certain fixtures. This information, with perhaps a bit of waffle about believing that the property is connected to the usual services but please rely on inspection for the route of the pipes, will satisfy most purchaser's solicitors; and in fact in the case of most houses there is not a great deal of further information which *can* be given. It is true that the form runs to three closely printed pages, but the majority of questions are either side-stepped or else simply ignored.

Even if, as sometimes happens, the purchaser's solicitor dreams up scores of additional enquiries – and some firms have their own sheets of questions which they add to the printed form, presumably under the impression that they are thereby doing a more thorough job – the net result in information obtained will be exactly the same.

2. Local Search

This is likewise done by means of a printed form or rather two printed forms, sent to the appropriate local Council. One form asks for particulars of any 'land charges'; the other consists of a list of questions. That the thought processes behind this questionnaire seem to be identical with those responsible for the preliminary enquiry form is not surprising if one reads the note in the publisher's catalogue: 'These forms are settled by the Law Society'.

The local search questionnaire is reproduced in appendix 4. The draftsman is evidently concerned to stuff the form with as many seemingly complicated questions referring to seemingly complicated Acts of Parliament as possible, whether or not they have any relevance. For instance there are fourteen questions on drainage, occupying three-quarters of a foolscap page, referring to S.21(1)(a), S.18, S.24(4) of the Public Health Act 1936; S.22 of the Building Act 1984; S.12 and 13 of the Public Health Act 1961. Yet these questions are relevant only to someone who is actually constructing the drains in the first place. In the case of ninety-nine out of a hundred houses, the only information the local Council can give about the drainage is that the house 'drains to a public sewer by combined operation' – which means there is a sewage pipe running under the front or rear of the property, serving several other houses as well, which at some unspecified point discharges into the mains sewer in the road.

Then there are twenty-four questions, occupying one and a

half foolscap pages, dealing with various provisions of the
Planning Acts; and again, in ninety-nine cases out of a
hundred the only information a local Council can give is
either that planning permission for a house was granted on
whatever date, or that there are no entries in the planning
register (depending on whether the house was built after or
before 1947). Incidentally, any information revealed by the
other local search form, which relates to 'land charges', would
also be duplicated in the answers to the questionnaire, e.g. a
smoke control order would appear on *both* forms.

The local search questionnaire runs to four closely printed
pages containing over sixty questions and subquestions. In
ninety-nine out of a hundred cases the sum total of
information elicited is: (a) the road abutting the property is
maintained by the Council; (b) drainage is 'by combined
operation' into the mains sewer; (c) planning permission was
granted on whatever date; (d) there are no Notices, or
proposals for compulsory acquisition on the register; (e) there
are no proposals on the register for new roads or road
widening within 200 metres of the property. Indeed so
standard are the replies, that local Councils invariably answer
the questionnaire by clipping a printed sheet of *answers* to the
form. Indeed so standard are the replies, that the Law
Commission's Conveyancing Committee has suggested
scrapping the local search questionnaire altogether!*

The time it takes for the purchaser's solicitor to send the
printed form of preliminary enquiries to the vendor's
solicitor, and get the replies, is generally two or three weeks.
The time it takes the local Council to return the local search
forms varies from two weeks to two months, and several local
Councils have been clocking up delays of *three* months.

Yet a bit of cold clear thinking applied to these forms, with
the consequent cutting out of unnecessary questions and
convoluted verbiage, and we would be left with two forms
each containing a dozen or so easily understood questions –
which the purchaser or his solicitor could either personally

---

* 'What we have at present is a standardised way to obtain information much of
  which is irrelevant to many of the transactions in question.' Consultation paper,
  December 1987.

present to the vendor and local Council respectively, and wait three minutes and half an hour, respectively, for the replies; or else if the forms were sent, the answers could be given by return of post. And with a bit more cold clear thinking we could not only speed up these two processes *but cut them out altogether*.

Most of the questions on the preliminary enquiries and local search forms, at any rate most of the relevant questions, ask for *fixed* information – whether the road abutting the property is maintained by the Council, whether the property has mains drainage, whether there is a direct mains water supply, whether planning permission was granted, and so on. Now if a house had mains drainage, mains water, and planning permission etc. when Pete Muggins bought it in 1962, it will have mains drainage, mains water, and planning permission etc. when Fred Nurkins comes to buy it in 1983. Yet in this day and age, when every bobby on the beat can radio-telephone our car number to a central computer and in a few seconds get our name and address (and probably blood group and political persuasion to boot), solicitors are still submitting these preliminary enquiry and local search forms, and getting this information three weeks to two months later, *each time a house changes hands*.

Not that we need computers to make the conveyancing system efficient, since we already have the basis for an efficient system in the Land Registry. All we need do is collect the few bits of fixed information about a house, which a purchaser needs to know, and put them on the land register – so the purchaser or his solicitor is automatically presented with them in the copy of the register which he receives with the draft contract.*

Similarly, instead of the purchaser's solicitor sending the local Council a printed form crammed with complicated questions about various Acts of Parliament under which the local Council *might* have issued a Notice or *might* have a proposal affecting the house, and waiting up to two months for the answers, the Council could exhibit a comprehensive

---

* The Land Registry would need extra staff to collect this information. What better source than the redundant local search clerks?

map (in the Town Hall or local library) on which it marks those relatively few houses and areas in respect of which it *has* issued a Notice or *does* have a proposal. The purchaser or his solicitor would then only need to look at this map to check that the house (and neighbouring land) are not shaded in red or spotted in green or whatever, and that therefore the Council has no designs on it.

This would not only give the purchaser the necessary information in a few seconds, but would afford him far *more* information than the present local search – which does *not* reveal any imminent development of adjoining or nearby property, or road widening schemes more than 200 metres away.

3. Mortgage Offer

During the weeks and months in which the purchaser's solicitor is bringing himself round to the task of submitting his preliminary enquiries, and the vendor's solicitor is bringing himself round to the task of answering them, and the various Council clerks are processing the local search forms, the solicitors and Council clerks can reassure themselves that they are not holding up the purchase, because the purchaser will at the same time be waiting for his mortgage offer. And here again we come up against the magic minimum period of three weeks which it takes a building society to offer a mortgage. In this case it is the survey which usually causes the hold-up.

The building society has the house surveyed (at the borrower's expense) to ensure that it is worth at least the amount of the loan, so that if the building society ever has to realise its security by selling the house, it will always be able to recover the amount loaned. At first sight this seems logical. Yet here again a bit of thinking could make this process redundant. The risk of (a) a defaulting borrower coinciding with (b) the building society finding that it could not sell his house for the amount of the loan then outstanding, is infinitesimal. Therefore each borrower, instead of paying £100 or so for the building society to carry out a survey, could pay £5 into a central compensation fund from which the building society would be reimbursed if one of its borrowers defaulted *and* his house failed, for whatever reason, to sell for the amount of the loan then outstanding. As this would be such an unlikely coincidence, and as approximately three-quarters of a million building society mortgages are granted every year, it would probably only need a £5 contribution from each borrower over one year to finance the fund for the next decade. If the building society survey were dispensed with on these lines, the building society would only need to consider the purchaser's income and status before offering a mortgage – which it could do before the purchaser even started looking for a house.

Thus with some minimal rethinking and reorganisation on the part of the Land Registry, local Councils, and building societies, these three pre-contract procedures – preliminary enquiries, local search, and building society survey – which traditionally take one or two months, could take one or two days, or one or two hours, or better still could be scrapped altogether.*

In fact this is what happened once upon a time in 1971/2, when it came to pass that the property market suddenly ceased to behave in its customary sedate and gentlemanly fashion. No sooner had a vendor accepted an offer, when another would come in for a thousand pounds more, and then another, and within a couple of days, or even the space of a few telephone calls, the price of an ordinary house might have leapt up several thousand pounds. During this period vendors and purchasers, to their solicitors' horror, refused to obey the rules. Vendors welshed on their initial verbal agreements, not unnaturally wanting to accept the highest offer. As for purchasers, they refused to wait for mortgage offers; they cared nothing about preliminary enquiries or local searches; they just wanted to secure the house before someone else put in a higher offer. Solicitors, who had been used to telling their clients that a month was the very shortest period in which contracts can be exchanged, were telephoned at 10 a.m. with

---

* The purchaser may want a survey, of course, but it would be for him to decide whether he delays exchanging contracts while he gets one; just as when I buy a secondhand car I have to choose between the risk of buying a faulty car, and waiting for a mechanical check and losing the deal. In any case, a reasonably thorough survey of an average house only takes an hour or so.

details of a purchase or sale, and given unambiguous instructions to get contracts exchanged by 1 p.m. that same day. To their disquiet they found that they could do so *without giving their clients any lesser service*. A contract would be typed out and delivered by messenger to the purchaser's solicitor; a clerk would be dispatched to the Council offices to make a 'personal' local search; and preliminary enquiries would be dealt with over the telephone. A couple of hours later the contract would be ready to be signed and exchanged. Even when, at the insistence of the purchaser, preliminary enquiries and local search were dispensed with altogether, or when the purchaser himself signed and exchanged contracts *before* consulting his solicitor, it did not seem to matter, or cause the purchaser any subsequent embarrassment.

It was an uneasy time for everyone, particularly solicitors who bewailed the immorality of 'gazumping', as it was called. I suspect they vaguely realised that had it continued on such a scale, the public might eventually tumble to the fact that preparing a contract for the sale of a house is five minutes work, and the two procedures the purchaser's solicitor traditionally carries out before exchange (preliminary enquiries and local search) could be done within a couple of hours, or could even be scrapped altogether without any adverse effects – and the elaborate facade, built up and preserved over a century or more, might have come crashing down. As it was, this period lasted only about six months, after which the market settled down and vendors and purchasers behaved themselves again. That is to say, they let their solicitors go back to their traditional conveyancing routine, i.e. a week or two to send out the draft contract, and a further month or two to exchange contracts. Sighs of relief all round.

In the previous chapter I suggested that the solicitor's pre-contract procedures, useless in themselves, nevertheless enable the solicitor to convince both himself and his client that he is doing something precise and esoteric. Now we see that they perform another even more valuable function: to drag out the conveyancing in order to obfuscate the fact that the solicitor has taken only three and a half hours to do it, and so conceal his rate of remuneration.

Now it is one thing to pretend you are doing something complicated and esoteric to justify a hefty bill. It is a totally different thing unnecessarily to extend the *time* you take over a job, to justify your bill. If a car repairer pretends he has replaced the big ends when all he has done is change the sparking plugs, the customer has merely been defrauded of a couple of hundred pounds. But if that car repairer unnecessarily strips the engine and sends the block to the factory to be rebored, which takes two or three months, the customer has not only been defrauded; he may also have had his holiday ruined.

Whereas the delay between exchange of contracts and completion is merely a transient inconvenience (often not even that), the delay between verbal agreement and exchange of contracts is potentially disastrous. This is firstly because delay (like war) once deliberately engineered is difficult to contain.

Solicitors have programmed the system to take about a month from verbal agreement to exchange of contracts – a week to take instructions and send out the draft contract, and three weeks for the preliminary enquiries and local search forms to be submitted and returned, and the purchaser to get his mortgage offer – and a month's delay may not seem too irksome. Unfortunately this programme can, at the drop of a hat, go berserk. For instance many local Councils, instead of taking two or three weeks to return the search forms, are now taking two or three months; and when either vendor or purchaser is simultaneously buying or selling *another* house, the pre-contract delay will be somewhere between one month and infinity. This is because someone who is buying a house, and at the same time selling his own house, cannot exchange contracts on his purchase until his own purchaser is ready to exchange on his sale. If that purchaser is similarly selling his house, he won't be able to exchange until *his* purchaser is ready to exchange, and so on. Therefore in a chain of dependent transactions, each can move only at the speed of the slowest – so if one of the local Councils involved happens to take three months to process the search forms, or if one of the solicitors involved goes on holiday leaving imprecise instructions with a dummy secretary, or whatever, the whole unwieldy caravan is stuck.

Meanwhile – and this is the chief reason why the pre-contract delay is of such significance – *at any time during this period either vendor or purchaser is free to call the deal off on any pretext, or none at all.*

Even if everything does eventually go according to plan, it is obviously a stressful time for the parties. But the longer the pre-contract period, the greater chance of one of the parties backing out. And if this happens, as it apparently does in a third of all transactions, the consequences to the other party can be ruinous. The vendor will have turned away other potential purchasers; the purchaser will have stopped looking and so will have missed other houses. Either will have wasted time and will have incurred heavy fees in vain. Moreover, in a chain of dependent transactions it is not only the other party who will be affected. The purchaser of The Laurels cannot proceed, because the person who had agreed to buy *his* house has withdrawn. The vendor of The Laurels therefore cannot proceed with his purchase of The Oaks. The vendor of The Oaks therefore cannot proceed with his purchase of The Elms, and so on. Each disappointed vendor may have lost other purchasers who *would* have proceeded; each disappointed purchaser may have lost other suitable houses. Each disappointed purchaser has incurred solicitors' fees, building society fees, and possibly surveyors' fees. And the longer the chain of dependent transactions, the greater the chance of one of the parties in the chain withdrawing, and the whole series collapsing like a row of dominoes.

Sometimes a party who withdraws has a good reason – a severe illness, a change of job. But an unscrupulous person can cynically exploit the system and withdraw at the last minute, happily oblivious of the havoc he thereby causes. Someone can make an acceptable offer and instruct solicitors, yet continue to look at other houses, hoping to find something he likes better but wanting to secure the original one in case he doesn't. A vendor having accepted an offer can continue to look for a purchaser with more money; or even if he does not actually look, someone can come along and offer him a few thousand pounds more. Alternatively, the system can be used as a smokescreen by one party to conceal the fact that he is not ready to proceed. Someone who has not found a purchaser for his own house, but who sees a house he wants to buy, naturally does not want to lose it, so he makes his offer and instructs his solicitor to start up the dance. The parties' solicitors pirouette happily, and only after the allotted span of four to six weeks has expired will the vendor's solicitor get round to asking the purchaser's solicitor when he will be receiving the signed contract. Only then does the would-be purchaser have to admit that he is still not ready to proceed – either because he has not even found a purchaser for his own house, or because his purchaser is himself not ready. The vendor in our example is then in a difficult position. Should he hang on in the hope that the original purchaser will eventually be able to exchange? Or should he start all over again with another purchaser, with another delay of another unspecified period, and no guarantee that the same thing will not happen again? Alternatively, it can be the vendor who uses the smokescreen, having accepted the purchaser's offer without having found a house to move to.

Under the present system there is no such thing as a 'quick sale', no means of distinguishing someone who can proceed quickly from someone who can't. The knowledge comes four to six weeks later, which may be four to six weeks too late. Nor is it the practice for the vendor's solicitor to send out draft contracts to more than one potential purchaser, so that the first out of two or more interested parties to sign and return the contract gets the house. This is because firstly, under normal market conditions most sales are effected through estate agents, who will take a house off the market once an offer for it has been accepted and try to interest a potential purchaser in another house on their books – hence there is not likely to be a multiplicity of offers. And secondly, even if there is more than one offer, solicitors actively discourage 'contract races' (as they are called), or even refuse to initiate them. The reason they give is that it is not 'ethical' or 'morally right' for someone to incur solicitors' and surveyors' fees if he is going to lose the property. Refreshing as it is to come across such concern for other people's clients, the real reason, I suspect, is that contract races threaten the sanctity of the month minimum pre-contract period.

Although gazumping has never returned to its 1971/2 level (when it reached such bizarre proportions as even to threaten the sacred conveyancing procedures), and although estate agents are generally content to play the solicitors' game and withdraw a property once a verbal offer has been accepted, gazumping is still the most common reason for the verbal agreement between the parties being broken before contracts are exchanged. According to *Which?* (April 1987) it affects one in three sales.

The problem of a vendor having agreed a price for his house, yet being free to accept a higher offer any time up to exchange of contracts, and the chaos which results from such freedom, has exercised many noble and learned minds in Parliament and elsewhere. Many wondrous solutions have been mooted. Parliament generally containing over a hundred lawyers at any given time, and the B.B.C. and other organs of the media being loath to question *professional* procedures, it is perhaps not surprising that the obvious solution has never been suggested: cut out the local search, preliminary enquiries, and building society survey, thus manifestly enabling contracts to be exchanged a few days – or even a few hours – after an offer has been accepted. The solution, in effect, is to remove the apparently plausible excuses solicitors have under the present system for not exchanging contracts as quickly as their clients forced them to during those few months in 1971/2 when gazumping was at its height.

This would put an end only to those delays caused by the unnecessary and artificially protracted procedures which we have examined. It would not end those delays consequent on a purchaser not having found a buyer for his own house, or a vendor not having found a house to move to. If someone buying a house is simultaneously selling his own house, and it takes him three months to find a buyer, then his vendor will have to wait three months, whatever the system – or sell elsewhere. But the smokescreens would be dispersed. Under the new system, the purchaser in our example would have to declare his true position at the outset, or at any rate after a couple of days when he would have to admit that he *still* was not ready to exchange; and it would be up to the vendor to decide whether to wait for him or look for another purchaser.

Moreover, once our purchaser *did* find a buyer for his house, that dependent contract could be exchanged in a matter of hours, instead of only after another delay of another unspecified period – and so on all the way down the line of a series of dependent transactions.

Thus the main indictment against solicitors is not that they charge at the rate of £200 an hour (there is, after all, no reason why they should love money any less than their fellow men); nor even that they find out nothing useful about the houses their clients are buying (in the case of ninety-nine out of a hundred houses there is nothing useful to find out anyway). The main indictment against solicitors is that in order to *conceal* the fact that they charge at the rate of £200 an hour, and that they find out nothing useful, they have foisted on the public a ludicrously inefficient system which makes moving house at best a time of great stress, at worst a nightmare.

7

New houses
Restrictive covenants
Leases
The typing industry

Conveyancing when a new house on an estate is sold

So far I have dealt with the conveyancing processes involved when a secondhand freehold house changes hands. When new houses are bought and sold, although the processes are basically the same, some of them take on a different aspect. For instance, the solicitor acting for the vendor/developer will usually be dealing not just with one house, but with a whole estate of houses, and as each house on the estate finds a purchaser he will send out the same form of draft contract to each purchaser's solicitor. This contract will be a more elaborate affair than the contract used for the sale of a secondhand house, and will contain certain additional clauses. These additional clauses will usually provide: (1) for the vendor/developer to make up the roads on the estate to the standard required by the local authority (which will in due course adopt such roads and so convert them into ordinary public highways). (2) For the developer, on completion, to enter into a separate agreement with the purchaser, regarding building defects, in the form laid down by the National House-Building Council. (3) For the developer to give the purchaser a right of way over the roads on the estate until they become public highways, and the right to use the drains and pipes running under the rest of the estate. (4) For the purchaser to enter into certain restrictive covenants with the vendor. In fact these restrictive covenants, and the rights to be granted to the purchaser, will be set out in a separate transfer (or conveyance if the property is unregistered) attached to the contract. If the house will not be finished by the time the purchaser is expected to exchange contracts, as will often be the case, there will be a provision in the contract for the developer to finish it, and for completion of the sale to take place so many days after it has been finished.

The developer's solicitor, having to deal with twenty or two hundred houses on the same estate, will streamline his procedure. To each individual purchaser's solicitor he will send the same set of documents: contract with transfer attached, copy of the register of the developer's land if registered (as when a secondhand house is sold), copy of the relevant planning permission, and a sheet of answers anticipating the traditional form of preliminary enquiries. And with this set of documents, he will send a duplicated letter informing each purchaser's solicitor that because the contract is in standard form for the whole estate, no alterations or amendments to it will be permitted.

Therefore once the developer's solicitor has drawn up the contract and the form of transfer attached, and has had them duplicated or printed, all he has to do is to push out the same set of documents twenty or two hundred times, and wait for the signed contracts to come in. In other words, once the scheme has been set up, there will be no further work for the developer's solicitor other than routine typists' work.

Now one might think that in the case of a new estate comprising a hundred houses or so, there would be one solicitor appointed on behalf of all the purchasers, to check the set of documents which the developer's solicitor had drawn up. One would be wrong. Each purchaser will have his *own* individual solicitor. So if Wimpey or Wates or whoever build an estate of a hundred houses, Wimpey's or Wates's solicitor will send out a hundred sets of identical documents to a hundred different solicitors acting for the various purchasers. And some of these purchasers' solicitors will in due course send the documents to a *building society's* solicitor. And each purchaser's solicitor and each building society's solicitor will look through the documents, and charge the full solicitor's fee for doing so. So when an average sized estate is developed, there arises the bizarre situation of a hundred solicitors *each checking an identical set of completely stereotyped documents*, and each being paid the full fee for so doing.

As for their being able to confer any *benefits* on their clients, it is a waste of time for the purchaser's solicitor to try to make any alterations to the draft contract, just as it would be a waste of time for the purchaser of a new car to ask for the guarantee to be altered. If you want a new car you have to accept the terms on which the manufacturer offers it, and the same goes for a new house. The purchaser's solicitor can therefore do nothing for his client except to present him with the stereotyped contract which he has received from the developer's solicitor.

Any supposed checking by the purchaser's solicitor of quasi-legal defects is even more of a sham when that house is on a new estate, than when it is secondhand. A house being a solid and not an abstract object, the number of things there are to be found out about it is limited (apart from matters touching on its condition and structure, which are outside a solicitor's terms of reference). Such things as there *are* to be found out, however, include whether the drainage of the house is direct to the mains sewer; whether the water supply comes direct from the mains; if not direct, the route of the drain and water pipe, and where they do join the respective mains; whether there are any other pipes and drains under the house or garden, serving other houses. Now although the printed form of preliminary enquiries does contain questions on these points, such questions never elicit any precise information in the case of a secondhand house – one of the reasons being that the average householder probably does not know the route of the pipes and drains serving his house, or whether there are any other pipes or drains under his land.

But in the case of a new house, the vendor must know all about the pipes and drains, and where they join the mains, because he *put* them there. One would therefore expect that when the *developer's* solicitor answers the purchaser's solicitor's form of preliminary enquiries, he would give the precise information asked for. In fact he never does. As mentioned, a duplicated sheet of answers anticipating the standard enquiries is usually sent out with the draft contract, and these particular questions are invariably answered by some such formula as: 'please see form of transfer for particulars of rights granted'. This transfer form will indeed grant the purchaser the right to use whatever pipes and drains run under the developer's adjoining land, but it will not show where they join the respective mains; and although the route of the drains constructed by the developer is *sometimes* shown on the plan attached to the transfer, the route of the water pipe never is. If more than one in ten purchasers' solicitors pressed for more precise information on these points, developers' solicitors would find it worth their while to get such information from their clients at the outset, and give it as a matter of course to each purchaser's solicitor. The fact that they never do indicates that probably 99% of all purchasers' solicitors do not press for any exact information. Thus even when there *is* some precise information to be had, purchasers' solicitors do not bother to ask for it, but are content to assume that a developer will not build a house, or an estate of houses, without having the necessary access to a water mains and mains drainage. This may not invariably be a safe assumption to make (see p. 52); but even if it were, it could be made equally well by the purchaser himself without any assistance from a professional adviser.

Restrictive Covenants

When a new estate is developed, the vendor will invariably make the individual purchasers enter into restrictive covenants, and in fact most houses, whether new or secondhand, will be subject to restrictive covenants of one sort or another. Why are they imposed?

The idea behind restrictive covenants is straightforward, and we have already touched on this subject. Someone owning an area of land, and selling *part* of that land, might wish to restrict either the use of the land he sells or the sort of buildings to be erected on it. For instance, if I was selling part of my large garden, I might not want a block of flats built on it. Accordingly, in the transfer deed (that is, either the conveyance or land registry transfer) I might impose a condition that no more than one house should be erected on the land I sold, and that the plans of that house must first receive my written approval. Such a condition, or *covenant* as it is called, would be binding on whoever happened to own that land in the future; conversely the covenant could be enforced by whoever came to own the land I retained. Thus fifty or a hundred years later, provided the areas of land originally retained and sold were still identifiable, the current owner of the retained land could still insist that the current owner of the sold land did not build except in accordance with the covenant.

This useful device is extensively used, but not for its original purpose of enabling a landowner to control the use of adjoining land which he or his predecessor previously sold, but unhappily for a rather different purpose: to clutter up practically every conveyance and land certificate, and so cause conveyancing to appear more complicated than it need be.

As I said, most houses are subject to restrictive covenants. They would usually be imposed by the vendor when the land was originally sold for building purposes, or when the individual houses themselves were sold by their developer. Often a house is subject to two or three different sets of covenants imposed at different times, as when an area of land is split up and then further split up. Sometimes the covenants are simple, contained in a single paragraph – e.g. to use any buildings only as a private house. Sometimes they drool on for several pages, containing all manner of complicated provisions as to what sort of houses shall and shall not be built. As mentioned, once covenants are imposed on an area of land, they continue to bind that land and whoever owns a house built on it, until the end of time. At least, that is the theory. In practice, hardly any of the restrictive covenants, which are so slavishly copied out year after year, century after century, could be enforced – even in the unlikely event of anyone ever wanting to enforce them.

Sometimes it is obvious that certain covenants cannot be enforced. To maintain a certain fence shown on the plan by an inside 'T' mark, and not to build beyond a certain building line shown on the plan, are common covenants. Yet it is quite usual to see such covenants on a land certificate, with a note in the margin that there were no 'T' marks or building lines shown on the plan lodged with the Land Registry. To refuse to register a covenant to repair a fence or observe a building line, if no indication has been given of which fence or what building line the covenant refers to, would apparently be too great a responsibility for the land registry officials to bear. It is easier for the land registry clerks to copy out everything put in front of them, however palpably meaningless. From time to time one even sees an entry on a land certificate that the land is subject to covenants set out in a certain deed, with a note in the margin that no copy of this deed was ever lodged at the Land Registry – in other words, says the Land Registry, the land may be subject to covenants, but no-one has ever told us, and neither is anyone ever likely to tell us, what they are.

But the main reason why most restrictive covenants are unenforceable is that to be binding on future owners of the land, the covenants must have been imposed *for the benefit of certain identifiable land*; and the land intended to be benefited is hardly ever shown, whether by plan or adequate description. Sometimes the original deed (i.e. conveyance or transfer) imposing the covenants baldly stipulates that the purchaser covenants with the vendor, and with the vendor's successors in title, to observe restrictive covenants a. b. c. d. etc., without referring to *any* land retained by that vendor. Sometimes the deed imposing the covenants does state that they are imposed for the benefit of the vendor's adjoining land, but without defining such land. Even if the covenants are stated to be imposed for the benefit of the vendor's 'Woodlands Estate' or whatever, they will probably be equally futile, as forty years later no one will know what is or was the 'Woodlands Estate'.

As mentioned, developers selling new houses on an estate invariably make the individual purchasers enter into a sheet or two of fresh restrictive covenants, the most common being: to use the house only as a private house, to keep a certain fence in good repair, not to make any additions or construct additional fences without the vendor's consent, not to obstruct the highway, and so on. But for what purpose? After the last remaining house on its Phase IV Billericay development has been sold, is Wates Ltd. going to be interested in whether Bill Bloggs constructs a porch to enclose his front door? And after it has sold all its adjacent land, the developer would not be able to enforce such covenants in any case, even if it wanted to.

The only way such covenants can serve any useful purpose is if each of the owners of the houses on a certain estate could enforce them against all the other owners, thereby enabling each owner to preserve the character of his immediate neighbourhood. This can indeed be achieved if the covenants are worded in a special way so as to create what is known as a 'building scheme'. In fact not only is this special wording rarely used when imposing restrictive covenants, but often a clause is inserted expressly denying the intention to create such a scheme. Thus developers' solicitors, from force of habit, will always make every new house subject to restrictive covenants; but for some obscure reason they will go out of their way to ensure that such covenants, while not being able to benefit the developer in any way, will not benefit anyone else either.

There is a further technical reason why the most common covenant – to keep a certain fence in good repair – cannot be enforced. This is because it is a *positive* covenant, which means that it requires the spending of money; and positive covenants can be enforced only as ordinary contractual obligations – that is, only by and against the persons who originally entered into them, which in most cases will be the developer and the first owner of the house. Thus in the ordinary course of things, neighbours will *not* be able to enforce a covenant to repair a fence against each other.

But whether or not the covenants are capable of benefiting anyone, whether or not they are enforceable, whether or not they are nonsensical (e.g. a covenant to observe a non-existent building line), whether they were originally imposed in a deed a year old or a hundred years old, all restrictive covenants are faithfully copied onto the land certificate (in the case of a registered house) or referred to in every subsequent conveyance (in the case of an unregistered house). Every contract for sale will refer to them; every conscientious purchaser's solicitor will ask questions about them, to which questions the vendor's solicitor will be unable to give any meaningful answers.

As there will generally be no indication of the land intended to be *benefited* by the covenants, not only will the covenants be unenforceable, but no-one will know who might *try* to enforce them, or who should be approached for any consent required under them. Thus the owner of a house may want to build a sun lounge, and may remember that the house is subject to a covenant, imposed forty years ago, that no additions shall be built without the consent of Bert Muggins or his successor. The covenant is probably unenforceable. In any case, there will usually be no means of finding out who or where Bert Muggins or his successor might be. Alternatively, the covenant might stipulate that the plans of the house itself must first be approved by Bert Muggins or his successor, and there will probably be no written approval with the deeds, and no way of ascertaining whether Mr. Muggins or his successor ever *did* approve the plans.

While this area of uncertainty and lack of precision may not have been consciously engineered by solicitors, it is just this sort of uncertainty and lack of precision, with its attendant morass of meaningless but faintly menacing verbiage, which solicitors know how to perpetuate and exploit. The bogey of restrictive covenants dances around every account of solicitors' conveyancing work, and the complication thereof. I quote: 'The purchaser's solicitor's questions to the owner's solicitor will be directed to finding out mainly whether there are any restrictive covenants affecting the use of the property . . .' (Dudley Perkins, *Buying a House*.) 'Two of the most important matters with which the contract must deal are the nature of the title, and whether there are any restrictive covenants affecting the future use of the property.' (Dudley Perkins, again.) 'Some common defects in title – an obvious breach of a restrictive covenant which is not released at all, or is not effectively released.' (Ian Wright, *The Compleat Conveyancer*.) 'If special conditions are imposed, or if there are restrictive covenants in existence, the solicitor will require to know whether these have been observed up to the present date.' (G. Sanctuary, *Before You See a Solicitor*.) But for the last word on restrictive covenants let's go to the Consumers' Association's book, designed to show the layman how to do his own conveyancing without a solicitor: ' . . . the person buying a house should assume that all covenants set out in the charges register can be enforced against him when he becomes the owner. If they forbid the doing of anything which in any way affects what he proposes to do with the property, he should *either take legal advice on the point, or look for another house.*'

Leases

So far in this book I have dealt only with freeholds. Freehold is where the owner owns the house absolutely; leasehold is where he owns it only for a stated number of years. Most houses are freehold; but flats have to be leasehold. Thus when someone buys a flat, even if it costs £250,000, he will only get a lease for a stated number of years. When a lease of a flat is first granted and sold, the purchaser usually gets a term of 99 years, but of course during this period the flat may be sold and sold again, with the number of years left to run constantly diminishing.

Leases are more complicated than freeholds. In the case of a freehold house the owner owns it absolutely, and that's that. He drives up to his property along a public road. He does not usually need any rights over anyone else's land, and nobody usually has any rights over *his* land. Subject to planning laws, he can do what he likes in or with his house, and let it get as dilapidated as he pleases. The owner of a flat, however, is in a much more restricted position, as he does not own the land itself but only part of a building, and then only for a stated number of years. The lease will therefore grant him rights to use the common parts of the building, and the drains and pipes in the building; and will impose on him certain obligations, the most important being to keep the flat in good repair and/or to contribute a certain proportion towards the cost of repairing the whole building.

But although leases are necessarily more complicated than freeholds, and although the scheme required for a large block of flats will be different from that appropriate to a terrace house which has been converted into two flats, the number of possible variations is limited. In fact there are only two basic kinds of flat lease. One is for each individual flat-owner ('the lessee') to keep his flat both inside and outside in good repair.

The owner of the ground floor flat will have to repair the drains; the owner of the upper flat will have to repair the roof. This is a rough and ready arrangement suitable for when there are only two or three separate flats in the building. The other scheme, which is more suitable for a block of flats, is for each flat-owner to have to keep the *inside* of his particular flat in good repair; and for the person who originally granted the lease ('the lessor') – or else a separate management company – to be given the task of keeping the *structure* of the building in good repair, with each flat-owner contributing a proportion of the total cost. Now it might be thought that although the latter scheme is more sophisticated than the former, it is really not all that complicated. Nevertheless, if a solicitor can add forty words to a postal description of a house without increasing its meaning one jot, he will be able to do wonderful things with a lease.

I have an example of a lease in front of me. Let's see if we can find out who is responsible for repairing the structure of the building of which the flat in question forms part. First of all, what is the flat in question? Start at page 2, where the substantive part of the lease begins: 'The lessor hereby demises unto the lessee all and singular the demised premises to hold the same unto the lessee for a term of 99 years from 29 September 1962'. That's all right; we just have to find out what the demised premises are. Turn to the definition section: 'the demised premises means the property hereby demised as described in the third schedule hereto'. On three pages to the third schedule: 'ALL THAT first floor flat forming part of the property and known or intended to be known as Block E Number 42 Muggleton Close'. So all we have to do is to find out who is responsible for repairing the structure of Block E. Usually it is the lessor or a separate management company which keeps the structure in repair. In this case there is no management company, so it will probably be the lessor. Turn therefore to the lessor's covenants, set out in the ninth schedule: 'No. 7: To do all such acts and things as are set out in the sixth schedule hereto'. Back eight pages to the sixth schedule: 'Repairing rebuilding or otherwise treating as necessary and keeping the Maintained Property in good and substantial repair order and condition'. The Maintained

Property? Go back to the definition section on page 3: 'The Maintained Property means the property more particularly described in the second schedule hereto'. Turn three pages to the second schedule: 'all those structural parts of the Buildings'. The Buildings? Back to the definition section: 'The Buildings means (*sic*) the buildings shown coloured red and pink respectively on plan numbered 1 annexed hereto forming part of the Property'. Stay in the definition section for the definition of the Property: 'The Property means the property described in the first schedule'. On to the first schedule: 'The Property: all that piece or parcel of land registered at H.M. Land Registry under title no. — together with the buildings erected or to be erected on parts thereof comprising 58 self-contained flats all which said property is for the purpose of identification only delineated on Plan no.1 annexed hereto and thereon coloured red'.

This particular lease is perhaps more grotesque than the average; nevertheless it is by no means exceptional. I have come across several worse drawn leases, where the draftsman has become so lost in his own bog of nonsense that he has forgotten to include *any* effective provision for the repair of the structure, or where he has omitted to give the lessee a right to use the estate roads.

Now a block of flats in Richmond is the same sort of animal as a block of flats in Leeds; and whether it contains ten or a hundred flats, and whether the development consists of one or ten blocks, the principle is always the same. The flat-owner must be given the same rights, and must observe the same covenants,* in every case. In every case the structure must be kept in repair by the lessor or by a management company, and the cost of such repair repaid by the individual flat-owners. Leases could therefore be standardised. The Law Society could commission some reasonably competent legal draftsmen to work out a standard form of flat lease with one or two variations – e.g. form A for when there is no management company; form B for when there is; form C for when there are common gardens. The master leases would then be printed, and the entire exercise would take a couple of months.

---

* This sort of covenant should not be confused with a *restrictive covenant*, which binds freehold land.

Under the present system, however, there is no such uniformity. Some leases are reasonably concise; others run to thirty or forty pages. Each time a lease of a flat is granted the lessor's solicitor drafts a new lease. Hence the wording of each firm's lease is different from every other firm's lease, so that each time a flat is bought the purchaser's solicitor will have to look through the particular lease he has been sent. And each time that flat is subsequently sold, *another* purchaser's solicitor will have to look through that lease (although however wretchedly drafted, he won't be able to alter it by a syllable), and yet *another* solicitor acting for the purchaser's *building society* will have to look through that lease. And each solicitor who looks through the lease will charge a large sum of money for so doing.

It is as if the motor industry had so arranged it that no two sets of sparking plugs had the same thread. Consequently each time they needed renewing the sockets would have to be bored out and re-threaded – at a cost of £100 a set.

As for the actual wording of the lease, consider the following example: '*At the lessee's own expense to do and execute all such works as are or at any time during the term hereby granted shall be under or in pursuance of any Act or Acts of Parliament already or hereafter to be passed directed or required to be done or executed.*'

This is a standard clause found in every lease, obliging the lessee to carry out any works required by any existing or future Act of Parliament. Yet notice how, by inserting several subclauses before the operative verb and by omitting any punctuation, the draftsman has contrived to express this simple concept in terms of near gibberish; and only by reading the passage half a dozen times is one able to puzzle out what *is* the operative verb. As for the absence of punctuation, this is because of a rule that no punctuation shall appear in a legal document. Lawyers try to justify this – and their convoluted verbiage – by claiming that if their documents were written in straightforward everyday language they would not be sufficiently precise. In fact the reverse is true. Solicitors use wodges of barely comprehensible verbiage as a substitute for precise thought. They do this, firstly, because precise thought takes a bit of effort, whereas telling a typist to copy the firm's form of lease does not; but secondly, and more important, because precise thought, if carried to its logical conclusion, would spell the end of the whole conveyancing industry. Conveyancing solicitors like precision and clear thinking in much the same way as the master of hounds likes the Society for the Abolition of Blood Sports.

*

And that, O my gentle and astute reader, completes my exposition of the conveyancing industry. But before leaving it I will mention an important ancillary industry – the typing or secretarial industry. An articled clerk or junior clerk may well share a typist, but every solicitor or reasonably senior clerk must have a typist or secretary to himself. It is a status symbol by which a valuable member of the staff is distinguished from a less valuable one. Now, having got a secretary, the solicitor or clerk must give her sufficient work to do. Hence an important part of a solicitor's daily routine is the dictating ritual, when he feeds his secretary with sufficient work to enable her to appear reasonably well occupied throughout the day. Thus a large part of a solicitor's office will be devoted to producing letters which will read something like this:

Dear Sirs,
    We thank you for your letter of . . . and note that you have been instructed on behalf of the purchaser. We now enclose draft contract with copy for your use, together with office copy entries of the register.
    Accordingly we await to hear from you as soon as possible,
                                    Yours faithfully,

Dear Sirs,
    We thank you for your letter enclosing your client's signed part of the contract. We have accordingly sent our client's part of the contract to him for signature and will be in touch with you again as soon as this is to hand.
                                    Yours faithfully,

The Consumers' Association's book helpfully sets out a series of such model letters for its readers – who might not be able to aspire unaided to such literary heights – to copy, e.g. on p. 42

'Dear Sirs,
14 Twintree Avenue Minford.
Thank you for your letter of 18 March 1971 enclosing the draft
contract relating to my proposed purchase of the above property. I
am grateful for the copy for my use.
I enclose some preliminary enquiries, with a copy.
Yours faithfully,

M.J. Seaton'

The point is not that these letters contain unnecessary
padding. The letters themselves are unnecessary. If a solicitor
sends me a draft contract or a form of preliminary enquiries or
whatever, I do not need a letter telling me what he has sent me.
I can discover this for myself by looking at the thing in the
envelope.

Yet probably over a million such letters are sent daily from
solicitors' offices in England and Wales. As each letter costs £7
or £8 to produce (so we are told) we can presume they fulfil a
purpose.

Conveyancing is the art of making the simple complicated.
Some things about a house necessarily have to be left to
chance, like whether the local Council will at any time in the
future exercise its powers over the house or its environment.
Other things have to be left to chance because of the defective
system which has evolved as a result of the profession's policy
of eschewing the precise in favour of the uncertain, e.g. the
uncertainty regarding restrictive covenants. In practice,
however, these defects rarely seem to give rise to difficulties. A
house is a solid object built on an area of land, about which
there are a dozen or so things which could either briefly be
checked, or in the vast majority of cases can as well be left to
chance. As we have seen, under traditional conveyancing
practice these dozen or so things are, in fact, left to
chance.

In Britain, about two-thirds of all town and suburban
houses are modest dwellings, without garages or any other
extension or addition, with a common drain running along
the rear and an individual water pipe coming from the mains
under the pavement in the front – rows and rows of ordinary
monotonous houses built forty to eighty years ago. A brief

inspection of such houses would at once show that there was nothing about them which a solicitor, however erudite or conscientious, could query or make a show of querying (apart from a routine check with the local Council). Perhaps half of the remaining third of town and suburban houses, although more spacious and expensive, equally have nothing for the solicitor to query. They have garages obviously built when the house was erected, and a side access within the boundary. In the remaining sixth, there may be something which a solicitor could at least make a show of enquiring about: perhaps a garage or an extension was built after the house was erected, or a right of way might be needed over a passage at the side or rear. The solicitor will not usually do anything about such matters; nor, in ninety-nine out of a hundred cases, will he need to. My point is that in about five-sixths of all houses in built up areas, there is nothing which a purchaser's solicitor can sensibly make even a pretence of querying.

Now the secret of any successful sales technique is that its operators must be able to convince not only their customers, but also *themselves*, of the value of what they are doing or selling. In conveyancing, this is achieved by the solicitor removing himself as far as possible – both mentally and physically – from the realities of the house he is dealing with. If a purchaser asked his solicitor what he had to find out about the house he was buying, the solicitor would pull out some generalities about having to check whether there was any liability for road charges, or whether there were any rights of way, or restrictive covenants, or 'unusual obligations towards other people' (D. Perkins, *Buying a House*). Such statements might sound plausible enough when uttered in the solicitor's office. But if instead the client drove his solicitor to the actual house and put the same question, the solicitor would probably be nonplussed. He couldn't very well talk about liability for road charges if the house was on a bus route. Nor would it be sensible to mention restrictive covenants if the house was obviously thirty or forty years old, with a row of identical houses on either side. And if the solicitor muttered something about 'unusual obligations towards other people', he would risk the immediate rejoinder of 'such as what?'

To enable him to believe that he is dealing with something

fraught with legal and quasi-legal overtones, not only must the solicitor refrain from inspecting the particular house his client is buying: he must take refuge behind the murky screen of professionalism, which will prevent him seeing the house as a simple physical thing. The printed forms crammed with complicated verbiage, the ritual formulas, the letters with their stilted phraseology and the paraphernalia needed to produce them – secretaries and the busy clack of typewriters – each in its subtle way helps to make up this screen. Once erected it needs no maintenance other than woolly thinking and imprecise drafting. Once erected, the solicitor can regard himself as a useful member of the community, giving his clients a skilled and *professional* service.

Moreover once erected, the screen will be impervious to any disturbing *facts* there may be knocking around. For example, a book review in the Solicitors' Journal (22 August 1975) stated: 'With the aid of this book and a little basic knowledge, any junior clerk should be able to carry through registered land transactions.' Yet in an article in the same Journal, the following week, we read: 'Every conveyancing transaction, however humble, requires a knowledge of law and a degree of professional skill in dealing with people and their problems far greater than is generally realised.' I doubt whether any solicitor reading both within the space of a week would have noticed any contradiction in the two quotations. The first – any junior clerk with a little basic knowledge should be able to do registered conveyancing – is a statement of palpable fact; palpable because in most solicitors' offices there will be junior clerks doing just that. The second – every house conveyance requires considerable knowledge of law and professional skill – is what the solicitor has to *believe*.

8 Solicitors' defences

Every system is defended by its exponents, and in the first chapter I outlined some of the arguments by which solicitors have convinced the public that their services are well-nigh indispensable in the business of buying and selling a house. Let's look at these arguments again in the light of what we have learned.

When someone is making the biggest investment of his life/embarking on the most important commercial transaction of his life (etc.), he needs a highly trained expert/qualified solicitor (etc.) to look after it for him.

The fallacy of this argument is in assuming that the complexity of a transaction is proportionate to the sum of money involved. In fact buying a house for £100,000 need involve no more knowledge of the law than buying a washing machine for £200 (often it involves less).

In any case, the fallacy is exposed by the fact that it is *not* a solicitor but an unqualified and unsupervised clerk who does most of the conveyancing which comes out of a solicitor's office.

Only a solicitor has the necessary knowledge and expertise in the highly complex field of land law of which conveyancing is a part.

Academic land law is indeed complicated, but fortunately such complications rarely obtrude in house conveyancing. For instance, the subject of mortgages occupies ninety pages in the standard students' textbook. Yet the only thing a purchaser needs to *know* about his mortgage is that if he pays the instalments he'll be all right; and if he doesn't, he won't.

Similarly, whole books have been devoted to the study of easements (rights of way etc.), how they are created and how extinguished – an enthralling subject, but of little relevance to the owner of 15 Muggleton Close. In fact I suspect that most solicitors forget their laboriously acquired knowledge of the complexities of land law within a few months of passing the Final exam, and feel all the better for it. If once in a way a problem *does* occur involving the complexities of land law, the first thing our learned solicitor will probably do is to take Counsel's opinion.

Your solicitor is concerned to make sure that the local Council does not have any far-reaching plans which could affect the house; and that the present owner has not offended against our multitudinous laws and regulations in some way which might bring trouble to a future owner.

The implication here is that because the local Council has far-reaching powers over a house by virtue of complex laws and regulations – *therefore* it must be a complex process, requiring professional expertise, to find out whether the Council has any proposals afoot to exercise them.

Yet all a solicitor does under this head is to send a printed questionnaire to the local Council, and check that the printed sheet of answers which the Council attaches thereto are standard – a task which scarcely needs an expert. Indeed this is the most questionable of all the solicitors' conveyancing activities. I have mentioned (p. 55) reported instances of two purchasers' solicitors who failed to find out about an impending road going through the properties their respective clients were buying, because at the time they submitted their 'local search' the proposal was not actually on the register but still in 'committee' stage. On the other hand had those two purchasers, instead of employing a solicitor, *personally called* at the Council offices and made a few common-sense enquiries of the appropriate clerks, they would have got the necessary information in a matter of minutes. These two cases happened to have been reported. There must be hundreds of similar cases which haven't.

In ninety-nine out of a hundred cases everything may be straightforward and you could do your own conveyancing. But how do you know that your case will not be the one in a hundred where there is something to go wrong?

It is true that in the exceptional case there is something to be found out, or there is something to go wrong. Yet this is hardly an argument for using a solicitor, since it is the *solicitor's* procedures which are geared only to those ninety-nine cases in a hundred where there isn't anything to find out or go wrong, but which – as we have seen in the above and other examples – are inadequate to cope with the hundredth case where there is.

Conveyancing requires no special knowledge? Here are some typical problems: Can a vicar sell the vicarage by himself? Can Mrs. Brown's nephew, who says he has Mrs. Brown's authority, sell her house for her? Will you be able to insist that a neighbour, who uses a septic tank on the property you intend buying, constructs his own septic tank on his own property?*

These are not typical problems, of course. Nevertheless every now and again a problem might arise which a layman on his own would be ill-equipped to deal with. In that case it should be possible for the layman (if he cannot find the answer in a reference book) to consult the 'expert' when and if such a problem *does* occur. The fact that every so often a nut needs special equipment to free it because it is rusted on a bolt, does not mean that *only* someone with that equipment is competent to undo a nut.

If your solicitor makes a mistake you can sue him for negligence; whereas if you do your own conveyancing and make a mistake, you can't sue yourself for negligence.

This is the famous 'insurance' justification – that the client, in employing a solicitor to do his conveyancing, is buying insurance against anything 'going wrong'.

For this justification to be valid, a solicitor's job would need to be precisely defined, so the client would know exactly what was covered, exactly what was guaranteed. Not only is a solicitor's job not precisely defined; it is not defined at all. It is

---

*   These examples are taken from *The Compleat Conveyancer* by I.M. Wright.

not even clear whether a solicitor is *obliged* to make the usual searches and enquiries (*Emmet on Title* p. 2). Hence the disgruntled gentleman, who found that his house had no water supply, would probably be met with the bland statement: 'But my dear fellow, that's your *surveyor's* job to find out.' It is difficult enough to prove negligence against someone whose job is well defined. To attempt to prove negligence against a solicitor in the case of a house purchase is a mammoth and hazardous undertaking.

There are numerous things which do not usually, but which *can*, 'go wrong' in a house purchase. The vendor might not be able to give possession until two months after the stipulated completion date; the purchaser on moving in might find himself immediately involved in a boundary dispute; the house next door might be demolished and work started to erect a monstrous edifice in its place; the purchaser, on clearing a site for a new garage, might strike a drain from another house and so be unable to build his garage. The client may have some hazy notion that employing a solicitor will somehow protect him from this sort of happening. Not only will it do no such thing, but there would be no question of any claim for negligence in such cases, for the simple reason that his solicitor would not have been negligent. This is the advantage of encouraging the client to think that the solicitor's job covers the whole spectrum of house ownership (as the Law Society does in its pamphlet), while at the same time being careful never to state what it actually *does* cover. The client is led to believe that he is buying an expensive but eminently worthwhile insurance policy to safeguard him in the most important commercial transaction of his life. But this notional insurance policy, if it ever has to be referred to, will turn out to be written in invisible ink.

Even if the solicitor *has* been negligent, it's not a question of his former client writing to him and getting a letter of apology, enclosing a fat cheque, by return. There is first the little matter of proof – i.e. before he is entitled to any compensation, the client has to *prove in Court* that his solicitor was negligent. Allegations of professional negligence tend to be hotly contested; and the task of proving his solicitor was negligent has ruined many an aggrieved client with a seemingly open

and shut case. For instance, the most common form of
solicitors' negligence in domestic conveyancing is exchanging
contracts on a client's purchase without securing his sale, or
vice versa, so the client is either left with two houses or no
house at all. Here the solicitor's defence will be that the client
verbally instructed him to take the risk and exchange on the
one transaction independently of the other, and the client will
have to *prove* that he did not. Another form of negligence is not
warning the client about an adverse clause in the contract or
entry on a local search form. Here the defence will probably
be that when the client called at his office the solicitor went
through the contract and various matters with him, and *did*
warn him of the item in question; and again the client will have
to *prove* that he didn't.

In any legal action against a professional man, the client is
always at a colossal disadvantage. First, because such an action
takes *four years* or more to come to Court, so it is not so much a
legal battle as a war of attrition. Secondly, because if the client
loses, he has to pay not only his own but also his adversary's
legal costs. Anyone suing a solicitor therefore has to risk losing
£15,000/£20,000 in legal costs – and will probably have to put
a considerable sum up front before his new solicitor will bring
the case to Court. For some reason those apologists for the
system, who talk so glibly about being able to sue your
solicitor if he makes a mistake, fail to mention these little
facts.

*Solicitors are subject to the discipline of the Law Society which ensures
they observe the highest standards of professional conduct and
competence.*

This is the 'professional' argument: that the client is safe in
the hands of the professional, because the professional has to
observe higher standards of conduct and competence than the
tradesman – which higher standards are enforced by his
professional body. This claim is made in various forms, e.g. in
its evidence to the Royal Commission on Legal Services, the
Law Society stated: 'The Law Society has accepted for a great
number of years responsibility not only for the maintenance
of professional standards of behaviour but also for the
maintenance of professional standards of competence and

efficiency' (para. 25.22). Yet at the same time as the Law Society made that claim, it was sending out 9,000 letters a year to complainants, telling them that as their complaint concerned their solicitor's *incompetence* the Law Society had no powers to deal with it, and that the complainant's only remedy was to find *another* solicitor to sue the first one in the Courts.

If the complaint was of a solicitor's misconduct, the Law Society was equally dismissive. For instance, I once reported an eminent solicitor who had bribed a witness I intended calling, in proceedings before the Industrial Tribunal. Replied the Law Society:

'Your letter alleges the commission of a criminal offence. I think it would be quite improper and certainly contrary to the usual practice of the Law Society for the Society to comment on your allegations or to take any action in the matter. The proper authority to whom to refer the commission of a criminal offence is the Police. This is a matter entirely for you. You may think in all the circumstances that you will be well advised to take separate legal advice.'

A lady of my acquaintance complained to the Law Society that her solicitor was refusing to hand over the proceeds of sale of her house. Again the Law Society took no action – at any rate not until I telephoned the Law Society official in question some months later, and told him I was investigating the lady's complaint in my capacity as journalist. He promptly put the phone down but, surprise surprise, the day *after* my telephone call the lady received a cheque for her money (with interest) from her erstwhile solicitor.

The spuriousness of the Law Society's claims was neatly exposed by Mr. Leslie Parsons, a businessman, who complained to the Law Society that his solicitor tried to overcharge him by £130,000. His solicitor had submitted a bill for £198,000 which the taxing master had reduced to £68,000, finding that the bill had been based largely on fictitious attendance notes and bogus claims for time spent in perusing documents. The Law Society dismissed Mr. Parsons's complaint, who thereupon himself took High Court proceedings and had the solicitor struck off – which the solicitor did not even oppose.

Following the embarrassing publicity which resulted from

this case, the Law Society attempted to restore its tarnished image by setting up the 'Solicitors Complaints Bureau', a supposedly independent body. However, the Bureau is still churning out the same letters by the thousand as before – 'If you consider your solicitor has not handled your case properly this is a matter of law rather than professional conduct, and you should seek independent advice . . .' The only difference is they come from a different address.

The Law Society publishes a magazine called *Exchange Contracts*, the back page of each issue proclaiming the message that the Law Society ensures 'the highest standards of service by Solicitors to the public.' I tried to bring a private prosecution against the Law Society on the grounds that that advertisement infringed the Trade Descriptions Act. Although my application was thrown out by the High Court judges (p. 15), it was not entirely in vain: thereafter the Law Society changed the message to 'The Law Society welcomes Exchange Contracts' helpful advice to homebuyers'.

We don't just deal with the conveyancing but give the client a whole range of services, such as telling him how much he can borrow, who from and how it is best done; advising husbands and wives on the benefits of co-ownership; coping with the tax problems which will arise; advising on insurance, planning permissions and bye-laws etc.

Unable to state what his job entails, the solicitor frequently takes refuge in an account of what his job does *not* entail. This list of peripheral matters on which the solicitor claims a special expertise may appear plausible, but it collapses on examination. For instance, most purchasers have already put in their mortgage application *before* they get to a solicitor – either to the building society with which they have been saving, or to one suggested by the estate agents who arranged the sale (who will generally have a building society agency); insurance is invariably dealt with by the building society or other lender; there are no tax problems, and normally no questions of planning permission, which will arise, and so on. Of course there *are* a few nuggets of relevant information knocking around – e.g. the advantage of putting the house in the joint names of husband and wife is that on the death of one, the whole goes automatically to the survivor – but it is as ludicrous for a solicitor to claim that dispensing such information is his exclusive domain as it would be for a travel agent to claim that only he can advise on the advantage of taking travellers' cheques.

We have to charge handsomely for conveyancing to subsidise other unprofitable work.

Another much used argument. I remember the President of the Law Society, in a television debate on Austin Mitchell's Bill, claiming that if solicitors lost their conveyancing monopoly then High Street solicitors would go out of business – and *then* where would Mrs. Moo go to for legal advice on her violent husband or the Council's repossession proceedings? In other words, when the solicitor isn't doing conveyancing he is sorting out the legal problems of the poor – who, being unable to afford the economic rate, have to be subsidised by his more wealthy house-buying clients.

The trouble with this argument is that solicitors are notoriously *uninterested* in poor people, and those areas of the law most likely to affect them, e.g. relating to industrial tribunals, Rent Acts, immigration etc. Solicitors are business-men, and not unnaturally they set up their offices in those areas where there is most money around – e.g. commercial centres of big cities, High Streets of market towns, prosperous suburbs, seaside resorts such as Bournemouth (which incidentally has the greatest concentration both of wealth and of solicitors in the Country). On the other hand, in those vast, desolate, densely-populated outskirts of the large cities there is scarcely a solicitor's office to be seen. When a handful of 'Neighbourhood Law Centres' were set up in a haphazard attempt to cater for those areas, they needed Law Society waivers to allow them to advertise – which the Law Society granted on condition that they did *not* do conveyancing. In other words, the Law Society was happy enough to allow the Neighbourhood Law Centres to advertise as long as they confined their activities to those areas of law which were of no interest to the High Street solicitors, and did not encroach on their lucrative conveyancing preserves.

That this 'conveyancing is needed to subsidise other unprofitable work' argument can be seriously advanced, is a measure of the preferential treatment we accord the professional over the tradesman. Such an argument in the mouth of a *non*-professional – you see, guv, we have to charge you £350 for that routine service on your Sierra because we do such a lot of work on those old bangers whose owners just can't afford the economic rate – would merely get a well-deserved raspberry.

Well maybe you can do your own conveyancing if you've got the time and can follow a handbook, just as you can do your own plumbing and install your own central heating. But most people don't want the bother and would rather leave it to the professional.

It is true that most people *don't* want the bother, and *would* prefer to leave it to the professional – whether 'it' is their plumbing, car repairs, or conveyancing. Nevertheless the real argument is not: you *can* do your own conveyancing just as you can do your own plumbing and install your own central heating etc.; but that if you do your own conveyancing with a modicum of common sense *you are bound to do a better job than the professional,* because you have the necessary equipment to do the job properly – i.e. the time and interest to look at the property and call at the Council offices – which the professional doesn't have.

It takes a thorough knowledge of the law and many years experience to make sure your conveyance is absolutely foolproof. Only a solicitor has that knowledge and expertise.

Solicitor *A*, my first employer, was an elderly gentleman who spent most of his afternoons asleep or dozing (except for when someone asked for a 'Commissioner for Oaths' upon which he would spring to life, quivering with excitement at the thought of earning £1 12s 6d for putting his signature to an affidavit). He had a cupboard at the end of his room in which all his files were kept, current and dead, in no particular order. The files themselves were ungainly bundles tied up with pink tape. When acting for a purchaser he would ask two questions only of his client: 'The house is still there is it? You've seen it? No, I'm not being funny.' As a result of this he had a reputation for great wisdom and inaccessibility. When I was going on holiday and told a certain client that Mr. *A* would be dealing with her matter in my absence, she asked incredulously: 'But will he have time?'

Mr. *B* his partner, on the other hand, took a less cavalier attitude. In fact he was so cautious that he would never exchange contracts until every detail was cleared up to his satisfaction. One of his clients was buying a house subject to some old restrictive covenants, including one to maintain a chain-link fence along one of the boundaries. Mr. *B* insisted on an assurance from the vendor's solicitor that this fence was in position before he would exchange contracts, and in the week or so while he was waiting for this assurance (when he could have exchanged) the vendor got a better offer and sold elsewhere, and *B*'s client consequently lost the house. The covenant in question could not have been enforced in any case.

My next employer was another senior conveyancing partner in a different firm. He accepted a contract containing the clause: 'The property is sold subject to *all* the entries on the charges register' – one of which entries was a substantial mortgage.

I once attended a completion appointment on behalf of the vendor at the building society's solicitor's office, where I met a solicitor's clerk acting for the purchaser. The building society's solicitor duly produced the deeds, which the solicitor's clerk inspected and put in his briefcase. The building society's solicitor then realised he had mixed up his appointments, and had consequently given the clerk the *wrong* set of deeds, which the clerk had not noticed.

Of course, we don't know how typical these cases are because there has never been an independent survey to show how well or badly solicitors do their work. (For its report on car repairers *Which?* books in a car with deliberately induced faults to fifty unsuspecting garages, but evidently considers it would be unseemly to subject *solicitors* to an equivalent test.) Nevertheless I think that some sort of mistake is the rule rather than the exception.

I previously stated that it is common practice for solicitors, after completing the purchase of a registered house, to wait for the receipt discharging the vendor's previous mortgage, unaware of (or indifferent to) the fact that the protection given by their land registry search will be lost meanwhile. This conclusion is supported by a letter in the Law Society's Gazette (4 September 1974): 'A sample count showed that more than half the search certificates . . . had their priority expire without the protected application being lodged. These figures, if typical, are quite remarkable in showing that in over one half of the cases the protection given by the search has been lost.' This letter was not contradicted or even commented upon. Thus in the *profession's own magazine* there is a statement of evidence indicating that over half the conveyancing cases are negligently dealt with by the profession, which fact is not considered sufficiently interesting or noteworthy for any of its 20,000 readers to comment upon.

Then again, if I repay Bill Bloggs the money he lent me, it is obvious that I should get a receipt signed by Mr. Bloggs. Yet the house-buyer's solicitor, for all his professional expertise, does not get a receipt when he pays off the vendor's building society's mortgage: all he gets is a letter from the building society's solicitor *undertaking* to send him the receipt when that solicitor receives it from the building society – which is no guarantee that the purchaser's solicitor ever *will* get the receipt. That this practice is universally accepted by the profession indicates that conveyancing solicitors and their clerks are little more than automatons.

On the other hand, very rarely will anything actually go wrong however badly the work is done. And even if it does, the solicitor is still in a well-nigh impregnable position since his client will regard the whole process as a mystery and so can easily be fobbed off if necessary. For instance, solicitor *B*'s client would not realise that it was his solicitor's fault that he lost the house: he would merely be told that the vendor had withdrawn before the solicitor had completed the necessary searches and enquiries. And in the unlikely event he was not disposed to accept this, but tried to take the matter further, he would find himself at the same disadvantage as an Englishman querying a restaurant bill on his first trip abroad.

When it comes to domestic conveyancing, our solicitor is in an enviable position. Usually nothing will go wrong however badly the job is carried out.* If, exceptionally, something does go wrong, the solicitor will generally be able to claim that he carried out the traditional procedures with perfect correctitude – and that it is the *system*, if anything, which is to blame. Even if the solicitor is actually negligent, the client can probably be fobbed off – and the odd client who can't, but tries to pursue his remedy through the Courts, will find himself at an almost insuperable disadvantage. Neither will the Law Society take any action against a solicitor however incompetent; or if he bribes a witness, or attempts to defraud a client out of £130,000, or even refuses to hand over to the client the proceeds of sale. All in all, these are not conditions which make for high standards.

---

* Unfortunately, this isn't true of *commercial* conveyancing – e.g. shop leases. *Face the Facts* (Radio 4, 23 June 1988) had an amusing item on an enterprising gentleman who let out some thirty or more fish and chip shops (in Somerset and North Devon) on leases which enabled him to quadruple the rent within two years, and so bankrupt the tenants. None of the tenants' solicitors had spotted the rogue rent review clause.

9

A reformed
Land Registry

As a result of the surprise success, in December 1983, of Austin Mitchell's private member's Bill to break the solicitors' conveyancing monopoly, the Government promised to introduce equivalent legislation in return for Austin Mitchell agreeing to abandon his Bill. Accordingly in March 1986 the Council for Licensed Conveyancers was set up, under whose auspices 'licensed conveyancers' were allowed to do conveyancing in competition with solicitors, the Council itself being controlled by the Lord Chancellor.

The Consumers' Association – which had sponsored Mitchell's original Bill – hailed the step as 'a great leap forward for consumers'; the Government proudly added solicitors' conveyancing to its list of hitherto unassailable monopolies which it had fearlessly tackled; and the British public happily went about its business under the impression that the conveyancing system had somehow been changed, and consequently everything was now 'all right'.

Yet despite these earth-shaking events, nothing has changed. To become a licensed conveyancer a candidate has to serve the same period of articles, and pass almost the equivalent examinations, as a solicitor. Small wonder that, according to the lastest list in the Law Society's Gazette (25 May 1988), there are only 146 licensed conveyancers in England and Wales competing with 45,000 solicitors. The advent of licensed conveyancers is therefore a shattering irrelevance (and the decrease in solicitors' conveyancing fees – if such it is – probably had nothing to do with them but came about only because the Law Society panicked and allowed solicitors to *advertise*).

But even if licensed conveyancers *did* take over a significant proportion of conveyancing, and even if conveyancing fees were cut by half as a result, this is not what is needed. If Sicilian peasants are having to pay the Mafia a thousand lire for every barrel of water they get, the solution is not to set up a body of licensed water carriers who will charge only five hundred lire a barrel. The solution is to lay a water pipe. As I have tried to show in the foregoing pages, it is not so much the cost as the *inefficiency* of the conveyancing system which is ludicrous. Tinkering with the species of conveyancing operator is irrelevant. We need to change the system.

When in the middle of the last century a group of enlightened people had the idea of setting up the Land Registry, their aim was to provide a cheap and efficient system whereby houses could be bought and sold as easily and as simply as anything else.* That it took over half a century for the first significant step towards land registration to be taken, in the shape of the Land Registration Act 1925, testifies to the muscle of the lawyers opposing them in Parliament. Thereafter land registration proceeded at a snail's pace until the 1960s when, in response to criticism of the delay and expense of the unregistered system, it was accelerated at the behest of the Lord Chancellor. Now over three-quarters of houses in England and Wales are registered; and the time is in sight when *all* houses will be.

However, while such progress significantly assists solicitors – whose job is much easier if the house is registered – it makes little difference to their clients. Not only is the time it takes to convey a registered house exactly the same as for an unregistered house, but the solicitors' costs are now the same as well. In fact the purchaser is *worse* off if the house is registered, because on top of his solicitor's costs he has to pay a hefty fee to the Land Registry for crossing out the vendor's

---

* 'By what means . . . can we now obtain such a system of registration as will enable owners to deal with land in as simple and easy a manner as they now can deal with movable chattels or stock?' 1857 Report of Royal Commission on Land Registration.

name on the register and substituting his own.

Therefore if the original aim in setting up the Land Registry was to provide a cheap and efficient system of house transfer to replace the expensive and inefficient system of unregistered conveyancing, then something has gone wrong.

What has gone wrong is that the Land Registry has done half the job, but has left the other half untouched. It has cut out the need for investigating the vendor's title, by guaranteeing that the person whose name is typed on the register is the owner of the house in question; and it has substituted a simple transfer form for the traditional conveyance. Also it sets out on the register a note of the current mortgages. It has therefore cut out practically all the legal work which was traditionally done by solicitors after exchange of contracts. Unfortunately it has left untouched the solicitors' work *before* exchange of contracts. Consequently our solicitor, who cannot plausibly tell his client of all the complicated and difficult things he does *after* exchange of contracts, merely has to switch his account to all the complicated and difficult things he does *before* exchange of contracts – like the 'fifty or sixty questions which he is almost bound to ask on any house purchase' (*Buying a House* D. Perkins), the hundred and one things he has to check, the thousand and two things he has to investigate, which the layman wouldn't know how to begin to check or investigate on his own.

But the Land Registry *could* do as good a job with the pre-contract legal work as it has done with the post-contract legal work, in which event it would be manifestly unnecessary for the house-buyer to go to a solicitor, or other professional adviser, at all.

Solicitors' conveyancing work consists, broadly, in checking and finding out various things about the house before exchange of contracts; and investigating the vendor's title after exchange of contracts. As regards the latter, they traditionally checked the vendor's title by going through a pile of old title deeds – A to B, B to C, C to D, and finally D to the present vendor – and a pile of old receipted mortgages. The Land Registry, to its credit, did away with that procedure. The current owner merely has to show his purchaser a copy of the register with his name, and the name of his building society or other lender, in the appropriate spaces, and that's that. Hence investigating title is rendered unnecessary. But the pre-contract rigmarole, whereby the purchaser's solicitor purports to check and find out various things about the house, could be rendered equally unnecessary. Here's how:

Each time a house is bought and sold, before contracts are exchanged the purchaser's solicitor makes a show of finding out, by his preliminary enquiries, various things about it: e.g. whether the house is directly connected to mains drainage and mains water, whether there are any other pipes or drains going under the land serving adjacent houses, who owns the boundary fences, and so on. In fact, as we have seen, the purchaser's solicitor does *not* find out these things, but for his pains merely gets a series of stock formulas from the vendor's solicitor meaning 'I don't know'. *But with a bit of trouble, the Land Registry could find out the few items of fixed information about a house, and set them out on the register.*

Under the existing system, the purchaser pays his solicitor £250/£500 for finding out that the vendor believes that the house is connected to the usual services but does not know the route of the pipes or drains, does not know whether there are any other pipes or drains under the land but the property is sold subject to any there may be, and so on. Under the new system this fixed information would be clearly set out once and for all on the register and plan, a copy of which would be automatically sent to the purchaser. The land registry plan would show the route of the mains drainage and how the house connected to it, the route of any common drain, the route of the water mains, whether the road abutting the house was maintained by the local Council – if not, whether there was a public right of way for vehicles along it. A copy of the relevant planning permission would also be attached. Conversely, the perplexing and often voluminous but generally obsolete and unenforceable restrictive covenants would be cleared *off* the registers, and the Land Registry would refuse to register restrictive covenants, and similar, unless the person wanting them registered could *prove* that they were imposed for a useful purpose. As most of the existing registers have a page or two of useless restrictive covenants (as well as wodges of other verbal rubbish, such as exceptions re rights of light and air etc.), the actual material on the new registers would be less than on the old.

None of your claptrap either about the layman not being able to understand the significance of the entries without a solicitor interpreting them. There would be explanatory notes under each heading, e.g. 'Roads: (a) If the register shows that the road leading to the house is maintained by the Council, the purchaser has no need to enquire further. (b) If it shows that although the road is not maintained by the Council, there is a public right of way for vehicles along it, the owner has the right to use that road – but there may be a future liability for road charges when and if the Council take it over (as to the likelihood of which the purchaser may be able to get some information by enquiring of the Council). (c) If neither (a) nor (b) applies, but the register shows that a right of way for vehicles along the road goes with the house, then it is a *private road* which the owner has a right to use, subject to the same proviso as under (b). (d) If neither (a) (b) nor (c) apply, the purchaser should take legal advice before contracting to buy the house.' In ninety-nine cases out of a hundred (a) would apply; in perhaps one in five thousand cases (d) would apply. Most of the explanatory notes would not need to be so elaborate, e.g. 'Water mains: if the plan shows that a water mains runs under the pavement or road abutting the house, the purchaser has no need to enquire further. If not, he should take legal advice.'

The other thing the purchaser's solicitor does before exchange of contracts is submit a 'local search' to the appropriate local Council. This consists primarily of a printed form of questions, some of which ask for *fixed* information (e.g. whether the road is maintained by the local Council, whether the house drains into the mains sewer, whether planning permission was granted, whether there is a smoke control order). The other questions ask whether there are any outstanding *Notices* affecting the house (e.g. dangerous structure, public nuisance, infringement of building regulations); and whether the Council has any *proposals* affecting the house (e.g. for new roads, road widening, compulsory purchase).

As we have seen, the local search has two disadvantages.

Firstly, it can take up to two months (sometimes even longer) for the Council to return the forms; secondly, the questions relate only to the actual house being bought and not to the surrounding area – thus the local search will not reveal any imminent development of *neighbouring* property. The local search should therefore be scrapped. The fixed information would be noted on the register in the same way as that covered by the preliminary enquiry form. As for the other information, the Council exhibits (in the Town Hall or main library) a comprehensive map on which it marks those houses and areas in respect of which it *has* issued a Notice or received a planning application, or *does* have a proposal. Therefore instead of his solicitor submitting a local search form crammed with seemingly complicated questions referring to innumerable sections and subsections of various Acts of Parliament, and waiting three weeks to two months for the answers, the purchaser himself merely looks at this map and checks that the house he is buying – and adjoining land – are not shaded in red or spotted in green or whatever, and that therefore the Council has no designs on it.

With these improved land registers and Town Maps, the purchaser – without the assistance of any legal eagle – could find out all the available quasi-legal information about the house he is buying in a matter of *minutes*. This in turn would put an end to all delays; and would wipe out many of the grey areas of the existing system. In other words, the original aim in setting up the Land Registry – which was to provide a cheap and efficient system of house transfer in which professionals play no part – would be realised.

Now from time to time various bodies and individuals have expressed concern over the delay inherent in the present system, and its encouragement of gazumping, and have suggested various alternatives – the Scottish system whereby the highest bidder in a postal auction is contractually bound; the American system where the buyer takes out title insurance; computerising local Council records. Yet I have never heard any suggestion to reform the Land Registry on the the above lines. But although my proposals are apparently revolutionary, they are based on three scarcely controversial premises: (1) If there are a dozen or so items of fixed information about a house, it is within the wit of man to collect those items and set them out on the existing land register, thereby obviating the need for the purchaser's solicitor to *ask* about them each time that house changes hands; (2) If the local Council exhibits a map showing those few areas in respect of which it has a proposal, and those few houses in respect of which it has issued a Notice, then similarly there is no need for the purchaser's solicitor to submit a local search form asking about such matters, but the purchaser merely *looks* at the map and checks that the house he is buying is in the clear; (3) That unenforceable or meaningless restrictive covenants and other verbal rubbish, so beloved by solicitors, should no longer be allowed to clutter up the land registers thereby making conveyancing appear more complicated than it is. In short, we already have the foundations of an efficient system in the Land Registry – it just needs the superstructure to be added and the superfluous procedures taken away.

*

Yet despite the obvious nature of these reforms, the ease with which they could be implemented, and the benefits which they would bring to house buyers and sellers, I doubt they will ever come about.

Parliament contains over a hundred lawyers at any given time, who are bound to oppose any reform which deprives solicitors of their most lucrative work.

Nor is it only solicitors who are interested in perpetuating the present conveyancing system. So are the other powerful institutions involved – banks, building societies, estate agents – who, with solicitors, form a closely-knit cabal, each with their hands in the others' pockets.

As for the media, on the rare occasions when television or the press betrays any interest in conveyancing, it is only in respect of sensational *cases* (e.g. when shortly after moving into his £150,000 dream house the purchaser discovered that the Council was proposing to drive a road through it). Proposals for conveyancing reform do not sell newspapers, or appeal to television producers.

On the other hand conveyancing frequently crops up in

radio 'consumer' programmes (local radio as well as B.B.C.); but here the only people whose views are considered worthy of transmission are themselves professionals, either solicitors or members of related professions, who will never criticise the system or those who operate it – presumably subconsciously fearful that if the conveyancing system was toppled, their own particular racket might be next on the hit-list. So a barrister thinks solicitors 'generally are good value' ('Woman's Hour', 23 September 1987); so a chartered surveyor has 'a very high regard for the work solicitors do in conveyancing' ('Tuesday Call', 5 July 1983); so an architect doesn't advise D.I.Y. conveyancing because she's heard of 'too many cases of D.I.Y. purchasers coming unstuck because they found they didn't own the land they wanted to build that garage on, or grandma turned out to be a sitting tenant' ('Woman's Hour', 9 January 1984), and so on.

The independent commentators will also be professional people; and having invested heavily in professionalism themselves they too will be unable to see (let alone expose) solicitors' conveyancing for the sham it is – because to do so would raise disturbing questions on the whole concept of professionalism. So the Consumers' Association has no compunction in castigating car repairers for their 'appalling picture of incompetence, wastefulness and even dishonesty', or the Electricity Board for making 'disgracefully false and misleading claims' for off-peak electricity, or travel agents for giving 'outrageously bad advice or absolutely wrong information'. But when it smells professional man, particularly *legal* professional man, it sings a different song – and in all the *Which?* reports on solicitors and conveyancing you will not find a single line criticising the absurdities and swindles of the conveyancing system which I have chronicled. Indeed many of its utterances on this subject could have come straight out of the Law Society's publicity material.*

---

* 'To get an inkling of what is involved in buying and selling a house, imagine seeing a new freezer on sale in a store. On reading the sale particulars you discover that the store cannot define its exact boundaries, that Mrs. Brown has a right to put one block of ice-cream in the second freezing compartment every thursday (sic), that you must not use it for storing frozen peas, and that you need planning permssion to place a toaster on top of it. A solicitor or licensed conveyancer has to be fully conversant with these complexities.' *The Legal Side of Buying a House.*

Michael Zander, in his book *Lawyers and the Public Interest*, writes: 'Occasionally a difficult problem poses itself, but the work [domestic conveyancing] is well within the capacity of the average school leaver with a couple of 'O' levels, who has undergone a period of training on the job.' But he cannot face the disturbing implications of the fact that work which produces over half the profession's income is well within the capacity of a not very bright junior clerk – and so he falls back on the official party line for his overall conclusion: 'The average lawyer works hard for his clients and does so honestly and with no little skill.'

So the insidious tentacles of professionalism atrophy the critical faculties not only of the public, but of those who should be its watchdogs; and those who have the power to topple the existing system – MPs, the building societies, the media, the Consumers' Association, even the public itself – for their various reasons are not motivated to do so.

Moreover, the solicitors' profession has shown an uncanny ability not only to parry the few brickbats which have been lobbed in its direction, but to turn them into boomerangs.

For instance, setting up the Land Registry was a brave reform originally intended to provide the public with a cheap and efficient alternative to the expensive and inefficient system of unregistered conveyancing, thus making solicitors redundant. Yet in the event it is only solicitors who have benefited – in that their work has been cut by half – while the public suffers the same delays, and pays even greater costs under the new system than under the old.

Another example is the Administration of Justice Act 1985 which inaugurated the Council for Licensed Conveyancers. The resulting handful of mini-solicitors pose no threat to the profession. On the other hand the Act slipped in two handy little provisions. First, it made it illegal for an unqualified conveyancer, for a fee, to prepare the *contract for sale*, whereas hitherto it was only preparing the *transfer* which was illegal. Secondly, an unqualified clerk employed by a solicitor, who prepares contract or transfer, is deemed to be the *agent* of his solicitor employer and therefore is not guilty of infringing the Solicitors Act – so forestalling any further embarrassing attempts to prosecute solicitors' unqualified conveyancing clerks (see p. 30). Thus the only real effect of the Act of Parliament which was popularly believed to break the solicitors' conveyancing monopoly, has been to *strengthen* it. To attempt to tinker with the conveyancing system is to cut off the head of the mythological monster which promptly grew another – and even less attractive – one in its place.

It seems we are therefore stuck with the present system.

What to do? If my reader has stayed with me, and I have done a reasonable job in reporting how the system operates, the question will answer itself. We're stuck with an inefficient system, but that is no reason why you should be stuck with an inefficient and expensive solicitor.

In the preceding pages I have tried to show how the profession misrepresents its services, and the skills it employs, in a way which no magistrate would tolerate from a mere trade or business. I have tried to show how the solicitor (or more usually his unqualified clerk) finds out virtually nothing about the house his client is buying; how the solicitor or clerk neither inspects the house nor goes near the Council offices; how practically everything of importance is left to chance – e.g. if a vendor wishes to conceal the fact that he has had notice that a tower block is going to be built next door, or that he has to pay his neighbour £500 a year for his water supply, all he has to do is to write 'no' to the purchaser's solicitor's question asking him whether he has received any notices, and 'yes' to the question asking if the services come direct from the mains. In fact the vendor does not even have to do that, as his own solicitor will answer these questions with some non-committal waffle on his behalf. And I have tried to show how, when something does go wrong, the purchaser generally has no come-back on his solicitor.

Of course in ninety-nine cases out of a hundred nothing will go wrong however the job is done. The local Council won't be driving a road through the garden of your new house, the water-pipe won't run across a neighbouring farmer's field, the property next door won't be demolished to make way for a tower block, there won't have been a long-standing feud with an unbalanced neighbour, and so on. But conveyancing – if it is about anything at all – is about the one house in a hundred where there *is* something wrong, where there *is* something to find out.

The reason I suggest you do your own conveyancing is not only because you will save yourself a considerable sum of money; but because if you follow my instructions (and in particular if you spend half an hour at the property looking out for the few things I shall tell you to look out for, and another hour or so at the Council offices asking the few questions I shall tell you to ask) you will have a far better chance of finding out whether the house you are buying is that one in a hundred, than if your conveyancing was done by the most prestigious firm of solicitors in the land. You won't be able to do anything about the built-in defects in the system – the delays, the things which ideally you should know about but which are not visible and which are nowhere recorded. But at least you will check the things that can be checked; and at least you will be aware of the other things which under the present system cannot be checked or guaranteed.

Part II

How to do your own conveyancing

Chapters

Appendices

10 Preliminary Points

In the second part of this book I explain how to do the conveyancing on your sale or purchase – whether the property involved is registered or unregistered, freehold or leasehold, house or flat (which includes maisonette), secondhand or new. You will see the layout of the instruction chapters on the facing page.

The instructions apply only to property in *England* and *Wales* (Scotland is excluded because the system there is completely different); and only to property sold or purchased with *vacant possession* (because sales and purchases subject to tenants in possession are sufficiently rare as not to warrant specific treatment).

No forms are needed for the sale, but you will need some for the purchase, as explained on p. 168.

If you do your own conveyancing you will escape all costs and fees on the sale. However on the purchase you will still have to pay stamp duty and land registry fees, if applicable; and the building society's (or other lender's) solicitor's costs if you are getting a mortgage. This is because the building society (or other lender) always employs its own solicitor to deal with the mortgage and check the vendor's title etc., whose fee you will have to pay – which would be the case even if you had a solicitor acting for you. The building society's solicitor's costs, and land registry fee, are laid down in accordance with scales set out in appendix 9. Stamp duty is currently 1% of the purchase price if over £30,000.

If your interest in this book is solely to learn how to do your own conveyancing you should nevertheless read it from the beginning, as this will make the practical chapters easier to follow in that (hopefully) you will start them with some understanding of the system. Also you should read the *whole* of the relevant chapter(s) *before* starting on any of the procedures. This is important as otherwise you may be unprepared for an alternative which I subsequently deal with.

If you are selling and buying at the same time, you will of course have to apply the instructions in the relevant chapters/ appendices simultaneously.

I have tried to avoid the error of most handbooks I have ever picked up – 'make sure sprocket engages with cam shaft regulators before tightening lug nuts' – and hurriedly put down; but if on reading the relevant chapter(s) you are thoroughly confused and petrified, it does not *necessarily* mean that I have failed. A second reading, perhaps a day or two later, and all may yet be well.

Finally a more prickly point. Are you likely to meet obstruction because you are doing your own conveyancing – whether from the other party's solicitor, the estate agents, or your mortgagee? And how should you deal with it if you do? From the feedback I have had since this book was first published, it seems that the professionals' attitude to D.I.Y. conveyancers varies from the 'very friendly and helpful' on the one extreme, to the bloody-minded, on the other; from the faintly patronising to the downright mendacious. The chances are you won't meet anything worse than the faintly patronising; but if you do, I offer the following advice:

If the obstruction comes from a junior employee of a building society or firm of estate agents (e.g. a clerk or 'negotiator'), ask the person concerned to put his objections in writing and say you will take it up with Head Office. This often has the desired effect of changing the bullying: 'No, I'm afraid you won't be able to do your own conveyancing', to 'I was only trying to help by advising you in your own best interests'. In general building societies are O.K., and estate agents can, if necessary, be bypassed. Banks can be a problem in that they will sometimes refuse to lend money to a D.I.Y. purchaser.

But this is largely the public's fault for being so docile. If more than half a dozen such purchasers threatened to withdraw their accounts – and persuade their friends to do likewise – banks would soon change their tune.

As to obstruction from the other party's solicitor, this is easy to handle if the market is in your favour: simply tell your purchaser or vendor to instruct his solicitor to behave himself, or you will find another buyer or another house; or you could try persuading him to buy this book and likewise do his own conveyancing. (However some D.I.Y. conveyancers tend to be a bit paranoid, and mistake a solicitor's fussiness – or even normal meticulousness – for deliberate obstruction.)

Obstruction from the other party's solicitor, when the market is not obviously in your favour, is more difficult to deal with. Nevertheless you need not feel overawed. Remember, you will probably not be dealing with a high-powered solicitor, but with a low-powered solicitor or unqualified clerk; and if you have read and understood this book you will probably know as much, or more, about the subject than he does. Obstruction tactics such as might jeopardise the deal – as opposed to pedantic insistence on some footling formality to make you feel small or ignorant – are, I'm fairly sure, very rare. The vast majority of solicitors would rather put up with the occasional D.I.Y. conveyancer than admit to being cousins of the mafia. However, if anyone – whether solicitor, building society clerk, estate agent, or whoever – tells you you *can't* do your own conveyancing because you won't be able to give an acceptable undertaking to discharge the existing mortgage, or because it's illegal for you to draft the transfer document, or for whatever reason; or that your building society will need to instruct a solicitor whom you might just as well employ as it won't be any cheaper doing your own conveyancing – he is lying.

Anyway, if you do meet any obstruction – or indeed any other difficulty – don't give up. Refer to the 'consultation pack' (details on the inside front cover), and we'll probably be able to sort it out together.

So are you sitting comfortably? Then I'll begin.

11

How to do
the conveyancing
on your sale

The instructions in this chapter tell you how to do the conveyancing on the sale of your freehold house, whether it is registered or unregistered. (If you are selling a *leasehold* house or flat you will have to apply the additional instructions in appendix 6 simultaneously.)

I am assuming that the house you are selling is mortgaged; and for convenience I refer to your mortgagee, who will be holding the deeds, as a building society – although of course it may be a bank, insurance company or whatever. 'Building society' therefore means 'building society or other lender'. If the house is not mortgaged, you merely ignore all references to mortgages and building societies. You will yourself be holding the deeds, and your job will be that much easier.

The first step is for you, the vendor, to write out the contract. To do this you need a copy of the register, if your house is registered; or a sight of the deeds, if unregistered. Approximately 85% of all houses are now in 'registration districts'; but that does not mean they are all registered, as when a registration district is declared, the houses therein are registered only on a *subsequent sale*. Whether your house is registered or not will therefore depend on whether or not it was in a registration district *when you bought it*. If you are not sure, telephone the appropriate – or indeed any – land registry office, and ask. See appendix 1 for registration districts, which land registry office deals with each, and its address and telephone number.

As there may be some delay in obtaining either copy register or sight of the deeds, as soon as you put your house on the market:

If your house is registered: write to the relevant land registry office stating your full name, and the full name of your spouse if co-owner, and ask for an 'office copy of the register and filed plan' of your house, No. 15 Muggleton Close, Thong, Wiltshire. ('Office' copy means 'official' copy.) Ideally, you should also state the title number* of your house in your letter, but there is no need to enquire separately for this. Explain in your letter that you do not know the title number (if such is the case), and the department in the Land Registry which deals with title numbers will write it on the letter before passing it onto the department which deals with copying. There is no fee for supplying the copy register.

If your house is unregistered: write to the appropriate office of your building society (i.e. the office handling your account, or Head Office) saying that you are selling your house and doing your own conveyancing, and ask for the deeds to be sent to a *local branch* as near as possible to your address. It will be to this local branch that you will go to inspect the deeds.

Once you have got the copy register, or the deeds are available for inspection, you will be in a position to draft the contract as soon as you find a purchaser.

When you have found your purchaser and agreed a price, get his full name (and that of his spouse if he is buying jointly), and the name and address of his solicitor. If your purchaser offers to pay you something on deposit, accept it and give him a receipt; but make sure the receipt – and any other writing you give or send him or his solicitor until exchange of contracts – contain the magic words SUBJECT TO CONTRACT. This will prevent a binding contract coming into force until you are ready. Remember, a conveyancing transaction is in two parts: the first, up to exchange of contracts; the second, from exchange of contracts to completion.

Then, with your copy register, or having inspected the deeds, type out the following contract on an ordinary piece of paper, with two carbon copies or photocopies. Where there are two adjacent square brackets, the first only applies to a registered house, and the second only to an unregistered house. Thus if your house is registered, delete the second of such brackets; if your house is unregistered, delete the first.

---

* Every registered house has a separate register which has a reference number called the *title number*. This appears at the top of each page of the register.

This contract is made the   day of   19
BETWEEN GENTLE READER and MRS. ASTUTE READER
both of 15 Muggleton Close, Thong, Wiltshire (hereinafter
called 'the Vendors'), and BERT BLOGGINS and MRS.
BERTHA BLOGGINS both of The Hovel, Great West Road,
Middlesex (hereinafter called 'the Purchasers'),

WHEREBY IT IS AGREED the vendors will sell to the
purchasers and the purchasers will buy from the vendors: the
freehold dwellinghouse known as 15 Muggleton Close,
Thong, Wiltshire, and land, [as registered at the Land Registry
with title absolute under title number AB123456] [as the same
was conveyed by a conveyance to the vendors dated . . .], for
the sum of   THOUSAND POUNDS (£   ), and subject to
the following conditions:

1. A deposit of 10% of the purchase price shall be paid to
    Messrs. XY of 123 High Street, Thong (estate agents) on
    exchange of contracts, and shall be held by them
    pending completion as stakeholders.
2. Vacant possession of the property shall be given to the
    purchasers on completion, which shall take place on
    19 .
3. The vendors sell as beneficial owners.
4. The property is sold subject to the restrictive covenants
    and matters [referred to by or set out in entries Nos . . .
    of the charges register, and referred to by or set out in
    the property register] [referred to by or set out in the
    above-mentioned conveyance to the vendors], copies of
    which having been given to the purchasers' solicitor, no
    objections shall be made or questions asked in respect
    thereof.
5. The vendors' title shall [be shown by supplying office
    copy of the register and filed plan, together with an
    authority to inspect] [commence with a conveyance
    between AB and CD dated . . .]
6. National Conditions of Sale (current edition) shall
    apply to this contract, and the prescribed rate of interest
    shall be 4% above Barclays Bank base rate.

Some explanatory notes on the contract.

If your house is registered:

When you get your office copy of the register, it will look something like the office copy reproduced in appendix 2 (p. 244). It will probably consist of two or three pages, and a plan (called a 'filed plan'), and those two or three pages are divided into three sections. Section A is the *property register* which contains the address of the property, and a note that it is freehold. Section B (usually on the same page as section A) is the *proprietorship register* and sets out your name(s) as the current owner(s). Section C is the *charges register* which sets out any restrictive covenants and mortgages. Practically every registered freehold house is 'Title Absolute'. You will see these words above your names in section B.

Sometimes section A, the property register, as well as containing the address of your house, will have some such entry as 'a transfer dated . . . contains a declaration as to party walls', or 'by a transfer dated . . . rights of drainage were excepted'. The wording in clause 4 of my suggested contract automatically provides for any such matters. Just copy it out.

Section C, the charges register, will probably consist of two or three numbered items, the last of which will be a note of your existing mortgage. If you have two mortgages outstanding, there will be two such notes. The first items will refer to restrictive covenants and similar matters (e.g. a certain section of your land may be subject to rights of drainage in favour of a neighbour). In your clause 4, refer to *all* the numbered items on the charges register *except* the mortgage. Thus if your charges register had the same entries as the charges register in appendix 2, clause 4 of your contract would read:

'The property is sold subject to the restrictive covenants and matters referred to by or set out in entries Nos. 1, 2, and 3 of the charges register, and referred to by or set out in the property register, copies of which having been given etc.' You don't refer to the mortgage because you are not selling the house subject to it. If the restrictive covenants are lengthy, they may be set out in a separate schedule, still part of the charges register, or even in a completely separate document. No matter. Just refer to *all* the numbered items, except mortgages. Of course, if there are *no* entries on the charges register except mortgages, and no entries on the property register except the address, omit clause 4 altogether.

If your house is unregistered:

As mentioned, you will have to inspect the deeds before you can type out the contract. The conveyance referred to in that clause of the contract beginning 'Whereby it is agreed' will be the conveyance to you when you bought the house.

When it comes to specifying the conveyance in clause 5, this has to be a conveyance at least fifteen years old. Thus your title deeds will not be a single land certificate, as with a registered house, but will consist of a few previous conveyances, e.g. A to B 1946, B to C 1958, C to D 1977, D to yourself 1984. If these were the dates of the previous conveyances, your clause 5 would be 'The vendors' title shall commence with a conveyance between B and C dated 3rd June 1958'. In 1992 you could specify the conveyance between C and D dated 1977 because it would then be fifteen years old.

Whether your house is registered or unregistered:

Clause 2. Leave this date blank for the present. The completion date is inserted only on exchange of contracts.

Clause 3. The expression 'beneficial owners' is explained on p. 172.

Clause 6. The National Conditions of Sale are copyright but they can be *referred* to without infringing copyright. In any case, there is no magic in them, but they are a convenient summary of the general law which applies to such contracts. The reference to interest means that if the purchasers do not complete on the date which will eventually be inserted in clause 2, they have to pay you interest on the purchase price from this date until the date they actually *do* complete. (There will be a similar provision in your purchase contract.)

Having had the contract typed out, with two copies, send it (unsigned of course), with one copy, to the purchaser's solicitor. In the letter you write him incorporate the words SUBJECT TO CONTRACT.* At the same time, if your house

---

*   Dear Mr. Solicitor, I understand you are acting for Mr. and Mrs. Bloggins who have agreed to buy my house, as above, for £— subject to contract. I enclose draft contract and copy, and office copy of the register. Yours truly.

is *registered*, send him your complete office copy of the register and filed plan. It is usual practice, however, to cut out the price if it appears after your name in section B, so that the purchaser will not know the price you paid.

If your house is *unregistered*, I'm afraid it's a bit more difficult just at this stage. The purchaser's solicitor must be sent a copy of all restrictive covenants and similar matters, and a plan. But whereas with a registered house these are conveniently contained in a single document, a copy of which can be obtained from the Land Registry, in the case of an unregistered house various covenants might be set out in several different conveyances, and the plan itself might be on an old conveyance. Thus the conveyance to you, when you bought the house, might go something like this: 'the vendor hereby conveys ALL THAT piece or parcel of land together with the dwellinghouse thereon known as 15 Muggleton Close etc. as the same is shown edged red on a plan attached to a conveyance dated 1st April 1977 TO HOLD the same unto the purchasers in fee simple *subject to the restrictive covenants set out in the schedule hereto and subject to the declaration as to light and air and the restrictive covenants set out in the conveyance dated 3rd June 1958*'. Clause 4 of my suggested contract automatically provides for any variety of restrictive covenants and other matters, as they must necessarily all be contained in – or referred to by – the conveyance to you when you bought. The difficulty is that when you inspect the deeds you will have to root out the plan, and the various restrictive covenants in the previous conveyances, which are referred to in the conveyance to you when you bought. Thus in my example, you should obtain (1) a copy of the entire conveyance to you when you bought (because it contains restrictive covenants in the schedule); (2) a copy of the plan attached to the conveyance dated 1st April 1977; and (3) a copy of the conveyance dated 3rd June 1958.

Sometimes it will be easy. There will perhaps be just one set of covenants referred to, plainly set out in a certain conveyance. Sometimes the conveyance to you will not refer to *any* covenants at all, so there won't be any problem. But just occasionally the job of locating one or two sets of covenants from a pile of unfamiliar documents will call for a certain acumen. Such difficulty as there may be is not intrinsic to the job, but merely because you will be moving on such unfamiliar ground. But even if you make a mistake here, and omit to send some covenants or whatever, all that will happen is that the purchaser's solicitor will subsequently ask you for a copy.

When you have found the restrictive covenants etc., ask the building society clerk to make a copy of the entire conveyance containing them. You will have to pay for such copies, unless there are *spare* copies among the deeds, which you will be able to have without paying for (remember they are *your* deeds). Alternatively, you may find the necessary copies in the file kept by the solicitor who acted for you when you purchased – and in any case you would probably find this file helpful. If convenient, call round and ask him for this file, which is *your* property.*

Once you have obtained the copy conveyances containing any covenants etc., and a copy of the plan, you send your contract and copies to the purchaser's solicitor in the same way as with a registered house. You send the letter in the footnote on p. 152, but substitute the words 'plan and copy conveyances containing covenants' for 'office copy register'.

Now relax. You've done all the difficult work. By and by, in a week or two or three, the purchaser's solicitor will send you a printed form of preliminary enquiries. You can answer them either in a 'professional' way, that is by employing a series of rhythmic inanities which give away no information at all – 'the deeds are silent but inspection may reveal', 'we know of none but the property is sold subject to any there may be', 'please rely on inspection', etc. – or you can give as informative answers as you can. I set out the current form, together with vendors' solicitors' typical replies, in appendix 3 (p. 246). Let's go through it.

Q.1. asks who owns the boundary fences. Normally no-one knows. Answer can therefore legitimately be 'We do not

---

* An acquaintance of mine asked her former solicitor for her previous purchase file, but was told it would take at least a week to locate. She promptly returned to the solicitor's office with her three children, whom she invited to make as much noise as they wished. The file was produced and handed over in a few minutes.

know'. Q.2. Any disputes? Obviously this question covers only disputes which might have some relevance to the future owner. Q.3. Any notices? Notices are official communications from the local Council or whoever (answer, of course, is usually 'none'). Q.4. An example of how 'legal' drafting can be used to create a spurious impression of esoteric complexity. This splurge of nearly two hundred words makes no apparent sense, but can be understood only after you have played the game of matching each of the items lumped together in lines 3 and 4 with the appropriate 'matter' in lines 6 to 15. Thus 'bond' goes with 'construction costs of any road', 'guarantee' goes with 'any repair of the property', etc. Once you have done this, you will see that all you are being asked is whether there are any guarantees still in force in respect of any work done to the house; and, if the house is less than ten years old, whether it is covered by a National House-Building Council's warranty (which, if it exists, will usually be kept with the deeds). Q.5. asks whether the services are directly connected to the respective mains. Solicitors invariably sidestep this question by replying 'The property enjoys the usual services [or whichever services *are* connected] but please rely on inspection or survey for the route of the pipes etc.' There is no reason why you should not do the same. Alternatively, if you know that any of the services *are* directly connected to the mains (i.e. without the drain or pipes going under or across anyone else's land), there is equally no reason why you should not say so. Q.6. Another example of the draftsman's penchant for verbal diarrhoea. Most of the items mentioned here have little or no relevance, but merely show how far removed is the verbiage which purchasers' solicitors mindlessly push out, from the realities of the houses they are dealing with. For instance, if a house catches fire I don't think the householder consults his deeds in order to decide over which adjoining property – if any – he has the right to make his escape. Neither will you, the vendor, have been called upon to do any 'maintenance repair or replacement work on any land or fixtures affording any facility', whatever that means. In short, the more incomprehensible the question, the more likely it is to be spurious. Q.7. asks whether anyone else has any rights over or under the property. If you do know that someone else's drain runs under your land, or someone uses a right of way over it, or the drive is shared, say so. Otherwise use the solicitor's stock reply 'No, but the property is sold subject to any there may be'. As it's such a wide and woolly question, this qualification is legitimate. Q.8. asks whether all 'restrictions' – presumably meaning restrictive covenants – have been observed. Reply (if such is the case) that you have not received notice of any breach. Q.9. The only information you can give on 'planning' is either that you have not made any additions or alterations requiring planning permission or building regulations approval; or, if you have, give brief particulars. If the house is comparatively new, invite the solicitor to get a copy of the planning permission from the local Council if he wants one. Q.10. asks whether various items are included in the sale; and conversely what fixtures and fittings you are going to remove. Self-explanatory. Q.11. asks the rateable value. Q.12. (A) Self-explanatory; (B) Completion by post is not applicable to a D.I.Y. vendor as it implies an undertaking to send the deeds on receipt of the purchase price. And that's the end of the form.

If the purchaser's solicitor has added any extra questions in the space provided, these will normally be self-explanatory, e.g. Do you know who is entitled to enforce the restrictive covenants? or Has any contribution been asked for to maintain the passageway at rear? Answer accordingly – usually 'No', of course.

By the time you come to sell, you may find yourself faced with a different form of enquiries. These forms have a habit of changing every few years. No matter. You can only answer those questions which ask for information within your knowledge: 'Have there been any disputes?' No, there haven't. 'Have you had any Notices?' No, I haven't. 'Have you made any building additions or alterations?' No, I haven't; or Yes, I had a garage built. The questions which you don't understand, or which are too wide, you don't answer. E.g. Q.7(C) on the current form: 'Is the vendor aware of any other overriding interests as defined by the Land Registration Act 1925 S.70 (1)?' is traditionally answered by vendors' solicitors: 'This question is too wide to permit a specific reply.' There is no reason why you should not employ a similar answer.

Alternatively, a more intelligent reply would be: 'This question covers a wide range of matters. If you will ask me exactly what you want to know about the property, and such matters are within my knowledge as owner and occupier, I will give you a specific reply.'

Some solicitors add their own duplicated sheets of questions to the printed form, presumably under the impression that the more questions they ask, the more thoroughly they are doing their job; and the fatuity of some of these additional questions (I remember seeing one which asked for details of any *gymkhanas* held at the property) is even commented on from time to time in the correspondence columns of the legal journals. But whatever form of questions you may be sent, and whatever verbiage may wrap them up, don't be overawed. Remember that vendors' solicitors either ignore or sidestep most of the questions (see appendix 3); and however many questions there may be on the form, or additional sheets, there are in fact only a dozen or so quasi-legal points which a vendor can sensibly be asked about. However, a word of warning: if the form or forms you are sent contain any questions about the repair or condition of the property (or if the purchaser himself puts such questions to you verbally), make sure you answer them with a non-committal reply such as 'Please rely on surveyor's inspection' – as every vendor's solicitor would. Otherwise you may find yourself being sued for misrepresentation if the purchaser subsequently discovers some insidious defect. It is even unsafe to state that you do not *know* of any defect, as the purchaser may come across some dry rot behind a wardrobe, or whatever, and claim that you *must* have known about it.

At the same time as he sends his preliminary enquiries, or some time afterwards, the purchaser's solicitor will return *one* copy of your contract, either 'approved', or on which he may have written some amendments. As the contract is completely standard, I don't think there can legitimately be any significant amendments, except perhaps an additional clause providing for the inclusion of any agreed items. Any amendments, of course, have to be agreed if they are to be incorporated in the actual contract. If the purchaser's solicitor adds some verbiage you don't understand, do not accept it unless he explains it to your satisfaction.

So you've answered the enquiries, and had one copy of the contract returned approved, or with some acceptable amendments. All you have to do now is (a) wait for the purchaser's solicitor to send you the purchaser's signed part of the contract – that is, the contract or copy which you originally sent to the solicitor (with any agreed amendments), with the purchaser's signature, or if more than one purchaser *both* their signatures, at the bottom; and (b) check that the purchaser has paid the full 10% deposit to the estate agents (and that any cheque therefor has been cleared). Remember that this deposit is probably your only sanction against a defaulting purchaser – the contract on its own is just a bit of paper.

Up to now, either you or your purchaser can still call the deal off without giving any reason. The agreement becomes legally binding between you and the purchaser the moment when you, having received the purchaser's signed part of the contract,* post to the purchaser's solicitor an identical copy of that contract signed by yourself (and spouse if co-owner); so each party or his solicitor holds a copy of the contract signed by the other. This is called 'exchange of contracts'. *If your sale is dependent on a simultaneous purchase you must be careful at this point* because obviously you do not want to commit yourself to your sale until you have a binding contract on your purchase, and vice versa. Therefore do not post your signed part of your *sale* contract until you have received your *purchase* contract signed by your vendor. The procedure to be observed in exchanging contracts, when your sale and purchase are interdependent, is explained in detail in the next chapter.

Before you post your signed part of your sale contract to your purchaser's solicitor, you must date both parts of the contract (that is, the contract signed by the purchaser which you have received, and the duplicate signed by yourself which you send) with the date of exchange. You also insert the completion date in clause 2 of both parts of the contract. If your sale is independent of any purchase, the completion date will usually be four weeks from the date of exchange. If, on the

---

* But see footnote on p. 193.

other hand, you are buying simultaneously, the completion date you insert in your sale contract will be the same date as your vendor's solicitor will have inserted in your *purchase* contract. It is advisable to telephone the purchaser's solicitor to check that he agrees the completion date you propose inserting, before you actually insert it.

You have now exchanged contracts on your sale. It may be a month since you originally sent your purchaser's solicitor the draft contracts, or it may be several months. If the latter period, the delay will probably have been caused by you or your purchaser having to tie up a simultaneous purchase or sale. At any rate contracts are now exchanged. At once write to your building society saying that you are going to pay off the mortgage on the date in question – the completion date – and ask how much will be required to discharge the mortgage on that date. Also ask for the daily amount of interest to be added on, in case completion is delayed beyond that date for any reason. If the house is unregistered, the building society will already have sent the deeds to a local branch which you will have visited. If the house is registered, this will be the first intimation the building society will have had of your forthcoming sale, so at the same time ask for the land certificate to be sent to a convenient local branch. It will be at this local branch that completion will take place.

After exchange of contracts, the procedure differs according to whether your house is registered or unregistered, although from the vendor's point of view the difference is marginal.

If your house is registered: Send your purchaser's solicitor a letter authorising him to inspect the register (quoting the address of the house, title number, and full names of the owner(s)). In due course the purchaser's solicitor will send you a transfer form for you (and spouse if co-owner) to sign, in the presence of a witness who will also sign and add his address. This transfer form is on a single sheet of paper and states the address and title number of your house, and continues: 'In consideration of £—— Gentle Reader and Astute Reader as beneficial owners hereby transfer to Bert Bloggins and Bertha Bloggins the land comprised in the title above mentioned'. At the same time, the purchaser's solicitor may send you a further form of questions or 'requisitions on title'. In the case of a registered house there can be no question of your purchaser's solicitor investigating your title, which is proved simply by your names being typed on the register. Consequently any such 'requisitions on title' are even more of a formality (or farce) than in the case of an unregistered house. Most of the 'questions' on this printed form are either not applicable, or else are statements of the obvious, like 'Vacant possession must be given on completion'; 'All mortgages must be discharged on completion', to which you reply 'of course' or 'agreed'.

If your house is unregistered: Whereas if your house was registered you would have sent the purchaser's solicitor a copy of your title document (the copy of the register) at the outset when you sent him the draft contract, if your house is unregistered you send copies of your title deeds to the purchaser's solicitor *after* exchange of contracts. Thus after exchange, you send him copies of the conveyance specified in clause 5 of the contract, and all subsequent conveyances. You will have to ask your building society for these copies, although you may already have sent some of them containing restrictive covenants before exchange. As a house changes hands on average every six or seven years, there are unlikely to be more than two or three conveyances to copy.* When the purchaser's solicitor has looked at these copy conveyances, he will send you a list of questions on them which might be more difficult to answer than in the case of a registered house. You'll just have to do your best with these questions, but remember that the answers which vendors' solicitors traditionally give are: 'We cannot say', 'We presume so', 'We do not know' etc. Remember also that when you bought your house, two highly qualified experts minutely examined the title deeds – one acting for you, one acting for your building society – so there can't be anything wrong with them, can there?

---

*   When it was the custom to type out summaries of the previous title deeds, as distinct from merely photo-copying them, all previous *mortgages* were included. This, I think, is no longer insisted upon. You might however be asked for copies of the receipts, which are written on the back of the previous mortgages (which will be with the deeds held by your building society).

Instead of a simple transfer form, as with a registered house, there will be a slightly more elaborate conveyance to sign, which will be in the same form as the conveyance to you when you bought. The purchaser's solicitor will first send you a 'draft' for you to return 'approved'. Provided he has got the house and the price right, and it does follow the form of the previous conveyance, I can't think there will be any amendments for you to make. Send it back 'approved' and he will have it typed out again on stiff paper, and send it back to you for your signature(s) in readiness for completion.

Apart from these few differences, the remaining procedure is the same for both registered and unregistered houses.

One of the questions on the printed 'requisition' form asks for a 'completion statement'. This is a statement showing the exact amount you will require on completion: purchase price, less deposit, plus or minus an apportionment of *water* rate depending on whether it has been paid up to a date subsequent or prior to the completion date. Do *not* bother to apportion *general* rates, but after completion simply notify the rating department of the date completion took place; and leave them to bill you for, or refund, any amount unpaid, or paid in advance, as at that date. Some solicitors fiddle around with general rate receipts and apportionments and undertakings to be handed over on completion, presumably unaware that general rates are a personal debt on the occupier, and a purchaser is therefore *not* concerned with any arrears prior to the date of completion.

So you've answered the purchaser's solicitor's 'requisitions', and you are holding the transfer or conveyance which you have signed. You have also managed to work out that at the date of completion £50 water rate will have been paid in advance, which information you have relayed to the purchaser's solicitor.

Completion takes place at the local branch of your building society, where the land certificate or deeds will have been sent. Before completion, you have to notify your purchaser's solicitor of this address; also the name of your building society and the amount needed to discharge your mortgage, so he can split the purchase price into two bank drafts – one for this amount in favour of your building society, and one for the balance in your favour. Any second mortgage will have to be paid off out of the proceeds of sale in the same way. (Of course, if your house is not mortgaged you will be holding the deeds or land certificate, and completion will take place at your address. The whole of the purchase price will be in your favour.)

Having arranged a convenient time for completion with your building society branch manager and the purchaser's solicitor, trot along holding in one hand the signed transfer or conveyance, and in the other, the keys to your house. The procedure on completion is the same as in any sale: the thing sold, in this case the house represented by the title deeds and keys, is handed over in exchange for the purchase price.

Give the purchaser's solicitor your signed transfer or conveyance, and keys; and your building society's representative will hand him the deeds (land certificate or previous conveyances). When the purchaser's solicitor has checked these, he will hand your building society's representative a bank draft for the amount needed to pay off your mortgage; and he will hand you a bank draft in your favour for the balance. E.g. purchase price £70,000, less deposit of £7,000, plus apportionment of water rate (paid in advance) £50: amount required on completion £63,050. Amount owing to your building society as at that day: £17,560.48p. The purchaser's solicitor will therefore give your building society's representative a bank draft for that sum, in favour of the building society; and will give you a bank draft, in your favour, for the balance of £45,489.52p.

A bank draft, incidentally, is a cheque drawn by a *bank*. It has the advantage over a cheque in that it cannot be stopped and is unlikely to bounce. *On no account accept a cheque*. If you think you might not recognise the difference between a bank draft and a cheque, ask your own bank for a half minute's lesson beforehand.

The deposit (being part of the purchase price) is now yours, and the purchaser's solicitor will give you a letter addressed to the estate agents who are holding it, authorising them to release it to you.

Although the building society's representative will not hand over the sealed form discharging your mortgage (form 53), but will give the purchaser's solicitor an undertaking to send this within fourteen days, you should nevertheless get a written receipt acknowledging that your mortgage *has* been paid off. And the same applies in the case of a mortgage other than to a building society.

To sum up: on completion you *give* signed transfer or conveyance, and keys; you *get* bank draft for sale price (less deposit and outstanding mortgage) and letter releasing the deposit.

*

So that's it for the sale. However, before leaving it, there are one or two variations from the above account which you may come up against.

The most common concerns the deposit. If the deposit is held as 'stakeholder' it may not be released to the vendor until after completion; whereas if it is held as 'agent for the vendor' the vendor can require whoever holds it immediately to release it to him after exchange of contracts, so he can use it as his own money.

The normal practice is for a *10%* deposit to be paid, on exchange of contracts, to someone who holds it as *stakeholder*. However, either you or your purchaser (or – when you come to buy a house – you or your vendor) may want to vary this. The purchaser may want to pay a reduced deposit if he is getting a 100% mortgage or otherwise has no available cash, and so cannot raise a 10% deposit without incurring the heavy interest charges of a bank bridging loan. On the other hand, the vendor may want the deposit held as 'agent for the vendor' so he can use it as (or towards) the deposit on a simultaneous purchase. Both variations are therefore prima facie reasonable. The trouble is that either variation in favour of one party makes the position of the other more precarious. From the vendor's point of view, the deposit is the only effective sanction against the purchaser defaulting; and the smaller the deposit, the less effective the sanction. From the purchaser's point of view, if the deposit is held as 'agent for the vendor', he will have paid the vendor a significant chunk of the purchase price without getting anything in return, which he will find difficult or impossible to recover should anything subsequently go wrong.

Any such variations which you and the other party may agree are a matter of negotiation between you – not *custom* as some solicitors will claim. A reasonable compromise might be for the vendor to accept a 5% deposit provided that the purchaser allows it to be held as 'agent for the vendor'. In any event, before agreeing to a less than 10% deposit you, the vendor, should see the purchaser's mortgage offer.

Another slight difficulty is: if there are no estate agents, who holds the deposit as stakeholder? It would normally be held by the vendor's solicitor, but the purchaser's solicitor would not allow *you* to hold it as a stakeholder. The way round this is to open a joint account with a bank or building society in the name of yourself and the purchaser, and split the interest. (On completion you would not get a release of deposit but a bank draft, or a building society's cheque, in your favour.) Alternatively the *purchaser's solicitor* can hold the deposit, provided he gives you a receipt stating that he holds it as stakeholder – which he would be pleased to do as *he* would then get the interest.

I have assumed that your building society will agree to send the deeds or land certificate to a convenient local branch, where completion will take place. If for some reason it does not agree – or if it is a small society with no convenient local branch – then it will appoint a local solicitor to whom it will send the deeds, and at whose office completion will take place. In that case the bank draft to pay off the outstanding mortgage will be in favour of this solicitor, not the building society. Also you will have to go to this solicitor's office to inspect the deeds (before writing out the contract) if the house is unregistered.*

---

* Although from the procedural point of view it makes no difference whether completion takes place at your building society's local branch or at a local solicitor's office, there may be a practical difference: the solicitor will add his fee to the amount required to redeem the mortgage. And this fee (for typing a dozen words on a printed form to discharge your mortgage) is sometimes exorbitant – the philosophy being that you have no option but to pay. Therefore do your best to persuade your building society (such a malleable entity beneath its institutional exterior) to send the deeds to a *local branch* rather than to a solicitor.

We have dealt with the possibility of obstruction by the other side's solicitor generally, but he might try two specific things. He might refuse to accept your contract, saying it is not in proper form. Your answer will be that it is in impeccable form, and in what way does he think it should be altered? If he wishes to suggest amendments he is free to do so. As every contract is in more or less the same form, it will be obvious that he can have no valid objections. Another thing he might try is to claim that you have not answered his preliminary enquiries properly. If he does, ask him for a copy of the answers which *he* last gave to the printed form, and/or invite him to your house and tell him you will give whatever information he wants provided it is within your own knowledge.

Finally, what do you do if your purchaser asks for the keys before completion has actually taken place? It is often extremely inconvenient for the purchaser if he cannot get the keys before completion. For instance if he is selling his house simultaneously, completion of your sale may have to be in the afternoon, whereas the purchaser's removal van may arrive in the morning. It is common to get round this problem by the vendor 'unofficially' giving the purchaser the keys beforehand, or leaving them with a neighbour. Yet the danger of doing so is obvious. If anything should go wrong at completion (unlikely but always a possibility) you will have parted with possession; and it may take a lawsuit, or more, to recover it. Therefore, whether the request is made just before completion or at any other time, *do not release the keys until completion has taken place and the sale monies are safely in your hands*. If it is more convenient for the purchaser to collect the keys from a neighbour than from his solicitor, leave the keys with your neighbour, with instructions not to surrender them until you telephone.

*

Summary of steps to be taken on sale

1. If house is registered, write to the Land Registry asking for an *office copy* of the register; if unregistered, write to your building society asking for the deeds to be sent to a local branch, where you will go to inspect them (p. 149).

2. Type out draft (proposed) contract; and send it, with a copy, to purchaser's solicitor. At the same time send him office copy register (or copy plan and restrictive covenants, if house is unregistered) (p. 150-154).

3. Answer purchaser's solicitor's form of preliminary enquiries (p. 155-157).

4. Purchaser's solicitor will return one copy of your draft contract 'approved'.

5. Receive purchaser's signed part of the contract, and (having made sure total deposit has been paid) send purchaser's solicitor *your* signed part of the contract. There is now a binding contract between you (p. 158).

6. Notify your building society of completion date, and ask how much is required to discharge mortgage. If house is registered, ask building society to send the land certificate to a local branch, where completion will take place (p. 159).

7. Send purchaser's solicitor an authority to inspect register; or, if house is unregistered, copies of the deeds (p. 159-160).

8. Answer purchaser's solicitor's 'requisitions on title' (p. 160).

9. Receive transfer (or conveyance) from purchaser's solicitor, which sign in readiness for completion (p. 159/161).

10. Arrange completion appointment at building society's local branch.

11. Attend completion (p. 162-163).

12. Get deposit from estate agents (who will deduct their commission).

12

How to do the conveyancing on your purchase – up to exchange of contracts

And so to your purchase. The instructions in this and the following chapter tell you how to do the conveyancing on the purchase of a freehold secondhand house, whether registered or unregistered. (If you are buying a *leasehold* house or flat, or a *new* property from its developer, you will have simultaneously to apply the additional instructions in appendix 7 and 8 respectively.)

I am assuming that you will be getting a mortgage, and I refer to the lender throughout as a building society, although it may be a bank or other lender. If you are buying without a mortgage then ignore all references to the building society, and your job will be that much easier.

As previously mentioned, a conveyancing transaction is in two stages, and I devote a separate chapter to each. This chapter deals with the first stage, up to exchange of contracts – at which point both parties are legally bound to the deal. The next chapter deals with the second stage, from exchange of contracts to completion – when the money is handed over and the purchaser becomes the owner of the house.

If the house you are buying was in a registration district when the vendor bought it (see appendix 1) it will be *registered*, and approximately three-quarters of all houses in England and Wales are now registered. By way of reminder, each registered house has a separate register exclusively relating to it (usually consisting of two or three pages and always a plan), which is filed at the Land Registry. The deeds comprise a single land certificate, which in fact is a copy of this register. If the house is not registered, the deeds consist of a series of previous conveyances.

The procedure up to exchange of contracts is basically the same from the purchaser's point of view whether the house is registered or unregistered, so both are dealt with together in this chapter. When a particular item does apply only to a registered or an unregistered house, this is stated. Otherwise there is no distinction between the two in this chapter.

Still on preliminaries, whereas you did not need any forms for your sale, you will need some for your purchase as follows:

In EVERY case
(1) Local Search forms: one 'LLC1'; and two 'Con 29A' (for houses outside London) or 'Con 29D' (for houses in a London Borough).
(2) Inland Revenue 'LA' form.
PLUS
When house is registered*
(3) Land Registry forms: No. 94A (search of whole – one print which has duplicate attached)
No. 19 (transfer of whole – one stiff and two flimsy)
No. A4 (application to register purchase after completion – one print).
(4) K16 – Land Charges Registry form to certify you are not bankrupt (which will be required by your building society's solicitor).
OR
When house is not registered
(3) Land Registry form No. 96 (to confirm the house *isn't* registered).
(4) K15 – Land Charges Registry Search.

---

* and you are buying the *whole* of the vendor's land/property comprised in the register, as distinct from *part* (which would be the case if you were buying from a developer). Transfer of part requires different forms, as explained on p. 208.

If the house is not registered but *is* in a registration district, it will have to be registered *after* completion, either by your building society's solicitor, or by you if you are not getting a mortgage – for which you will need an additional form: Land Registry No. 1B in the former case, or 1A in the latter.

The Inland Revenue form is obtainable from the appropriate Stamp Duty office (the London one is at Bush House, Strand, WC2). The other forms can be bought by members of the public from the Solicitors' Law Stationery Society. The main shop is at 144 Fetter Lane, London EC4, and most big towns have a branch. Find out the most convenient branch from the telephone directory, and either call or write. If the latter, first telephone for the current prices.*

Now for the detailed instructions.

After you have agreed the price of the house, ask your vendor for the name and address of his solicitor; and introduce yourself to this gentleman by letter or telephone, telling him that you have agreed to buy the house from Mr. X, his client, and that you are acting for yourself. You give him your address for him to send you the draft contract. In any letter, up to exchange of contracts, be sure to include the magic words SUBJECT TO CONTRACT, which words prevent a binding contract coming into existence before you so wish it. (Dear Mr. Solicitor, I have agreed to buy the above house from Mr. X, your client, for £—, subject to contract. Please send me the draft contract, as I shall be acting for myself. Yours truly.)

The first step is for the vendor's solicitor to send you the draft (proposed) contract, with a carbon copy. This sets out the terms of the proposed agreement – broadly, that you will buy the house from the vendor for the price agreed; plus half a dozen standard clauses.

At the same time as he sends you the draft contract, the vendor's solicitor will also send a copy of the register, if the

---

* Alternatively, I can send these forms (including the Inland Revenue form) to you. Send me £4.50 for a set of purchase forms for a *registered* house (stating whether or not it is in a London Borough), £3.00 for a set of purchase forms for an *unregistered* house, and they will be sent by return of post. My address is on the rear cover.

house is registered. This should be an *office copy*, which is an official copy made by the Land Registry (with the words 'Office Copy' on every page including the plan).* It should also be a *complete* copy, as otherwise you cannot properly check the contract. You will know whether your copy is complete from the note of the total number of pages which that register comprises, which appears at the top of the first page. It is permissible for the vendor's solicitor to cut out the note of the price which the vendor paid for the house, but he should not cut out anything else. A typical office copy register is reproduced in appendix 2.

If the house is not registered, the vendor's solicitor will send you a copy of any restrictive covenants, and a plan of the house and land, taken from previous conveyances.

Draft Contract

The contract which you will receive will probably be either on a 'National Conditions of Sale' form, or a 'Law Society's Conditions of Sale' form. Each incorporates a mass of closely printed conditions. Alternatively the contract need not be on either form but can be typed on ordinary paper, in which case there will be a clause referring to one or other set of conditions. I don't think you need bother with the printed conditions, most of which are either irrelevant (dealing with auctions, tenancies), or unnecessary (dealing with apportionment of rates etc.), or statements of the general law which we have already examined (the house is at the purchaser's risk from exchange, the vendor is not obliged to show ownership of boundary fences etc.) Just confine your attention to the typing.

The 'National Conditions of Sale' is the most commonly used form, and the main provisions of the contract are typed on the front page: names and addresses of vendor and purchaser, address of house being sold (with title number if

---

* Some solicitors send a photo-copy of the land certificate with the draft contract, but an office copy is preferable for a number of reasons, e.g. it has the date on which it was issued (and the branch of the Land Registry which issued it) on each page – the significance of which will be explained later. *Therefore insist on getting an office copy.* As the vendor's solicitor can get one free of charge from the Land Registry within a few days, and as the contract will in any case entitle you to it on exchange of contracts, there is no reason why he should not send you an office copy at the outset.

registered), price, completion date. The remaining provisions are typed on the back page, with the two inside pages containing the printed conditions. But whichever form is used, or if no form is used, and however the lay-out may vary, every contract for the sale of a secondhand freehold house should contain basically the same provisions as the contract set out on p. 150 in the previous chapter – with clauses equivalent to the *first* of the two adjacent square brackets if the house is registered, or the *second* if it is unregistered.

As every contract for the sale of a secondhand freehold house is basically the same as every other contract for the sale of a secondhand freehold house, there should not be too much to worry you in the contract you receive from the vendor's solicitor. Apart from one or two possible alterations, your main concern is to check that the vendor's solicitor has drawn it up correctly. Therefore check the following points:

(a) Check that the house is correctly described. That is, it is described not only by its postal address, but (if *registered*) by reference to its *title number*. Each register has a separate title number, and this should appear in the contract – either separately, or as part of the description of the property being sold, e.g. 'the freehold dwellinghouse known as 12 Mustard Street, Thing, Yorkshire, *as registered at the Land Registry under title number YZ12345*'. This ties the description of the house to the plan which is part of the register.

If *unregistered*, the house should be described (in addition to its postal address) by reference to a plan showing the land which goes with it (edged red), preferably attached to the contract.

If there is no separate clause stating that the house is freehold, this word should be incorporated in the description of the property sold, e.g. 'the *freehold* dwellinghouse known as 12 Mustard Street etc.'

(b) There should be a clause providing for the purchaser to pay a deposit – either to the estate agents or to the vendor's solicitor. The deposit is usually 10% of the purchase price, and is held as *stakeholder*. I have dealt with the possible variations which either the vendor or you, the purchaser, might want to make to the usual practice, and the implications of such variations (p. 163).

The deposit is paid on exchange of contracts – although it is customary for estate agents to ask for a preliminary deposit (say £200/£300) at the outset, as a token of your seriousness in proceeding. This is returnable to you at any time up to exchange of contracts (and on exchange you merely pay the balance).

(c) If included in the purchase price there are some furnishings or other items which the vendor has agreed to leave, there should be a clause in the contract providing for this, e.g.: 'The following items are included in the purchase price [and £— thereof shall be apportioned thereto]: (1) curtains and carpets in all the upstairs bedrooms; (2) shelving units in the living room; (3) bathroom cabinet, etc.' If you did come to such an agreement with your vendor, he may not have mentioned it to his solicitor. If the contract contains no reference to the matter then write, or preferably type, in such a clause.

At present, stamp duty at 1% of the price of the house is payable if it is over £30,000. Therefore if the agreed price of the house is over that threshold by such an amount as could reasonably be apportioned to any separate items, then ask the vendor's solicitor to agree to a separate price being apportioned to these items, in accordance with the words in square brackets. This will reduce the price of the house itself to £30,000 (or below), and so no stamp duty will be payable. (Stamp duty is further explained on p. 197.)

(d) There is usually a clause stating that the vendor or vendors sell as 'beneficial owner(s)'. These words imply certain assurances, for instance that the vendor owns the house and has the right to sell it. These implied assurances may have had some relevance in the last century, when wicked uncles went round dispossessing their nephews of their rightful inheritance, but they have little relevance today, especially if the house is registered. Nevertheless, I suppose it is best that the traditional words are in the contract. However, if the vendor is the *executor* of the person who formerly owned the house, the clause in the contract will read 'The vendor sells as "personal representative" ', which means that he does not give these implied assurances – but as mentioned, it does not really matter one way or the other.

(e) The contract should state that vacant possession will be given on completion; and it should provide for a completion date, which is left blank at this stage.

(f) There will be a rate of interest in the contract – usually 4%/5% above bank 'base' rate. This is the rate at which you will have to pay interest on the purchase price (less deposit) should you delay completion *beyond* the completion date which will eventually be inserted in the contract. Except in the unfortunate case where you are selling your own house simultaneously and your purchaser himself delays, you should never have to pay interest.*

If the house is registered, you will see that the copy register which you will have been sent is in three sections (see appendix 2). Section A is the 'Property register' which contains the address of the house. Section B (usually on the same page as section A) is the 'Proprietorship register' which sets out the name or names of the owners. Section C is the 'Charges register'; a slight verbal confusion is that the charges register sets out particulars of restrictive covenants, and also particulars of 'charges', which in this context mean *mortgages*.

Check the following points on the copy register:

(i) That the address stated in section A is the address of the house you are buying; and the property is described as 'freehold land' – land being legal terminology for land and any building on it.

(ii) That the owner whose name is set out in section B is the vendor in the contract, and if there is more than one owner (e.g. husband and wife) then they are all stated to be the vendors in the contract.

(iii) That the words 'Title Absolute' appear under the heading 'B. Proprietorship Register'. These words mean that the Land Registry guarantees that the person or persons whose names are set out in section B *are* the owners of the house.†

(iv) That the clause in the contract which states that the house is subject to certain entries on the charges register refers

---

* If you are selling simultaneously, make sure you insert the *same* rate of interest in your sale contract as appears in your purchase contract.

† If, exceptionally, the house is not 'title absolute', it will be '*possessory* title' or '*qualified* title' – in which case do *not* proceed except under expert advice.

only to restrictive covenants and similar, and does not inadvertently include reference to any *charge* (that is, mortgage). The last entry on the charges register, section C, will usually be a note of a *charge* (mortgage) which will be paid off on completion.

(v) That the title number, which appears at the top of each page (including the plan), tallies with that in the contract.

If the house is unregistered, there will be no copy register to check; any checking of the vendor's title documents comes after exchange of contracts. There will be a clause similar to clause 5 of the contract on p. 150, and the conveyance specified in that clause should be at least fifteen years old.

Thus you look through the contract and also, if the house is registered, the copy register, and you check the above points. Some of them are technical, but for the most part this checking is no more than common sense. A prudent purchaser of a secondhand car would check that the numbers in the log book tally with those on the car, that the mileage stated in the advertisement agrees with that on the mileometer, that the vendor's name on the receipt is the same as that in the log book, and so on. Apart from the possible reduction of the amount of the deposit, or the addition of a list of furnishings and items which the vendor may have agreed to leave, there should not be any amendments to make to the contract – unless the vendor's solicitor has inadvertently left out a standard provision.

If there *are* any additions or alterations to be made, it is best first to agree them over the telephone with the vendor's solicitor; then write or preferably type them in both the contract and the copy which you are holding.

Finally the contract may contain an additional rather forbidding clause to the effect that the purchaser takes the property subject to all Town Planning Schemes, Local Land Charges, easements, wayleaves, restrictions etc. etc. In fact such a clause adds nothing to what would be implied in any case. As with any secondhand purchase, you buy the house with all its defects, physical and quasi-legal. It is up to you, the purchaser, to find out as best you can whether there are any before you exchange contracts.

Restrictive Covenants and similar

With the draft contract, the vendor's solicitor will have sent you a copy of any restrictive covenants to which the house is subject – and the contract will contain a clause stating that the property is subject to them. These covenants will be set out in section C of the copy register which you will have received, if the house is registered;* or they will have been copied from a previous conveyance or conveyances, if the house is unregistered. Perhaps the house you are buying will not be subject to any covenants, but the chances are that it will be. What should you do about them? The most common covenants are:

(1) To keep a particular fence in repair;
(2) To use the house only as a house and not for any trade or business;
(3) Not to do anything which causes a nuisance;
(4) Not to erect any buildings and/or not to make any alterations or additions except in accordance with plans previously approved by X or his successors (X being a previous owner who sometime in the past sold the land on which the house is built, and has probably since vanished without trace).
(5) A variation of (4) is where the covenant itself stipulates what sort of houses may and may not be erected, e.g. no house may be erected which costs less than £x to build, no part of any building may project beyond a certain building line, or exceed a certain height, and so on.

Of these covenants, (1) is unenforceable because it requires the spending of money; (2) this is what you want to use the house for anyway; (3) adds nothing to your ordinary common law obligations. Only (4) and (5) seem to call for consideration.

Now it would be reassuring to have proof that the house you are buying has been built in compliance with any restrictive covenants which may have been imposed on it. And if you see that your house is subject to a covenant similar to (4) above, you can *ask* your vendor's solicitor for evidence that the plans of the house, or any addition, were duly approved. The chances are, however, that all you will get is a statement that:

---

* Sometimes they are set out in a separate document which is *referred* to by an entry in section C, in which case you should ask for a copy, if you are not sent one with the copy register.

'there are no approved plans with the deeds, but the vendor has not received notice of any breach of covenant.' Had you employed a solicitor, that is all *he* would get. This is one of the many grey areas of the conveyancing system (registered and unregistered) where nothing is precise; and nobody can even be sure whether such a covenant is enforceable, and if so, who would be entitled to enforce it. The practical answer is that if the house is more than a few years old you can accept the situation – because even if any building had been carried out in breach of covenant, the covenant in question would almost certainly be held to have been waived, provided no objection had been raised at the time the house or addition was actually being built. On the other hand, if the house or addition has only just been built – apparently in breach of such a restrictive covenant – then you could buy an insurance policy indemnifying you against any risk. Once the house has been built, the risk is negligible and would diminish as each month passed. But apart from advising you to insure against the risk, a solicitor can do nothing to alter it. When it comes to assessing the significance of restrictive covenants, there is a vital distinction between virgin land which a developer is buying to build on, and an existing house. For practical purposes when it comes to buying an *existing* house, the bogeys of restrictive covenants, which are the main weapons in the solicitor's armoury, turn out to be so many red herrings.

Conversely, if you yourself will want to build some addition or garage, and you see that the house you are buying is subject to some such covenant as (4) above, how will you know from whom you need consent? Again you can *ask* the vendor, but again he probably will not know, and there will be no indication from the wording of the document which originally imposed the covenant. If you adopted a cavalier approach and ignored the covenant, you would probably be 99% safe. Alternatively, you might think it worth spending a modest sum on an insurance policy indemnifying you against this 1% risk.

Just as developers' solicitors impose restrictive covenants on every house they sell, to little purpose, so do they make each house on a newly-built estate subject to certain rights in favour of the developer and other house-owners on that estate. These rights enable other house-owners, for example, to use all drains pipes and cables running under the property in question, and/or allow the developer to build to any height on adjoining land notwithstanding any resulting loss of light or air to the property. Such conditions are generally imposed indiscriminately, whether or not there *are* any drains pipes or cables running under the property which anyone else may need to use; or whether or not there *is* any possibility that the developer will want to build on the adjoining land. And as with restrictive covenants, there is nothing you can *do* about these chunks of faintly ominous verbiage which you may find littering the register, or previous conveyances. A typical entry will be worded: 'The property is subject to the exceptions and reservations contained in the transfer/conveyance dated . . . ' which may appear, if the house is registered, either in section C ('Charges register') or section A ('Property register'). The contract will likewise state that the property is subject to any such matters.

If the house is registered, you may also see on the copy register some such entry as: 'No disposition of the property may be made without the consent of the proprietor of charge no.—'; or a declaration that the walls between the property and its neighbour are party walls. You need not bother with either – the first because all charges (mortgages) will be paid off on completion, the second because such a declaration is merely stating the obvious.

To sum up, in the case of a *registered* house, apart from the address of the house and the name of the owner, the entries which you are most likely to see on the copy register you are sent will be: (1) restrictive covenants, (2) particulars of rights 'excepted and reserved' in favour of owners of adjoining houses, (3) a note of the vendor's mortgage or mortgages, (4) the two items mentioned in the preceding paragraph. None of these matters need cause you any concern. However, if you see some *other* entry on your copy register, see p. 210 for my advice.

In the case of an *unregistered* house there is no register for these matters to be noted on; but the house will be subject to the same sort of restrictive covenants, and rights 'excepted and reserved', as a registered house. The only difference is that you will be sent copies of whatever covenants and rights there may be affecting the house, taken from a previous conveyance or conveyances, instead of being sent a copy of a single register.

If the house is unregistered, you should now send form 96 to the appropriate land registry office which deals with that area (see appendix 1). This is called an 'index search', and its purpose is to *confirm* that the property has not been registered (and there is no pending application to register it). In the highly improbable event that the vendor was purporting to sell you an unregistered house which had in fact been registered in someone else's name, you obviously would not proceed. This search will also reveal whether the house is in a registration district, and so will have to be registered after you complete your purchase. Remember it is quite likely that an unregistered house will be in a registration district, because when a registration district is declared, the houses therein are registered only on a *subsequent sale*. The procedure is that after completion the purchaser sends his recent conveyance, and all the previous conveyances, to the Land Registry, which issues a new land certificate in their place.

So you have received the draft contract – which either required no amendment, or else the one or two amendments which you have made; and the restrictive covenants, and other matters to which the house is subject, turn out to be the standard ones which clutter up 99% of all land registers and conveyances to no purpose except to make your job seem more difficult than it really is.

Your Inspection of the House

At this stage the purchaser's solicitor would send the vendor's solicitor a printed form of preliminary enquiries. You will likewise send him some enquiries; but before you do, and before you return one copy of the contract to the vendor's solicitor, your next step is to visit the house. For the reasons already stated, you will probably not get any useful information in the vendor's solicitor's answers to your written enquiries. Neither, if you had instructed a solicitor, would *he* get any useful information in reply to *his* questionnaire. The only useful information you will get about the property you are buying is through your own eyes when you inspect it, and through your own ears when you call at the Council offices. If you want to know whether the clutch of a secondhand car you are contemplating buying is in good condition, you drive the car; you don't write to the vendor: 'Please confirm the clutch is in good condition.' Solicitors, who never bother to inspect the property, do not seem to have twigged that little fact.

When you inspect the house what do you look for? You simply try to find out everything there is about it of a quasi-legal or general nature, which might be important. There may be some important things which you *won't* be able to find out, because they are not visible, and are nowhere recorded, e.g. the route of a common drain, or whether anyone else's drain runs under the garden. Under an efficient system these few bits of information would be clearly set out on a single register. Under the existing system, you will just have to check the following points as best you can:

1. Do the water and gas pipes, and electricity cable, come to the house direct from the respective mains under the road or pavement? You will normally see a little iron plate in the pavement, just beyond the front boundary, which covers the water stop-cock, but in the case of gas and electricity there is no such indication. You need not worry too much in the case of town and suburban houses fronting ordinary made-up roads. However, if the house fronts onto an *unmade* road or track, or is in the *country*, get written confirmation from the appropriate authorities (whose address will be in the telephone book) that the house is directly connected to the various mains – i.e. that the connecting pipes/cable do not go across or under anyone else's land. If gas is not connected, check that a mains supply is available.

2. Does the drain of the house go directly into the mains sewer in the road? A manhole may reveal whether it does or not. If it does not, it will most likely be a common drain. Your inspection may not tell you much, but again this point is probably not important in built-up suburban districts, especially if the house is more than a few years old. In country areas – where the house may not even drain to a mains sewer –

check this point more particularly when you get to the Council offices.

3. Are the boundary fences firmly in position? If there is an unfenced section, or the fence is falling down in one place, this could lead to a dispute with your neighbour. No-one is obliged to keep a fence in good repair – even if there is a covenant to do so. More important, if there is an unfenced section, the dispute might not be about who should erect a fence but where any new fence should be. Boundaries are the most frequent subject of dispute between neighbours, as to which see point 10.

4. You will have received a copy of the deed plan with the draft contract (either being part of the register, or else taken from a previous conveyance). *It is only the land shown on this plan which you will get.* Is it what you expected, and do the physical boundary fences agree with this plan? The plan does not purport to be accurate, but obviously there should not be any significant discrepancy. If this plan shows less land than appears, from your inspection, to go with the house, the neighbour may try to reinstate the boundary in future. An obvious point to check is that the garage is *within* the boundaries shown on the plan.

5. Is a right of way needed over a drive at the side (or part thereof if it is a shared drive between two houses), or over a track or roadway at the side or rear – to get to the garage? Normally the drive to the garage will be within the boundaries of the property itself, and the owner will neither need any rights over anyone else's drive, nor will anyone have any rights over his drive. Sometimes, however, there will be a shared drive between two houses; or there may be a track or roadway at the side or rear leading to the garage. In such cases, unless the track is a public right of way, there must be a note in the deeds (i.e. register or previous conveyances) that a right of way for vehicles over this common drive or track goes with the house. You would expect to see this note after the address of the house, either in section A of the register, or in a previous conveyance (e.g. 12 Mustard Street etc. *together with a right of way for vehicles over the roadway/drive coloured brown on the plan*). Similarly a right of way is sometimes needed over a track at the side or rear leading to the back garden.

If, however, the track is a public right of way, the house-owner as a member of the public automatically has a right to use it, so no specific right need be included. The local Council should be able to state whether it is or not.

6. Does any neighbour or member of the public use any rights of way over the land which goes with the house? This will usually be obvious on inspection.

7. What items, whether 'fixtures or fittings' or furnishings, are included in the purchase price? Go through each room (and, if applicable, the garden) with the vendor and make a list, so that when this list is added to the contract there won't be any subsequent dispute. This will be your most likely amendment to the contract, see p. 172 (c).

8. Are there any drains going under the land which serve any other house? There might easily be if the land on which the house was built was originally part of the garden of another house; and the point may be material if you want to build an extension or garage. The deeds probably won't reveal anything; neither can the vendor be relied on, because he may not know about it. You should therefore look out for, and uncover, all *manholes* – which may reveal such a drain. On the other hand, any manhole may be buried under a few feet of soil or undergrowth. This is something which often has to be left to chance.

9. Has the vendor, or his predecessor, erected any extension or garage without planning permission and/or building regulations approval? It is not every extension or garage which needs planning permission: if it is less than 70 cubic metres, generally it does not. Thus the average garage will not need planning permission, but every garage and almost every extension will need *building regulations approval* (which is dealt with by a different department).

Therefore you look out for anything which looks as if it might have been built subsequently to the house, and if you see such an addition, check with the Council that the necessary planning permission and/or building regulations approval was granted; and that the building inspector has given it a final inspection, and has passed it.*

---

* This will be under the *building regulations*. Curiously, there is no machinery for the *planning* department to inspect and pass a new building or extension.

10. As neighbour trouble is the most likely quasi-legal defect in a house, it would be prudent to introduce yourself to the neighbours and ask them whether they have had any disputes with your vendor. If any of the boundary fences or walls look a bit dodgy, or there is an unfenced section, this could give rise to a future dispute, so try to come to an agreement with the neighbour in question. You will probably introduce yourself to your new neighbours sooner or later, so do it sooner, as (just once in a while) later may be *too* late.

It should not take long to check the above points. The vast majority of houses are suburban dwellings fronting ordinary made-up roads, whose owners will have lived in them for the previous three to eight years without any kind of legal adventure. The boundary fences will be in position; there will be a mains water supply from the front, and a common drain at the front or rear; no-one will use a right of way over the garden land; the drive to the garage will be within the boundaries of the land being sold – or else access to it will be over a track at the side or rear and a right of way will be duly noted in the deeds; and the vendor will have got on perfectly well with his neighbours.

But what do you do should you discover something which seems *not* to be in order? The first thing you should do is to put the defect to the vendor's solicitor. It may be that he will be able to explain it to your satisfaction, or else be able to rectify it (which he should do *before* exchange of contracts). For example, a fence might have been erected in what is obviously the wrong position, or there may be no proper right of way over the track to the garage; but the vendor may be able to sign a declaration that that fence has been in its present position *for the past twelve years*, or that he and his predecessors have used the track without query for the past *twenty years*. Such a declaration (called a 'statutory declaration') would generally be considered to be a satisfactory resolution of this sort of problem.

However, if the defect cannot be put right – or if the vendor's solicitor offers no constructive suggestion to put it right – what should you do? It depends, of course, on what the defect is. If the irregularity appears to be a mere technicality, for instance if three years ago the vendor erected a perfectly ordinary garage without obtaining building regulations approval, you would be foolish to let that fact deter you from your purchase. On the other hand, if the house enjoys its water supply only by the grace and favour of a neighbouring farmer, obviously you would be unwise to buy it. You will have to exercise your own judgement in such a case. Sometimes the decision may not be clear cut: e.g. access to the garage, built five years ago, may be over a track at the rear, but there is no right of way noted in the deeds and the Council has no records that it is a public right of way. You see that garages of neighbouring houses are served by this track, and you consider it unlikely that anyone is going to interfere with your use of it. You therefore decide to accept the position. On looking at the garden land more closely, with the aid of the plan, you notice that a certain unfenced area which you thought was included is, in fact, not included, and this will make an appreciable difference to the garden. The vendor will not lower the price. You decide *not* to accept the position, and so you withdraw your offer. These two decisions would be based on a common-sense appraisal of the situation. However, if having found what seems to be a defect, you do not feel sufficiently confident to assess its significance, or whether the vendor's solicitor, who claims to have rectified the defect, has in fact done so – see p. 226 for my advice. A house with a quasi-legal defect serious enough to make a potential purchaser withdraw is, of course, very rare.

As important as your inspection of the house you are buying, is a look at the houses and gardens next to it. Owning a house anywhere carries a certain risk because you never know what will happen to the house or garden next door. No land is proof against the developer's lascivious eye, but some is more obviously attractive. Old and dilapidated houses are what he is looking for, especially when surrounded by a large and unkempt garden. If the house you are buying is next to such a house or garden, be alive to the greater possibility of a drastic upheaval in the environment. If the *windows* of your house directly overlook someone else's garden, or scrubland, and the house is less than twenty years old, remember that the adjoining owner can build so as to obstruct all light to those windows, provided he gets planning permission – and in some cases without planning permission. Also there is no right to a *view*, however long it may have been enjoyed.

If your dream house happens to be in a street in which most of the other houses have broken or boarded-up windows, or are otherwise obviously derelict, it is more likely to be next on the list for a compulsory purchase order by the Council, than if it is in a respectable residential road.

Preliminary Enquiries

After inspecting the house, submit your preliminary enquiries. Although I think it is unlikely that any written enquiries to the vendor's solicitor will elicit any useful information, your building society's solicitor will in due course ask you for such enquiries and answers. And there is just a chance that such enquiries *might* pick up something which you would not otherwise have known about. For reasons already given, I advise against using the solicitors' printed form, but suggest that you type out the following questions on the left-hand side of a sheet of foolscap paper (with copy), leaving the right-hand side blank for the answers. You head the paper with the address of the house, your name, and the vendor's name:

(1) Do the water and gas pipes, and electricity cable, come to the house direct from the respective mains in — Road, without going under or over anyone else's land? (2) Does the drainage of the house go direct to the mains sewer in — Road? If not, can you indicate the route of the drain, and where it does join the mains? (3) Who owns the boundary fences? (4) Is a right of way needed by the house-owner over a drive or track at the side or rear of the property, to get to the garage? (5) Does a neighbour or member of the public use a right of way over the land which goes with the house? (6) Are there any drains or pipes which serve any other houses, running under the house or land being sold? (7) Has the vendor made, or does he know whether his predecessor made, any building alterations or additions? If so, please supply copy planning permission and building regulations approval. (8) What fixtures or fittings, if any, is the vendor going to remove? (9) Has the vendor

received any Notices from the local Council, or in respect of breach of covenant, or otherwise? (10)(a) Has the vendor had any disputes of any kind with the neighbours? (10)(b) Has the vendor had any disputes with anyone else in connection with the property? (11) Is any work which has been done to the property still covered by a guarantee? (12) If the house is less than ten years old – (a) Is there a National House-Building Council warranty in force? (b) If so, has the vendor made any claim in respect thereof? (13) Are there any periodical payments in respect of the property other than general and water rates? *

Dispatch this sheet of questions (with copy) to the vendor's solicitor. *At the same time also return one copy of the draft contract – unsigned, but with any amendments.*

The answers you will get to (1) to (6) of your questions will probably be of the 'please search' or 'the vendor has no information' variety, but these questions will have been answered, so far as it is possible to answer them, by your inspection. But as questions (7) to (13) must be within the vendor's knowledge, insist on proper answers being given. Thus if the vendor's solicitor answers any of questions (7) to (13) with a non-committal reply, write to him e.g. 'Q.(7) asks whether the vendor has made any building alterations or additions. Either he has or he hasn't. This question is repeated.'

Also put these questions *verbally* to the vendor. For all you know, he may be selling *because* of a long-standing feud with an impossible neighbour, and it is more difficult to lie face to face than in writing. It is also worth asking the vendor (verbally) whether he knows of any *physical* defects relating to the house.

Your visit to the local Council

And so to the Council offices. You will of course have to find out which is the Council for your house. Sometimes it will be obvious; if the house is in Lewisham, the appropriate Council will be the London Borough of Lewisham. Where it is not

* The only such payment I can think of is a 'rent charge', which mercifully is virtually unknown outside Bristol and Manchester.

obvious, you will have to ascertain the nearest Council to the house with the aid of Yellow Pages – in which the Councils are listed under 'Local Government Authorities'. Telephone the Council first to make sure it is the right one. Then call round.

The fixed bits of information you require are:

(a) Is the road leading to the house maintained by the Council?

If it is, as it will be in 999 cases out of 1000, no worries. You will have an automatic right to drive along such road, and there will be no future liability for road charges.

If it is *not*, ask whether it is nevertheless a public right of way for vehicles. If it is, then as a member of the public you have an automatic right to use it, but there is a potential liability for road charges should the Council at any time decide to make it up into a standard road. The Council clerk may be able to tell you whether, and if so when, this is likely.

If the road is neither maintained by the Council nor a public right of way, then it is a *private* road. In that case there must be a note in the deeds that a right of way for vehicles over such road goes with the house – which you would expect to see after the address of the house, either in section A of the register, or in a previous conveyance. There will likewise be a potential liability for road charges if the Council decides to take over the road.

At the same time as you enquire about this road, ask about any track at the side or rear which you need to use. If there is such a track, it will usually not be maintained by the Council, so you will need to check that it is either a public right of way, or else a right of way (for vehicles) over it is included in the deeds.

(b) Does the house drain into a mains sewer? In country districts, especially, check where the mains sewer is, and how the house drains to it. If the drain goes under a neighbouring garden or gardens, theoretically there should be a right to use such drain noted in the deeds. Often there is not, and the house-owner has to rely on the right having been established by long user, or else on the fact that it is unlikely that anyone will try to interfere with a common drain.

(c) If the house is comparatively new, ask to see a copy of the planning permission, and building regulations approval; and ask the clerk if it can be accepted that all conditions have been complied with. The planning permission itself will not tell you much – in fact it could be a composite permission for an estate of fifty or more houses, e.g. 'Take Notice that the XY Borough Council has granted permission for development of land between Park Road and Imperial Drive, being residential development for AB Development Co. Ltd. in accordance with plans lodged with the Council on . . . '

If there is a garage at the property, ask the clerk whether the original planning permission included such garage; if it did not, ask to see the subsequent building regulations approval relating to it.

Some peripheral information you could usefully pick up:

(d) Ask how much the current rates are.

(e) If there are open fireplaces at the house, ask if there is a Smoke Control Order in force. If there is, it means that you are not allowed to burn smoke-producing fuel.

For the rest, and more important, you should check:

(f) That there are no outstanding *Notices* in respect of the property, e.g. dangerous structure, public nuisance, public health, or breach of planning/building regulations.

(g) That there are no proposals for road widening, or new roads, which might affect the house – either because of their proximity, or because they involve the compulsory acquisition of the house or any part of the garden.

(h) That there are no planning applications, or planning permissions which have not yet been implemented, in respect of the houses and land *adjacent* to the house you are buying.

(i) That there are no redevelopment schemes in the offing which might involve the compulsory acquisition of the house or garden, or otherwise affect it – e.g. for a new school, the extension of an existing school, or a new shopping precinct.

(j) That the house is not, nor is likely to be, in a *redevelopment area*. A redevelopment area comes into being when the Council considers that an individual street or area is so dilapidated that it decides compulsorily to acquire all the properties therein, and comprehensively redevelop such area. Councils have also been known to acquire and demolish quite sound houses to make way for new council housing estates.

(k) That there are no other proposals for the compulsory acquisition of the property.

Each of the above points will be dealt with by different departments, and you will be directed from one to the other. The set-up will vary from Council to Council, but I have always found the clerks helpful, as has everyone I know who has adopted this personal approach.

In addition to this 'personal' search, you should *leave* the two search forms – LLC1 (which is a search for 'local land charges'), and CON 29 (which is a questionnaire containing some of the questions you will already have asked the clerks), together with the appropriate fee, which is stated on the forms. You have to fill in the address of the house you are buying and your own address on each form. Both forms have to be delivered in duplicate, but LLC1 has a duplicate attached.

In the fullness of time* the Council will return the forms duly answered. Any entries which appear on the 'local land charges' search form will usually be duplicated in the answers to the questionnaire form, e.g. Smoke Control order and planning permissions. In appendix 4, I reproduce the questionnaire together with answers which will apply to ninety-nine out of every hundred houses. *Indeed, so standard are these answers that the Councils have them printed on sheets which they simply attach to the questionnaire.*

However, if when the forms are eventually returned to you, you are doubtful about any answer or entry, ring up the Council, and the appropriate clerk will explain it – just as he will be pleased to explain the significance of anything out of the ordinary revealed by any of your questions when you call round. Many entries, although out of the ordinary, give no cause for alarm: for instance, there may be a tree preservation

---

*   The time it takes a Council to return the forms varies from two weeks to two
     months. As this is likely to be the chief delay, if you do not plan to visit the Council
     offices within a few days of receiving the draft contract you should *send* these forms
     to the Council at the outset.

order, or the house may be in a 'conservation area'. Only a developer would find these entries onerous; the ordinary house-owner would, in fact, welcome them.

On the other hand, just occasionally something may be revealed which cannot be explained away so easily, and in respect of which the Council clerk may not be able to offer much help. For instance, you may learn that a new main road is planned to pass within 200 metres of the house, and that it is intended to start work in, say, six months. In such a case you will have to make up your own mind whether you want to proceed with your purchase. It may be a difficult decision, especially when there is a proposal in the offing which *could* be disastrous, but – as is often the case – no-one can say when it will be implemented or even, if implemented, whether it actually *will* affect the house you are buying. Again, you will have to make up your mind whether to proceed or withdraw – but you would have had to make exactly the same decision had you employed a solicitor.

In fact, by calling at the Council offices, rather than employing a solicitor, you will place yourself in a far better position to make such a decision. A solicitor will rely exclusively on his local search forms. Yet some important points which you covered on your visit to the Council offices are not included in the forms – e.g. planning applications in respect of the adjoining property. Moreover, you are more likely to get useful information by speaking to a human being, than you are from the monosyllabic answers to a printed questionnaire. In particular, the local search forms will not pick up matters until they have been put on one of the Council's registers. A proposal for, e.g., a new road or a redevelopment area can hang like a black cloud over a district for several years or more, while the various departments push it backwards and forwards, investigate it, postpone it, re-open it. Meanwhile the proposal is *not* on any register – although everyone at the Council offices will know about it. So will all the local residents. The purchaser's solicitor sitting in his office perhaps a hundred miles away will, however, know nothing about it – even *after* his local search forms are returned.

You have now returned one copy of the contract to the vendor's solicitor; you have inspected the house and visited the Council offices; you have received your local search forms back from the Council, and your page of preliminary enquiries back from the vendor's solicitor. You have discovered nothing to deter you from proceeding. You have therefore done all the pre-contract work. And as the post-contract work is negligible in the case of a registered house, or is an academic nonsense in the case of an unregistered house, it follows that you will have now done the most important work.

It may occur to you that nothing you have done so far has been 'legal' work, or has required much knowledge of law. In fact, apart from understanding a few technical points on the contract, what you have done has been merely to follow the dictates of common sense. A house needs water. If the water pipe comes direct from the mains, no-one can interfere with it; on the other hand if it comes across a farmer's field, perhaps someone *can* interfere with it. You therefore check where the pipe does come from. If access to the garage is by a track which is a public right of way, no-one can prevent you using it. However, if that track is not a public right of way, and there is no right to use it included in the deeds (register or previous conveyance), then perhaps someone *can* prevent you using it. Therefore you check that the track is either a public right of way or else a right to use it is noted in the deeds. A proposal for Orbital Ringway III, which may disastrously affect the house, may be awaiting the Borough Engineer's feasibility report. The answers to the local search forms won't reveal anything about this proposal. The Council clerks will. You therefore ask the clerks, *as well as* submitting the forms. Neighbour trouble is the most likely quasi-legal defect of a house. Therefore you don't rely on the vendor to tell you whether there is any, but you *ask the neighbour*.

Of course in ninety-nine cases out of a hundred the net result – whether you call at the Council offices or send the printed search forms or do both or neither, or whether you inspect the house or send a form of enquiries or do both or neither – will be the same. The road will be maintained by the Council; the house will drain to a mains sewer; there will be no Notices or proposals; there will be a right of way to the garage if such is needed; Orbital Ringway III, even if approved, will be going nowhere near the house. Nothing will have been planned to disrupt the suburban peace of your new abode. What you are doing, when you inspect the house and call at the Council offices, is merely to check – so far as the defective system permits such matters to be checked – that the house you are buying is not the one in a hundred which *does* have something about it to make you reconsider your purchase. To spend a few hours checking such matters seems to be sensible. To spend a few hundred pounds employing a solicitor who, for all his forms and verbiage, will *not* check such matters but will leave them to chance, seems not to be sensible.

Survey

Remember, you take the house not only with all quasi-legal defects but all physical defects as well; and a vendor is under no obligation to disclose either variety.

Many, perhaps most, purchasers rely on their building society's surveyor; but this is unwise as the building society's sole interest in the house is that, if necessary, it will sell for the amount of the mortgage advance. Should you therefore spend several hundred pounds on a separate survey? I confess I do not know how to advise you. I have seen numerous survey reports devoted chiefly to telling the purchaser about the state of decoration and the size and number of the rooms, coupled with a blanket escape clause at the end – that as all timbers, foundations and drains were covered up, they were excluded from the report. This sort of report is completely valueless. But then unaided, you may not notice that the house is subsiding, or riddled with dry rot or whatever. A good surveyor has no magical qualities, only a pair of eyes which he knows how to use – but how do you find one? I suppose the ideal solution is to have a knowledgeable friend/relative in the building trade, who will go round the house with you.

Mortgage Offer

If you are getting a mortgage, you should not exchange contracts (which binds you to the deal) until you have received a written mortgage offer. If your mortgage is coming from a Local Authority or Finance House, you will usually have to get a report on damp, woodrot and woodworm from a specialist firm; and a retention may be made from the advance, of whatever sum that firm estimates for any remedial work.

By way of digression, the way such a firm tests for damp is by a damp-meter. A positive reading does not necessarily mean that the wall in question is damp or that the damp proof course is defective, as the instrument could be picking up surface moisture (condensation). A positive reading, however, usually means that the unfortunate borrower is going to have to pay a considerable sum for that firm to drill the wall full of holes at damp proof course level (thereby possibly ruining a perfectly adequate *existing* damp proof course), in order to inject a *chemical* damp proof course. A situation where the firm which gives the report is generally the same firm which does any work it considers necessary – and where the purchaser *has* to accept the lender's conditions – is open to abuse. A surveyor friend of mine suggests that damp-meters should be used only under licence granted to applicants of proven intelligence and honesty. A more practical suggestion is that you should be present when the 'specialist' visits. When he makes with the damp-meter, dig the skirting boards in the relevant area with a penknife or screwdriver. If the woodwork is sound, put it to the specialist that this shows the damp proof course is *not* defective, and that his meter is picking up condensation. If necessary, get half a dozen firms to give reports.

Exchange of Contracts

A contract, you will remember, consists of two identical documents; and exchange of contracts is when one party (or his solicitor), having received the other party's signed contract, posts to that other party (or his solicitor) his signed contract. Any agreed amendments should have been inserted in both parts of the contract, prior to signature. By tradition, it is the purchaser who sends his signed contract first. At the outset, you received a contract and copy from the vendor's solicitor. You returned the copy unsigned. The contract you retained will be the contract which you – and your spouse if a joint purchaser – will sign and send to the vendor's solicitor. If your purchase is not dependent on a simultaneous sale, you can send off your signed purchase contract as soon as you have completed your inspection and searches etc., and have received your mortgage offer. Exchange of contracts is achieved by taking steps 2 and 3 described below.

However, if your purchase is dependent on a simultaneous sale, you should not exchange contracts on your *purchase* until you have received your *sale* contract signed by your purchaser. This is no more than common sense. Obviously you should not be in a position of having contracted to buy your new house before you have a contract to sell your existing house; or of having contracted to sell your existing house before you have a contract to buy your new house. Therefore in the case of an interdependent purchase and sale, when it comes to exchanging contracts the following steps must be taken strictly in the order stated:

1. *Receive* your purchaser's signed contract on your sale* (having made sure he has paid the deposit);

2. *Send* to your vendor's solicitor your signed contract on your purchase, with balance of deposit (sending a bank draft will save time as a cheque has to be cleared);

3. *Receive* your vendor's signed contract on your purchase.* If there is more than one owner (e.g. husband and wife)† make sure that all of them have signed. This completes exchange on your *purchase*; and without any delay

4. *Send* to your purchaser's solicitor your signed contract on your sale, thereby completing exchange on your *sale*.

This procedure ensures, as far as possible, that your sale and purchase contracts are exchanged simultaneously. If either your sale or your purchase falls through at the last minute, you simply cancel the dependent purchase or sale. Thus if you never receive your purchaser's signed contract on your sale, you never send your own signed contract on your

---

* Sometimes a solicitor will send a signed contract with a letter stating that it is to be *held to his order* pending his telephone release of this proviso. This is for administrative convenience, so that a chain of dependent contracts can all be exchanged within the space of a few telephone calls rather than having to wait for the post. If you get such a letter, you haven't 'received' the signed contract for the purpose of these instructions *until* you receive the solicitor's telephone release of the proviso.

† In the case of a registered house this is easily checked because the owners' names appear on the register. In the case of an unregistered house it cannot be checked without a copy of the latest conveyance. For this reason, it would be a good idea to ask for a copy before exchange.

purchase. If you never receive your vendor's signed contract on your purchase, you never part with your signed contract on your sale.

When you receive your vendor's signed contract on your purchase, you will see that his solicitor has inserted a completion date, which will usually be four weeks from the date on which he posted it to you. If you are selling your house simultaneously, insert this same date in your sale contract before sending it to your purchaser's solicitor.

As soon as your purchase contract is exchanged, telephone the building society with whose assistance you are buying, and ask it to arrange immediate insurance cover. Send a confirmatory letter. If you are not getting a mortgage, arrange this insurance yourself, as the house is now at your risk.

*

Summary of steps up to exchange of contracts

1. Receive draft (proposed) contract, with carbon copy, from vendor's solicitor.

With the draft contract the vendor's solicitor will send you *office* copy of the register (if the house is registered); or a copy of the plan and any restrictive covenants (if unregistered).

2. Check the draft contract and copy register (p. 170-174).

3. Send 'local search' forms to Council – or if you propose visiting the Council offices within a few days *leave* them there – [and check replies] (p. 188).

4. If house is *unregistered* send form 96 to Land Registry (p. 178).

5. Inspect house (p. 178-184).

6. Send preliminary enquiries to vendor's solicitor [and check replies] (p. 184).

At the same time return one copy of the draft contract, unsigned – having typed in any agreed alterations or additions (which you also type into the copy contract which you retain).

7. Visit local Council offices (p. 185-188).

8. Having received written mortgage offer and tied up dependent sale (if applicable), send your signed part of the contract to vendor's solicitor. At the same time pay the deposit (either to the estate agents or the vendor's solicitor, as the contract provides) (p. 193).

9. Receive the vendor's signed part of the contract. The contract is now legally binding between you.

13

How to do the conveyancing on your purchase – from exchange of contracts to completion

(I) when house is registered

The previous chapter dealt with the steps leading to exchange of contracts. This chapter deals with the procedure from exchange to completion. Except in matters of detail, the pre-contract procedure is the same whether the house is registered or unregistered. Both were therefore dealt with together. After exchange of contracts some of the steps do vary; hence this chapter is in two parts, the first applying when the house is registered; the second containing *additional* instructions for when it is unregistered.

Whereas the pre-contract work consisted mainly in checking various things about the house, the post-contract work (registered and unregistered) consists in getting ownership of the house from vendor to purchaser, and getting the purchase price from purchaser and his building society to vendor.

As we saw in Chapter 9, the Land Registry has taken away practically all the post-contract work in the case of registered houses, leaving but a few formalities. As stated in a book published by the Solicitors' Law Stationery Society, *Practical Conveyancing* by E. Moeran, 'Registered land conveyancing is delightfully simple.'

Transfer

This is the document which, when signed by the vendor, legally transfers the house to you. You, the purchaser, have to prepare it. Among the forms which you bought at the outset was a 'transfer of whole' (form 19). In the spaces provided type the postal address of the house, title number, purchase price (excluding any part apportioned to furnishings and separate items), full names and address of vendor(s), and your – and if co-purchaser, your spouse's – full names and address as purchaser(s).

Make sure that you insert as vendor or vendors *all* the owners in section B of the register; and that the names you insert in the transfer correspond exactly with the names in section B of the register.

There is a chunk of verbiage at the end of the transfer called a 'certificate of value', which relates to stamp duty. If the price of the house (excluding any sum apportioned to furnishings etc, see p. 172(c)) is £30,000 or less, no stamp duty is payable provided you insert '*£30,000*' in the 'certificate of value'. If the price of the house is *more* than £30,000,* you will have to pay stamp duty of 1%* of the total purchase price of the house – in which case the 'certificate of value' has no relevance and should be ignored.

Type the transfer with two (flimsy) copies and send it, with one of the copies, to the vendor's solicitor, who will get it signed in readiness for completion.

Building Society

Immediately after exchange of contracts, send your building society's solicitor the following documents (in fact he will probably have already sent you a letter asking for them):

Local search forms, with the Council's replies.

Preliminary enquiries, with vendor's solicitor's replies.

Original contract signed by vendor.

Copy of register. (Make a photocopy before sending this.)

Vendor's solicitor's authority to inspect the register. (Ask the vendor's solicitor to send you *two* such authorities – one in favour of your building society's solicitor; and one in your favour, to enable you to do the search described in the next section.)

Copy of transfer. (This was why you made *two* copies.)

When the building society's solicitor has looked through these documents he will send you three things:

---

* As they can be varied in any budget, check the current threshold and rate with your building society's solicitor, or Stamp Duty office.

(I) The mortgage for you (and spouse if co-purchaser) to sign, in the presence of a witness who should add his signature, name and address. Check that the amount of the mortgage advance, the rate of interest, and the monthly repayments correspond with the mortgage offer. Apart from that, there is nothing to be done with it except to sign it, but if you have any queries ask the society's solicitor.

(II) A statement of the building society's solicitor's fees (which are laid down by a scale, set out in appendix 9). This will also include land registry fees and any stamp duty, and the total will be *deducted* from the advance.

(III) A sheet of 'requisitions' – that is, questions about the house you are buying covering the same sort of points as your preliminary enquiries. As far as possible, repeat the answers that you were given to your own preliminary enquiries. Any questions that appear on this form which you yourself did not raise can usually be answered with a bit of waffle. Sometimes a building society solicitor's clerk will make a great song and dance about needing to see a building regulations approval for a garage erected ten years previously, but normally the questions should present no difficulty. In any case, they are raised purely as a matter of mindless routine: will it really matter to your building society who owns the boundary fences? The important thing is to get the documents to the society's solicitor as soon as you can after exchange of contracts, so that any points can be settled in good time, rather than tripping you up at the last minute. If you don't hear from him with the mortgage etc. within, say, a week, chase him up – and *keep* chasing him until you do.

Included with the 'requisitions' will be a list of documents which the building society's solicitor will require on completion. This list is basically always the same, viz:

(1) Vendor's land certificate, (2) transfer signed by vendor, (3) vendor's building society solicitor's undertaking to send form discharging vendor's mortgage. These three documents will be produced and handed over by the vendor's solicitor on completion. The other documents on the list will be supplied by you: (4) mortgage signed by you, (5) land registry search form (described in the next section) – and three other rather

irritating forms as follows: (6) K16, which you send to, and which will be returned by, the Land Charges Registry at Plymouth, certifying that you (and spouse if co-purchaser) are not bankrupt. You write your name(s) in the spaces provided, and send it, with postal order for 50p. for each purchaser, to the address printed on it. (7) Inland Revenue LA form, which is presented to the Stamp Duty office, with the transfer, after completion. (8) Form A4 to accompany the documents when they are sent to the Land Registry after completion. These last two formalities will be dealt with by the building society's solicitor.

The last two forms should take only a few minutes to fill in, but if they cause you any difficulty take them along blank to completion, and your building society's solicitor will do it for you. However, there is an important point on the last form, A4. When husband and wife are joint purchasers, the usual arrangement is that on the death of either, the whole house automatically goes to the survivor. If you are buying jointly and this is what you want, answer Q.8 on this form (Can the survivor give a receipt for capital money?) 'YES'. The alternative is where the deceased's half share of the house is added to his or her estate, and distributed in accordance with his or her will (e.g. to children of a former marriage). If *this* is what you want, answer Q.8 'NO'.*

Land Registry Search

This is done by sending form 94A to the Land Registry a week or so before completion – and although this is one of the building society solicitor's requirements, you should still do it even if you are not getting a mortgage. At the outset the vendor's solicitor sent you an office copy of the register, which will have a date stamped at the bottom of each page (including the plan), being the date on which it was issued. This search form is a device to warn you of any adverse dealing with the property *after* this date, and which therefore would not appear

---

* Where the deceased's share is to go automatically to the survivor, the joint owners are called 'joint tenants'; where it is to be added to the deceased's estate, they are called 'tenants in common'. In the case of a 'tenancy in common' there will be a restriction on the register to the effect that the survivor cannot give a receipt for capital monies. Joint tenants necessarily have an *equal* share, but tenants in common can own *any* fraction of the property.

on the office copy you were sent. Thus the last entry on the 'charges register' of your office copy will probably be a note of the vendor's building society mortgage, but after the date of the office copy the vendor might have entered into a *second* mortgage with a finance company, which your office copy would not show. You therefore send this search form to the appropriate branch of the Land Registry, *which will be stated on the office copy*, having filled in the necessary particulars on it: title number, full names of vendor(s), *date* of the office copy, full names of purchaser(s), and address of property. With this form you also have to send the vendor's solicitor's written authority to inspect the register. In a day or so the Land Registry will return the form with the words 'since [the date of your office copy] no adverse entry has been made thereon' stamped on the reverse side. You can therefore complete your purchase with a light heart and a clear conscience knowing that firstly, the vendor has not created any second mortgage or whatever; and secondly, that even if he does so *after* your search, you will still take the house free of it – provided that your building society's solicitor sends the documents to the Land Registry after completion (in order to register you as owner in place of the vendor) *by a certain date stamped on the search form*. This date will be six weeks from when the Land Registry returns the form to you.*

The procedures described above may appear complicated. This is inevitable when trying to explain a slightly technical subject to the uninitiated. The work, such as it is, is indeed fiddly and irritating but, like the pre-contract work, it requires no skill or legal knowledge. If you were doing this work for a living, and had the services of a typist, the post-contract work involved in the purchase of a registered house would not take more than half an hour.

---

* But what if the vendor or his solicitor has tampered with the office copy itself, before sending it to you – e.g. by blanking out a mortgage or two? As this would be so easy to do, it would be a prudent precaution for *you* to obtain an office copy of the register *direct* from the Land Registry after exchange of contracts, which you can do (free of charge) with the vendor's solicitor's authority to inspect the register.

Finances

In fact, the most complicated thing in the whole business is bringing the right amount of money with you to completion – and the complication has nothing to do with law but derives from the diversity of your financial sources. You are buying a house for, say, £65,000 (having paid £6,500 by way of deposit), with the aid of a mortgage of £30,000, from which the building society will be deducting £800 costs and stamp duty; and perhaps the balance of the purchase price will be coming partly from the sale of your present house for £55,000, on which there is £27,560.45p. still owing to the building society. If you were buying a car with the aid of a hire purchase agreement, supplemented by the proceeds of sale of your present car which was subject to an existing hire purchase agreement, the arithmetical processes would be the same – except that the figures would not be so frightening.

A week or so before completion, your vendor's solicitor will send you a 'completion statement' showing the exact amount he will require on completion: purchase price less deposit, plus or minus an apportionment of water rate, depending on whether at the date of completion it will have been paid in advance or arrears. Ask him – perhaps by telephone ten days before completion – *not* to apportion general rate, because it is not necessary (see p. 161).

Your vendor's solicitor should also notify you (and if he does not volunteer this information ask him for it, say, a week before completion) whether he wants all the purchase money by way of bank drafts* in his favour, or whether he wants some of it in favour of the vendor's building society's solicitor. If the latter, you will have to arrange accordingly with your building society's solicitor. Thus if the purchase price, less deposit, comes to £58,500, you and your building society's solicitor together have to bring bank drafts totalling this sum to completion. If the vendor's solicitor does not require the purchase price to be split, these bank drafts will be in his favour. On the other hand, if he wants £25,432.52p. to be in favour of Blink & Co., then you and/or your building society's solicitor will have to hand over bank draft(s) for this sum in

---

* For a definition of bank draft see p. 162. Cheques, of course, are not acceptable.

favour of Blink & Co., and separate bank draft(s) for the balance in favour of the vendor's solicitor. If part of the purchase price is coming from the proceeds of a simultaneous sale of your own house, ask your *purchaser's* solicitor to make sure the bank draft you get on your sale is not crossed 'account payee only' – so you can use it for your purchase (by endorsing it) without having to put it through your bank; or ask him to split the proceeds of your sale into whatever bank drafts are required by your vendor's solicitor.

Before completion you therefore have some finances to work out, involving rather alarming sums of money. But you would still have had to work out these sums if you employed a solicitor, and in any event you must have had a clear idea of your finances before you even made your offer of purchase.

Before completion you also have some liaising to do. If you are buying and selling simultaneously, you have to arrange with your present building society's branch manager (or solicitor), and your purchaser's solicitor, the time and place at which your *sale* will be completed. Then you have to arrange with your vendor's solicitor, and your new building society's solicitor, the time and place your *purchase* will be completed. This will be either at the vendor's building society solicitor's office; or if, as usually happens, the vendor's building society instructs the vendor's solicitor to act for it, it will be at the vendor's solicitor's office.

Finally you have to make arrangements with your removal firm. You will have instructed removers as soon as you knew the completion date, that is, after exchange of contracts. It will greatly assist you if your vendor will let you have the keys before completion, so that your furniture van can drive straight from your old address to you new address and unload your furniture; but if he is properly advised he will not do this – just as you would not part with the keys of your old house until the sale monies were safely in your hands. You must therefore try to arrange for completion of your purchase to follow as soon as possible after completion of your sale. Again, this administrative problem would be the same if you had a solicitor acting for you, except that he would attend the completion appointments, leaving you free to supervise the loading and unloading of the furniture van.

If you are not selling simultaneously, it will be that much simpler. You merely have to arrange with your vendor's solicitor, and your building society's solicitor, the time and place at which your purchase will be completed.

Completion

On the appointed day and at the appointed time, you go along to the office where completion is to take place. You bring with you documents (4) to (8) listed on p. 198/9; bank draft(s) for whatever balance of the purchase price is needed; and a letter addressed to the estate agent who holds the deposit, authorising him to release the deposit to the vendor. (No letter is needed if it is held by the vendor's solicitor.)

But before you and your building society hand over the purchase money, you want to make sure that the house has been totally vacated, and that there are no dear old ladies – or indeed ladies of any description, particularly the vendor's wife or 'common law wife' – peacefully knitting in any corner. Under the conveyancing system many things have to be left to chance; and this is one of the things which your solicitor would have left to chance. However, as this is the most likely encumbrance that a house can have, you (who are doing the job so much more thoroughly and intelligently than the experts) are *not* content to leave it to chance. Just before you complete, you – or someone on your behalf – should therefore check that the house is empty and void of furniture; also that any items which the vendor has contracted to leave *have* been left. If you've managed to obtain the keys before completion, this won't be difficult. Otherwise you, or your representative, will have to borrow the keys from the estate agent or neighbour. This should be arranged between you and the vendor. If you do find someone apparently still living there, or any evidence thereof, do *not* complete.

At the completion appointment itself you will meet your building society's solicitor, and you give him the documents he has previously asked for. The vendor's solicitor produces the transfer and land certificate.* You check that this land certificate is the same as your office copy which you were sent

---

* Actually, if there is a mortgage on the house it is called a 'charge certificate'.

at the outset. You also check that the transfer is the same document as you yourself typed out; and that the vendor or – if more than one – *all* the vendors have *executed** it at the bottom. Both land certificate and transfer you hand to your building society's solicitor. (You would, of course, keep them yourself if you were not getting a mortgage.)

If there is only one charge (mortgage) on the charges register, and this is to a building society, it is the accepted practice for the vendor's building society's solicitor to give a written undertaking to send the form discharging the vendor's mortgage (form 53) within fourteen days *after* completion. This undertaking should read: 'As solicitor for XY Building Society, I undertake to discharge the mortgage dated — on the above property, and to send you form 53 executed by the building society within 14 days.'† Although the practice is to give this undertaking direct to the purchaser's building society's solicitor, it should be addressed to you, the purchaser, as you are directly concerned that the vendor's mortgage is paid off; and the vendor's building society's solicitor should give a further undertaking to your building society's solicitor. (Of course if the vendor's building society could execute the form in readiness for completion, the whole bothersome business of these undertakings would be unnecessary.)

If the vendor's mortgage is *not* to a building society, you should not accept an undertaking, but insist that the form 53 executed* by the mortgagee (lender) is handed over *on completion*. The form is very simple. After quoting the address of the house and title number, it continues '[AB Insurance Co. Ltd.] of . . . hereby admits that the charge dated — and registered on — of which it is proprietor, has been discharged.'

---

* This is a convenient technical word. In the case of an *individual* execute means to sign, with a red disc after his signature, in the presence of a witness who also writes his name and address. In the case of a *company* or *building society* execute means to affix the company or corporate seal (thus impressing its name in raised lettering on the document), in the presence of a director and secretary (or other authorised officers) who also sign.

Thus if, exceptionally, your vendor was a limited company, the transfer would bear the latter type of 'execution'.

† Although this undertaking will come from the vendor's building society's solicitor, this will usually be the *vendor's* solicitor – who for this purpose will have been instructed to act for the vendor's building society as well.

You will see from the register whether there is any charge other than to a building society. If so, inform the vendor's solicitor immediately on exchange of contracts that you will not accept an undertaking, but will require the executed form 53 to be handed over on completion.

Your building society's solicitor then produces the mortgage money split into whatever bank drafts have been previously requested by the vendor's solicitor, and you produce your own bank draft(s) for any balance needed. You also hand over the letter releasing the deposit.

The vendor's mortgage has been paid off, and the vendor's solicitor has received the balance of the purchase price. The deeds (land certificate and transfer) and new mortgage have been handed to your building society's solicitor as security for its loan. It remains for the vendor's solicitor to release the keys, either by giving them to you, or by telephoning instructions to whoever has got them. Also he should give you the NHBC warranty, if applicable (see Q.12 p. 185). And that's it. The house is yours.

After completion there are two further formalities which will be dealt with by your building society's solicitor: (I) The transfer has to be stamped with any stamp duty payable – and (whether or not any stamp duty is payable) with an Inland Revenue stamp (see (7) on p. 199). (II) The documents have to be sent to the Land Registry for your name(s) to be entered on the register as owner(s) in place of the vendor.

If you are buying without a mortgage, you will have to attend to these two formalities yourself. As to the first, this is done at a Stamp Duty office, which is a branch of the Inland Revenue – address in phone book; as to the second, when you send the documents (land certificate, transfer, search form 94A) to the Land Registry, form A4, duly completed, needs to accompany them.

If you are buying with a mortgage, write to the Land Registry three months or so after completion, quoting the address of the house, title number, and your full name – and ask for an office copy of the register. This will show that your registration as the new owner has been effected (and if it hasn't you will want to know why); and it will be useful for when you come to sell. If you are not buying with a mortgage, the land certificate will be automatically sent to you when registration has been effected.

*

I have assumed that everything about your vendor's register is commonplace: that is, the vendor will have his name on the proprietorship register; that apart from restrictive covenants and rights of drainage etc., the only other entry on the charges register will be a single mortgage; that there will be no entry on the other sections of the register to cause you any qualms; that your land registry search will be returned with the words 'Since . . . no adverse entry has been made thereon'. This will usually be the case, but there are a few other possibilities as follows:

1. The vendor may be the executor or administrator of the person who owned the house, and who has since died. In that case the proprietor (owner) on your office copy will be AB, whereas the vendor, who will sign the transfer, will be XY. If this is so, on completion you will require a sealed copy 'Probate' or 'Letters of Administration', which is an official one-page document stating that XY is the executor or administrator of AB – see appendix 5. You are not concerned with the will of the previous owner, or any question of Inheritance Tax (Estate Duty).

2. If there is a second or subsequent charge (mortgage) on the charges register, it should be dealt with as previously explained; that is, in addition to the building society's solicitor's undertaking in respect of every *building society* charge, you should get a separate executed form 53 for every charge which is *not* to a building society. Also there will be a separate 'charge certificate' in respect of any second or subsequent charge, which should be handed over with the form 53.

Occasionally you will see on the charges register an entry headed 'Notice of Deposit'. This is an informal mortgage, usually to a bank; on completion you must get a written release called 'Withdrawal of Notice of Deposit' signed on behalf of the bank, which will be on a printed form.

If your land registry search form is returned with particulars of an adverse entry entered on the register since the date of the office copy in your possession, such an adverse entry will probably be a second charge, and you will deal with it in the same way as if it had been shown on your original office copy, in accordance with the above.

3. Sometimes, very rarely, the word CAUTION will appear on the proprietorship register (or on your land registry search form), which means that someone has registered a hostile interest in the property – e.g. someone might claim a prior contractual interest. Or the vendor's wife, not being a joint owner, might register a NOTICE claiming an interest in the property as the matrimonial home (which would appear on the charges register). The effect of either entry is that the property may not be sold without the consent of whoever registered it. Therefore if you see such an entry, do *not* complete unless you get a form signed by the person who registered it (whose name will also appear) stating that he/she *withdraws* it. It is partly for this reason that you should obtain a complete copy of the register at the outset, because in the rare case of a Caution or matrimonial Notice being registered, you will need to be satisfied that the vendor can get it released *before you sign contracts* – particularly if you are selling simultaneously.

4. More problematical is the right of someone other than the registered owner (usually the owner's 'common law wife') to remain in the house by virtue of having contributed to the purchase price *and* being in occupation. Because this right does not have to be registered (as distinct from a *wife's* right), it is less easy to find out in advance whether there is someone claiming such a right. Of course, you don't complete unless and until the property is vacant; but it will be more than inconvenient if you discover such a claimant only at the last minute. Therefore on your visits to the house try to find out (by asking the vendor and looking around) who is living there *other* than the registered owner(s), and check that they consent to the sale. Some solicitors insist that any such person – even children – join in the contract to *confirm* they consent to the sale, which seems to make rather a meal out of a problem

which probably occurs less than once in a thousand cases. Nevertheless, it would be prudent to get a note signed by everyone over 18 who is living in the house (but who is not a registered owner) consenting to the sale – which should not be too difficult.

5. I have assumed that – with the assistance of your spouse and/or other representative – you are able to attend completion of your sale, check that the house you are buying is empty, and attend completion of your purchase, within the space of a day. This should normally be possible; but it might not be if one or other of the houses, or solicitors' offices, is a great distance away. Solicitors get round this problem by completing through the *post*, and getting their bank telegraphically to transfer the purchase monies to the vendor's solicitor's bank. There is no reason why you should not do the same, but it will need a bit of planning beforehand; and you will need the vendor's solicitor's written undertaking to send the same documents which he would have handed over on receipt of the funds if you had personally attended completion. Alternatively, you could ask your *building society's solicitor* to act as your 'agent' on completion of your purchase, so you do not have to attend yourself. If he agrees, give him clear written instructions to do on your behalf everything which you would have done yourself had you attended.

6. Although in this chapter I am not dealing with the purchase of new houses from a developer, it may happen that you are buying only *part* of the land (remember land means land and any building on it) comprised in the vendor's register. This will be the case if the vendor is retaining some of the garden land, or if he owns some adjoining property; and it calls for a slight variation in some of the procedures.

The land registry *forms* will be different. Instead of 'search of whole' (94A) and 'transfer of whole' (19), you will need 'search of part' (94B) and 'transfer of part' (20). Also instead of A4 (application to register purchase after completion), you will need A5. On completion the vendor's solicitor will not hand over the vendor's land certificate, but will himself send it to the Land Registry, which will take the land you have bought *out* of the vendor's register and issue a separate register/land certificate in your name. The vendor's solicitor will give you an undertaking to send the vendor's land certificate to the Land Registry and notify your building society's solicitor of the reference number (which will be inserted on the A5, so the Land Registry can tie up your application with the land certificate).

However, the main difference when you are buying part only of the vendor's land is that you need an accurate plan (preferably with measurements) showing (usually by red edging) *which* part. This plan should be attached to the contract, search of part, and transfer of part; and in the latter case the vendor should *execute* the plan. Moreover, whereas when you are buying the whole of the vendor's land there is no doubt that he owns all the land shown on the office copy of his land registry plan, when you are buying part only, you must check that the part you are buying (as shown on the transfer plan) falls *within* the vendor's land (as shown on his land registry plan). A particular reason for doing the land registry search (94B) is that it will confirm that no part of the land has been sold off to anyone else after the date on this land registry plan; and will protect you from any such sale *after* the date of your search.

Any mortgages on the charges register will, of course, have to be dealt with as previously explained (except that form 53 will have a plan attached, showing your plot edged red, which plan should also be executed by the mortgagee).

7. I have mentioned the possibility of a 'Caution', or a Notice in favour of the vendor's wife, appearing on the register (or search form), and what you should do about it if it does. Unfortunately these are not the only entries of this nature, but there are also such things as NOTICES and RESTRICTIONS which may appear either on the charges register or proprietorship register. Even more unfortunately, the Land Registry has a habit of registering completely routine items under these headings which are of no concern to the purchaser. You may therefore see a wodge of faintly ominous verbiage, or a cryptic one-line note, *anywhere* on the register. I have mentioned three of the more common ones (p. 177/199), but cannot deal with

all of the possibilities. How will you know, therefore, whether such an entry is the one in a thousand which should make you stop in your tracks, or whether it is one of the other 999 which you can safely ignore? The answer, happily, is simple. You ask the experts in the enquiry department of any Land Registry.

Each land registry office has a department which will answer any reasonable enquiries – whether from solicitors or members of the public – concerning registered property, its conveyancing procedure, and the significance of any entry on the register. You can either telephone or call personally – any branch, not just the one for your area (see appendix 1 for the addresses and telephone numbers). The staff of these enquiry departments are trained in land registry practice, although they are not solicitors. If they are asked a question to which they do not know the answer (which one assumes would be rare), they have access to qualified legal staff. You do not pay for having your questions answered. Yet the service should not be regarded as free: you pay for it in land registry fees levied when the Land Registry registers you as owner after completion. The service was set up in those far-off and forgotten times when the purpose of the Land Registry was to enable members of the public to buy and sell their houses without solicitors. As we have seen, solicitors, building societies, and even the Land Registry itself have (wittingly or unwittingly) combined to defeat this purpose. However, the enquiry service remains – although used almost exclusively by solicitors, while being paid for by the public. The public also pays for setting up the local Council offices . . .

If you should ever want information on your purchase or sale – if an entry should appear on the copy register, or your local search, which you are not sure about – go to the experts, the people who spend their lives answering questions such as yours will be: the land registry clerks and local Council clerks. You are already paying for these services in land registry fees and rates. Use them.

On the other hand, if a problem arises which is outside the scope of the Council clerks or the land registry enquiry department, see p. 226 for my advice.

Finally a reminder. In Chapter 5 I listed various things which a purchaser's solicitor, in following the conventional conveyancing procedures, leaves to chance. These items fall into two broad categories: first, those consequent on the fact that the purchaser's solicitor neither inspects the property nor calls at the Council offices; secondly, those items consequent on defects in the *system*. By doing your own conveyancing in the manner suggested, you will eliminate the first group but not, of course, the second.

Finally finally, if you come across any variation from my account of the procedure, or you think there is any point I have not sufficiently emphasized, or (perish the thought) there is anything I have got *wrong* – please let me know. This will help keep future editions up to date.

*

Summary of steps from exchange of contracts to completion (registered house)

1. Type transfer form, and send to vendor's solicitor (p. 196).

2. Submit documents to building society's solicitor (p. 197).

3. Receive mortgage form (and other documents) from building society's solicitor (p. 198).

4. Answer building society's solicitor's 'requisitions' (p. 198).

5. If required by building society's solicitor, submit form K16 (to confirm you are not bankrupt) (p. 199).

6. Submit Land Registry search form (94A) (p. 199).

7. Arrange completion (p. 202).

8. Attend completion (p. 203-205).

9. If purchasing without a mortgage: (a) stamp transfer, and (b) send documents to Land Registry for you to be registered as new owner (p. 205).

(II) Additional instructions when the house is unregistered

It is only *some* of the post-contract work which varies if the house you are buying is unregistered, rather than registered. Most of the procedures described in the first part of this chapter apply to both. Therefore if you are buying an unregistered house, apply the procedures in the first part of this chapter but with the modifications and additional instructions contained in this part.

The basic difference between the two systems is that if the house is registered, the vendor has a single land certificate bearing his name as owner, and the State guarantees that he *is* the owner; whereas if the house is unregistered, the vendor has a series of conveyances (title deeds) going back at least fifteen years. The vendor's solicitor will send you copies of these title deeds after exchange of contracts.*

Whereas in the case of a registered house there is no such thing as investigating the vendor's title, in the case of an unregistered house investigating the vendor's title – i.e. making sure the vendor really owns the house – is traditionally the most important and mysterious of the purchaser's solicitor's tasks. The way he does it is by looking through the copies of the vendor's title deeds – A to B, B to C, C to vendor – and sending the vendor's solicitor a list of questions, called 'requisitions on title', asking for further information or clarification on any points on which he is not satisfied. This is the part of the job which is 'very technical and skilled' (according to Cockshutt, *The Services of a Solicitor*); and which is 'extremely complex and demands a detailed knowledge of the law relating to the title to land' (according to Sanctuary, *Before you see a Solicitor*). What advice do I give my reader at this point, who has neither skill nor detailed knowledge? The advice I

---

*   It used to be the practice to send a typed summary called an 'abstract of title', but vendors' solicitors now find it easier to send photo-copies of the two or three relevant conveyances.

give is that investigating the vendor's title is an academic nonsense.

It is by examining the vendor's title deeds, and sending 'requisitions', that the purchaser's solicitor satisfies himself that the vendor owns an unregistered house. Now in the case of a tangible object, be it house or typewriter, there is no wholly satisfactory way of proving ownership. The best way is to have an official register of ownership. A less satisfactory way is for the manufacturer or retailer of an object to issue some sort of document testifying that a certain person purchased it – less satisfactory because such a document, being in the possession of the individual rather than being filed at a central registry, might not be authentic. Nevertheless, a manufacturer's or shopkeeper's invoice is *some* proof of ownership, perhaps secondary proof. In the case of registered houses we get primary proof of ownership, that is, the official register. But in the case of unregistered houses we do not even get secondary proof of ownership, because the land on which those houses are built is neither manufactured nor retailed. It is true that the vendor will have a series of title deeds going back at least fifteen years – but these are documents which are typed on ordinary paper with ephemeral names written at the bottom of them. The plan showing the land does not even have to be *signed*. They are therefore not as good evidence that someone owns a house as a stationer's invoice is that someone owns a typewriter.

No amount of investigation by the purchaser's solicitor of the vendor's title deeds will make any difference. If all someone has to do to prove ownership of a house is to type out a conveyance to himself and backdate it fifteen years, or else substitute one plan for another in a genuine conveyance, then it follows that title deeds are not worth a great deal.

But leaving aside any question of trickery, a previous conveyance to the vendor is no proof of the vendor's ownership. It is merely proof that sometime in the past the vendor paid a certain sum of money to someone who purported to convey the house to him. In fact, in the absence of an official register, *no-one* can prove ownership of a house. All anyone can do is prove that he paid some money for the house to some other person, who paid some money for the house to some *other* person, and so on. A series of conveyances amounts to no more than a series of receipts.

Now it is generally acknowledged by legal theorists that there is no such thing as proving ownership of an unregistered house;* but they argue that the longer the period over which a vendor can prove his or his predecessor's possession of a house, by producing previous title deeds, the less likely will anyone else be to come along and claim ownership of that house. This may be true in theory, but I doubt whether it makes any odds in practice. On 31st December 1969 no purchaser's solicitor would have accepted that a vendor had shown satisfactory evidence of his ownership of a house if all he could produce by way of title deeds was a fifteen year old conveyance to himself. Title deeds going back thirty years was the traditional requirement, and thirty years it must be, for the purchaser's protection. Then along comes the Law of Property Act 1969 which, in effect, lays down that instead of having to inspect the vendor's title deeds going back *thirty* years, the purchaser's solicitor need inspect deeds going back only *fifteen* years – and hey presto! on 1st January 1970 a fifteen year old conveyance to the vendor is suddenly perfectly acceptable evidence of the vendor's ownership. As far as I know, no purchaser has since suffered one jot from this dramatic measure. If the period covered by the title deeds, which the purchaser's solicitor has to inspect, can be safely cut from thirty years to fifteen years, then presumably it can be cut still further from fifteen years to ten years or five years.

These questions on the nature of proof of ownership, and how far back a purchaser's solicitor should investigate the vendor's title deeds, fascinating as they may be to legal theorists, are rapidly losing their importance as land registration progresses, and eventually they will be wholly academic. Meanwhile, if you are buying an unregistered house my advice to you, O reader, is to check the conveyance to the vendor, be it one year old or fifteen years old, but not to bother with the previous title deeds.

---

* 'It is clear from the foregoing analysis that English law knows no abstract "ownership" as opposed to the right to recover possession.' *The Law of Real Property* – Megarry & Wade.

Before the Law Society excommunicates me for making such a dangerous suggestion, it should remember that it has itself made a very similar one. In 1965, in response to pressure from the Lord Chancellor's office to cut the cost of conveyancing, the Law Society came forward with a proposal for an alternative conveyancing procedure, known as the 'Title Certificate scheme'. Under this scheme, a purchaser's solicitor would certify that he had examined a particular vendor's title deeds, and that they were in order. A *subsequent* purchaser's solicitor would be able to rely on that certificate, and therefore would not need to investigate any title deeds prior to its date. The Lord Chancellor turned down the scheme on the grounds that there was no room for a *third* system of conveyancing, and decided that the answer to the conveyancing 'problem' was to extend Land Registration as quickly as possible. The suggested scheme – probably the most sensible idea ever to come out of the Law Society – amounted to a proposition that there is no need to duplicate a professional man's work; that if the purchaser's solicitor sees a certificate that the vendor's solicitor examined the previous title deeds and found everything in order, then the purchaser's solicitor can safely rely on that certificate. It is true that under *my* suggested scheme you won't see a solicitor's certificate. Nevertheless, there will be an equivalent *notional* certificate, in as much as your vendor will have employed a solicitor when he bought, who presumably found all the title deeds in order; and for your added protection you will have an additional notional certificate from your vendor's *building society's* solicitor, who will *also* have investigated the title deeds when your vendor bought, and who presumably will *also* have found them in order. And if you are getting a mortgage, your lender will in any case employ a solicitor – at your expense – making a total of three highly qualified professional men, all of whom will have investigated (or will investigate) your vendor's title deeds, and all of whom will have found (or will find) them in order.

In short, either the traditional conveyancing procedure, whereby the solicitors acting for the purchaser and his building society investigate the title deeds, is valuable in that they thereby make certain that the vendor really owns the house – or else it is a nonsense. Either way you do not need to repeat it.

However, there will always be a theoretical risk if you are buying an unregistered house, because although a vendor may be able to prove he has had *possession* of a house, he can never prove that he *owns* it. How often this risk actually causes trouble, if indeed it ever does, I do not know, but presumably it is diminishing all the while as land registration continues apace.

Therefore, if you take my advice, you simply check the copy conveyance to the vendor, as you would check the copy register had the house been registered. If, after exchange of contracts, the vendor's solicitor sent you a typed summary of this conveyance, ask for a photo-copy. The operative part of this conveyance will read as follows (your vendor being, of course, the *purchaser* in the conveyance):

> The vendor as beneficial owner hereby conveys to the purchaser ALL THAT piece or parcel of land together with the dwellinghouse erected thereon known as 12 Mustard Street in the parish of Thung in the town of Thing in the County of York as the same is more particularly shown edged red on the plan [attached hereto] [attached to a conveyance dated . . . between . . . and . . .] TO HOLD the same unto the purchaser in fee simple subject to the restrictive covenants set out in [the schedule hereto] [the conveyance dated . . . between . . . and . . .]

You check that the purchaser(s) in this conveyance are the vendor(s) in your contract; that the address of the house you are buying is correctly stated; that the plan referred to, either attached to this or a previous conveyance, is the same plan as the vendor's solicitor sent you at the outset, and which is attached to the contract. The words 'fee simple' are important because they denote that the house is freehold as opposed to leasehold. In the rare case of the road which leads to the house, or garage, being a private road (i.e. a road which is not maintained by the Council and which is not a public right of way), the words 'together with a right of way for vehicles over the road coloured — on the said plan' should appear after the description of the house – which is a point you will have checked before contracts were exchanged. The restrictive covenants referred to will be those of which you were sent a copy before exchange of contracts. Any stamp duty paid on the conveyance will be shown by a stamp impressed on the top left-hand corner. As the rates have been altered several times over the past twenty years, ask your building society's solicitor, or else the Stamp Duty office, to confirm that the correct duty was paid – or else that none was payable. Finally, check that the vendor (that is, your vendor's vendor) has *executed* the conveyance at the bottom, and if there was more than one vendor, that they *all* executed it.*

After you have checked the conveyance to your vendor, type out the conveyance to yourself on ordinary paper, with two carbon copies. (This is the equivalent of the 'transfer' in the case of registered property.) You can either use the conveyance to your vendor, or the following conveyance, as your model. Make sure that the names of the vendor or vendors which you insert in this conveyance correspond exactly with the names of the purchaser, or purchasers, in the previous conveyance which you have just checked; and that *all* the purchasers in the previous conveyance are inserted as vendors in your conveyance.

THIS CONVEYANCE is made the   day of   19
BETWEEN EDWARD MUGGINS and EDWINA MUGGINS of 12 Mustard Street, Thing, Yorkshire (hereinafter called 'the vendors') and GENTLE READER and MRS. ASTUTE READER of 15 Muggleton Close, Thong, Wiltshire (hereinafter called 'the purchasers')
    WHEREAS the vendors are the owners in fee simple of the property hereinafter conveyed and have agreed to sell the same to the purchasers for   pounds (£   )
    NOW THIS DEED WITNESSETH that in consideration of   pounds (£   ) paid by the purchasers to the vendors (the receipt whereof the vendors acknowledge) the vendors as beneficial owners hereby convey to the purchasers ALL

---

*   See footnote on p. 204 for a definition of 'execute'.

THAT land and dwellinghouse known as 12 Mustard Street, Thung, Thing, Yorkshire as the same is shown edged [red] on the plan attached to a conveyance dated . . . between . . . and . . . TO HOLD the same unto the purchasers in fee simple [as joint tenants in law and equity] [as tenants in common (in equal shares)] subject to the restrictive covenants set out in or referred to by the conveyance dated . . . to the vendors.

It is hereby certified that this transaction does not form part of a larger transaction or series of transactions in respect of which the amount or value or aggregate amount or value of the consideration exceeds £30,000.

IN WITNESS whereof the vendors have set their hands and seals on the date above written

SIGNED SEALED & DELIVERED
BY EDWARD MUGGINS and
EDWINA MUGGINS in the presence of:

Apart from minor optional variations, the wording of this conveyance is used on the sale of every secondhand freehold house, and the content is basically the same as a transfer of a registered house. As regards the square brackets, these are technical expressions which have nothing to do with 'tenants'. The first of the square brackets means that on the death of either purchaser, the whole house automatically goes to the survivor; the second means that the deceased's share is distributed in accordance with his or her will (see p. 199). If buying jointly, insert whichever square bracket is appropriate; in the case of a sole purchaser omit both.

It is not necessary to attach a plan or copy out the restrictive covenants, as both are incorporated by reference to the relevant previous conveyance. However, if a right of way goes with the house, then this should be added to the description of the house in your conveyance, viz: '12 Mustard Street etc. as the same is shown edged red on the plan etc. *together with a right of way for vehicles over the road coloured brown on the said plan.*' The final clause is inserted only if the price of the house (excluding any sum apportioned to furnishings and other separate items, see p. 172(c)) is £30,000 or less, in which case no stamp duty is payable. Otherwise this clause is omitted (and you will have to pay stamp duty, the current rate being 1% of the total purchase price).

So you have checked the conveyance to your vendor, and instead of a transfer, you have typed out a conveyance. The remaining procedures are pretty well the same as described in the first part of this chapter for the purchase of a registered house, and you should therefore carry out the instructions as from the heading 'Building Society' on p. 197, but with the following modifications:

Building Society

You send your building society's solicitor the documents listed, except that instead of a copy register you send the copy deeds you will have received from the vendor's solicitor; and instead of copy transfer you send a copy of the conveyance you have typed.

The building society's solicitor will send you the three documents mentioned: mortgage, statement of fees, and 'requisitions'. But whereas in the case of a registered house any requisitions would be purely a formality, which you would consequently be able to answer yourself, in the case of an unregistered house some of them may be 'technical' questions on the vendor's title deeds. Any such questions you pass straight on to the vendor's solicitor. Strictly, any questions on the vendor's title deeds have to be raised within eleven days from when you received the copy deeds, so the sooner you get all the documents to the building society's solicitor after exchange of contracts, the better.

When you send the building society's solicitor's requisitions (or so many of them as relate to the title deeds) to the vendor's solicitor, you also send him the conveyance you typed out, plus a copy.

The vendor's solicitor will in due course return the requisitions with his answers, which you pass on to your building society's solicitor.

Some of the documents listed on p. 198, which the building society's solicitor will require on completion, will be different if the house is unregistered: for (1) land certificate and (2) transfer, substitute (1) previous title deeds and (2) conveyance; for (5) and (6), substitute Land Charges search form (described in the next section); (3), (4) and (7) will be the same.

There is an extra little terradiddle to do with the conveyance. You sent your conveyance to the vendor's solicitor. In due course he will return a copy to you, either without alteration or with some alterations which he will make in red. As a conveyance for a secondhand house is almost as straightforward as a transfer, I cannot think of any significant alterations which the vendor's solicitor is likely to make. However, if your vendor entered into any covenants in *his* conveyance, the solicitor might add a clause making you indemnify your vendor against any future breach of such covenants – which addition is an academic nicety. If your vendor's solicitor has made any other alteration or addition, other than obviously formal ones, telephone him – or your building society's solicitor – and ask him to explain its significance.

After any alteration or addition to your conveyance has been settled, you type out a fair copy on stiff 'engrossing' paper;* and you send this fair copy *back* to the vendor's solicitor for him to get executed by the vendor in readiness for completion. However, if he has made the addition mentioned, then you (and spouse if co-purchaser) have to execute the conveyance before you send it to the vendor's solicitor.

Land Charges Search

Whereas if the house was registered you would have sent a search form to the Land Registry a week or so before completion, when the house is unregistered you send a different search form (K15) to the *Land Charges Registry* in Plymouth. Although there is no central register of unregistered houses, there is nevertheless a register of miscellaneous interests which various third parties can have in an unregistered house, and which are registered against the *name* of the owner of the house. For example, the vendor's wife, if not a joint owner, might have an interest in the house as the matrimonial home, or XY Finance Ltd. might have an interest in it as security for a second mortgage. If the vendor's wife or XY Finance fail to register their interests, then a purchaser takes the house free of them. If they do register their interests, then a purchaser takes the house *subject* to them. You must therefore

---

* This is obtained at a Law Stationers. Alternatively, it is included in the 'forms pack' (see inside front cover).

make sure that no-one has registered such an interest, which you do by sending form K15 to the Land Charges Registry (whose address is printed on the form), having filled in the names of your vendor or vendors, and the vendor(s) who sold to them – which you get from the copy conveyance you checked. You send 50p. (in postal orders) for each name to be searched against. In a few days the result will be sent on a *separate form* – usually 'No subsisting entries', which means that no-one has registered any interests against the names listed. Alternatively, if your vendor(s) bought the house from a developer, they will have entered into the usual splurge of restrictive covenants, which will be shown as: 'Edward Muggins, D (ii) 14th October 1984. Edwina Muggins, D (ii) 14th October 1984.' D (ii) is the code for restrictive covenants, and the date is when the entry was registered, which is usually a few days after the date of the conveyance imposing them. In the rare case of any entry *other* than 'D (ii)' appearing on the form, see p. 224/5 for what to do.

Before sending this form to the Land Charges Registry, check with your building society's solicitor that he does not want you to add any other name. As each purchaser's solicitor will have made a similar search against the current vendor, there should be a series of 'results' against all the previous owners, but some might have got lost. In any case your building society's solicitor will require you to add *your own name* (and spouse's if co-purchaser) to confirm you are not bankrupt.

Completion

Having arranged your finances, made the completion appointment, instructed your removal firm, and checked that the house is empty – as described in the first part of this chapter (p. 201-203) – you attend completion, where you will meet your building society's solicitor.

In his 'requisitions' to you, your building society's solicitor will have told you that he requires certain documents on completion: (1) vendor's title deeds, (2) conveyance executed by vendor, (3) vendor's building society solicitor's undertaking to discharge vendor's mortgage, (4) mortgage executed by you, (5) land charges search form described above, (6) Inland Revenue LA form, which is presented to the Stamp Duty office, with the conveyance, after completion. Your vendor's solicitor will supply (1), (2) and (3); you will supply the rest. You also bring bank draft(s) for the balance of the purchase price.

The vendor's solicitor will produce the original title deeds – the latest being the conveyance to the vendor, which you check is the original document of which you were sent a copy.

There is something else you should check on this convey-ance: that no note appears on it, either in the inside or on the cover, stating that part of the land has been sold off. If the vendor had sold part of his garden he would still keep the title deeds, but a note of the sale would (or should) have been written on the latest conveyance.

As for the rest of the deeds, although I have said that I do not think they are of much value you should nevertheless make sure that they are all present, as they will be required when you come to sell; or alternatively, they will have to be sent to the Land Registry for the house to be registered if it is now in a registration district.

The deeds should comprise a series of original conveyances – in the same form as the conveyance to your vendors, and executed – going back at least fifteen years: A to B, B to C, C to D, D to Mr. and Mrs. Muggins. This is provided that during this period the plot of land had not been split off from a *larger* plot owned by, e.g., a developer. If it had been, when the developer sold off the plot you are now buying he would have kept all the previous title deeds, because they would include *other* land. In that case you would get original conveyances only from the date when the area of land which you are now buying was first separately sold, and *copies* (typed or photo) of any previous ones. Any such copies should bear a note that they were 'examined with the original' (see p. 60).*

---

* This is another reason why the unregistered conveyancing system, plausible in theory, often breaks down in practice. It is by possessing a series of original title deeds going back over at least fifteen years that your vendor proves that he owns the house. Yet whether he has got them, or whether he has just one original conveyance a few years old, is a matter of chance depending on the date when the land happened to be split up.

The vendor's solicitor will produce the conveyance to you, which you check is the same document as you yourself typed; and that the vendor or – if more than one – *all* the vendors have executed it at the bottom.

This conveyance, together with the previous title deeds, you pass to your building society's solicitor. You would, of course, keep them if you were not getting a mortgage.

Whereas in the case of a registered house all current mortgages are set out on the charges register, in the case of an unregistered house there is no such register. With the deeds there will be some previous mortgages with the mortgagee's receipt endorsed thereon; and the vendor's solicitor will have sent a note with brief particulars of the vendor's mortgage (or even a complete copy of the mortgage itself) when he sent you the copy deeds after exchange of contracts. But it is primarily by getting the original title deeds – albeit they may comprise only one conveyance to the vendor – that you have to assume that any *first* mortgage has been discharged. By getting a clear land charges search (against the vendor and his immediate predecessor) you know that there is no *second* mortgage. Assuming the vendor has only one mortgage, and that this is to a building society, the vendor's building society's solicitor will give a written undertaking to discharge it. This should read: 'As solicitor for XY Building Society, I undertake to discharge the mortgage dated — on the above property, and to send you the mortgage with the receipt endorsed thereon executed by the building society, within fourteen days.' This undertaking should be addressed to *you* (and a similar undertaking given to your building society's solicitor).

If the vendor's mortgage is *not* to a building society, you should not accept an undertaking, but insist that the receipted mortgage is handed over *on completion*. The receipt is endorsed on the actual mortgage, and should read: '[XY Insurance Co. Ltd.] hereby acknowledges receipt of all money intended to be secured by the within-written mortgage, payment having been made by Mr. & Mrs. Muggins' – executed by the mortgagee.

The remaining procedures – handing over the bank drafts, releasing the deposit if held by estate agents, getting the keys (and the NHBC warranty if applicable) – are the same as for a registered house. Also the procedure for stamping the conveyance with any stamp duty, and with the Inland Revenue stamp, is the same as for stamping a transfer.

If the house is now in a registration district (see appendix 1) it will have to be registered at the Land Registry, with your name as the owner. To this end your building society's solicitor will send all the accumulated deeds and documents to the Land Registry after completion, together with form 1B. If you are purchasing without a mortgage you will have to do this yourself, in which case the form is 1A.

*

So there we are. The purchase of your unregistered house has been completed, and everything has gone smoothly. There may, however, be some variation from the above account, in which case it will most likely be one of the following:

1. Your land charges search, instead of revealing 'No subsisting entries', or D (ii) (restrictive covenants), reveals some *other* entry. This is not likely to happen but if it does, such entry will most probably be either 'C (i)' or 'F'.

'C (i)' is the code for a second or subsequent mortgage. If it appears on your search form, you must receive on completion the actual mortgage deed endorsed with the receipt, executed by the mortgagee, as previously explained. If there is more than one C(i), you must receive the receipted mortgage in respect of *each*.

An 'F' entry means that the vendor's wife, not being a joint owner, has registered her interest in the house as the matrimonial home. If this appears on your search form, do not complete your purchase without a form signed by the wife applying to cancel the entry, which you send to the Land Charges Registry after completion. If the vendor's wife is not a joint owner (and therefore does not have to join in the contract), it would be prudent to make a land charges search at the outset (as well as just before completion), so that this possible impediment to the sale would come to light *before* you exchange contracts.

If the name of your vendor happens to be John Smith or

Frank Williams, you may well find that your land charges search reveals numerous entries denoting that John Smith or Frank Williams is bankrupt, and his property therefore vests in his trustee in bankruptcy. The code for this is PA (B) or WO (B).* In such a case, it is the custom for the vendor's solicitor to certify on the form that the John Smith who has the entry against him is not the same as the John Smith who is selling you the house. Exactly what legal rights a purchaser would have against the vendor's solicitor if he subsequently discovered that it *was* the same John Smith is not clear. Because there is no central register of unregistered property, anyone having an interest in such property which is capable of binding subsequent purchasers – e.g. a second mortgagee, a wife, a trustee in bankruptcy – can register these interests only against the *name* of a person. As a name can be common to several thousand different people, this is just another area where the unregistered conveyancing system, plausible in theory, breaks down in practice.

2. Your vendor is the executor or administrator of the previous owner. In that case, the link between the previous deceased owner and your vendor, instead of being a conveyance, will be the 'probate' or 'letters of administration' (see appendix 5); and you will get a sealed copy of this document on completion.

In the conveyance (p. 217), *instead* of the paragraph beginning 'Whereas the vendors are the owners . . . ' insert: 'Whereas Dick Deadman, who owned the freehold of the property hereinafter conveyed at the date of his death, died on — and probate/letters of administration of his estate was/were on — granted to the vendor(s) who have agreed to sell the said property to the purchaser for the sum of £— NOW THIS DEED WITNESSETH etc.'

3(a) Although at the moment I am not dealing with the purchase of a new house from a developer, it may be (exceptionally) that you are buying only *part* of the land (property) comprised in the conveyance to the vendor. In that case follow the additional instructions in paragraphs (1)-(4) on p. 269/270 (substituting 'vendor' for 'builder').

---

* Pending Action (Bankruptcy); Writ or Order (Bankruptcy).

3(b) Similarly, in the unusual event that you are buying a secondhand house from a *limited company*, an additional search in the Companies Registry is necessary, which is explained on p. 270.

Points 4. and 5. on p. 207/208 are equally applicable to unregistered property.

The above variations from the norm are the most likely ones to occur. However, once in a while a problem arises which I have not covered, and which *does* require legal advice. It could arise in connection with unregistered property, in which case there will be no 'free' advisory service as there is with registered property. Or the problem might be outside the scope of the advisory service, even if the house was registered. Solicitors, when defending themselves and the system, often make out that difficulties are likely to occur in the most routine conveyancing transaction. For instance, in his booklet *The Compleat Conveyancer* Ian Wright lists some 'typical' problems – 'Mrs. Brown is not really capable of looking after her affairs. Her nephew Tom says he has her authority to sell her house for her. Can he do this?' This of course is not a typical problem. Nevertheless, it is possible that you may come across a problem or a situation which I have not covered.

So what do you do in such a case? It seems that you have four choices: (a) With your new-found quest for knowledge you go to your local reference library (or university Law Library, if accessible) – and in a book on conveyancing (e.g. Emmet on Title) you look in the index and hope to find the answer. (b) You consult with the solicitor acting for your building society – whose interest in your getting a good title to your new house coincides with your own – and you are guided by his advice. (c) You avail yourself of the 'Consultation Pack' (see inside front cover); or otherwise try to find a solicitor who will advise you on the specific point which has arisen. (d) You throw your hand in, and ask a solicitor to take the whole matter over.

To take the last course would, I think, be a pity – especially as the first thing your new-found solicitor will probably do is to thumb his way through the index of Emmet; and in any case the point which has thrown you may be quite simple to resolve. Nevertheless you need not feel embarrassed to do so, any more than you would feel embarrassed had you begun a routine repair to your car, but discovered that as a nut had rusted in, you had after all to give the job to a garage having the necessary equipment to deal with the problem. Neither need you worry about finding a solicitor who, at £200 an hour, will take on the job.

*

Summary of steps from exchange of contracts to completion (unregistered house)

1. Receive copies of vendor's title deeds, and check conveyance to vendor (p. 216).

2. Type conveyance to yourself with two copies (p. 217/218).

3. Send documents to your building society's solicitor (p. 219).

4. Receive mortgage form, and 'requisitions', from your building society's solicitor (p. 219).

5. Send such 'requisitions' which you cannot answer yourself, plus the conveyance to yourself with copy, to vendor's solicitor.

6. When vendor's solicitor returns conveyance, type out fair copy, and send it back to vendor's solicitor for him to get *executed* in readiness for completion. Relay vendor's solicitor's answers to 'requisitions' back to building society's solicitor.

7. Send search form to Land Charges Registry (p. 220).

8. Arrange completion.

9. Attend completion (p. 221-223).

10. If purchasing without a mortgage: (a) stamp conveyance, and (b) *if the house is in a registration district* send documents to Land Registry to register the house and your ownership thereof (p. 224).

14

In conclusion: a look at some other branches of the law

Commercial Conveyancing

The abuses I have described in the preceding pages are not confined to domestic conveyancing. Commercial conveyancing, where the sums involved often run into millions, is sometimes extremely complicated; and sometimes it is extremely simple. I have personally attended to the conveyancing involved in selling a registered property in the City of London for the equivalent of several million pounds in today's money. The work was exactly the same as for the sale of a registered house – that is, an hour's not very arduous activity. The legal fee was the equivalent of £10,000. I have done the conveyancing where a client granted a mortgage of a million pounds. The work involved was *less* than that for an ordinary purchase of a house. The fee was £8,500. If Centre Point changes hands, and provided it was empty at the time, the conveyancing would be exactly the same as when 'The Laurels' changes hands. The solicitor's fee would probably be a hundred thousand pounds. These are the plums which usually fall, ripe and luscious, into the laps of the big City firms.

When it comes to the more routine commercial conveyancing, solicitors still work their alchemy, although to a less dramatic extent. For instance, shop leases invariably contain a covenant by the tenant not to do any alterations without the landlord's consent. If the tenant wants to make alterations – e.g. install a new shop front – and the landlord agrees, the document embodying such consent is drawn up by the landlord's solicitor. Consequently it runs into several pages, with provisions obliging the tenant to obtain all planning permissions and building regulations approvals, to comply with all local authority regulations and notices of any and every description etc. etc., although none of these things may be relevant. The time it takes for such a document to be typed by the landlord's solicitor, agreed by the tenant's solicitor, fair copied in two parts, executed, might be two or three months; and at the end of it the tenant has to pay both his solicitor's *and* the landlord's solicitor's costs. Yet in most cases a simple letter of consent is all that is necessary, especially as the landlord's property will probably be improved by the alterations.

Sometimes several different parties have to join in a licence, where there is a headlease and one or more underleases – that is when A grants a lease to B and B grants a further lease (or underlease as it's called) to C. If C wants to make alterations or sell his lease or whatever, he will probably need not only B's consent but A's consent as well. The more parties involved, the more complicated will the licence be, and the longer will it take to get settled – especially in the case of an office building where there may be a veritable pyramid of underleases. This is the sort of solicitors' work which is generally given to the office dude (and most solicitors' offices boast at least one), because it does not really matter to the various landlords whether a licence is ever granted or not. I have come across several files where a desultory correspondence has been going on for over a year between three or four different firms of solicitors, with no-one knowing who is supposed to be giving a licence for what, or why. And if the licence is ever completed, the wretched undertenant finds he has to pay the bills of all the solicitors involved.

So much for conveyancing. But let me add a few notes on some other branches of the law.

Company Law

In 1976, Companies House moved from its premises in London to Cardiff. The company files were put on microfilm so that inspection can still take place in London, although less conveniently and at much greater cost. The London premises were no longer sufficient to house the ever increasing mounds of paper spawned by the 700,000 limited companies registered in England and Wales. Yet most of that paper is as unnecessary as the conveyancing forms we have examined, and could as profitably be scrapped. For example, each company has to have a 'memorandum' which sets out the objects of that particular company; and by virtue of a certain rule (the 'ultra vires' rule), a company cannot engage in any activity *outside* those specified objects. Company lawyers therefore have a nice profitable time drawing up the company's memorandum, making sure they list every activity that company could conceivably and inconceivably ever want to carry on. You never know when a property company will want to start selling leather goods; you can never be sure that a purveyor of soft drinks will not at some future date want to set up as a finance house. Therefore every activity, likely and unlikely, must be set out in every company's memorandum, which document consequently drools on for nine or ten pages. If the ultra vires rule was abolished, and with it the necessity for this document, that little reform alone would save seven million pages having to be drafted, printed, examined, filed, carted about, microfilmed, inspected, and stored.

By cutting out the unnecessary documents, and arranging the information in the remaining documents in a more economical manner, the paper work involved in company law could be reduced by two thirds. Ironically, those solicitors who bemoaned the inconvenience of moving Companies House to Cardiff were those very gentlemen whose financial interest in proliferating company documents made the move necessary.

Divorce

The two areas of the law which are most likely to affect the average person are conveyancing and divorce. Before the Divorce Reform Act 1969, someone wanting a divorce had to prove that the other party to the marriage (respondent) had been guilty of a matrimonial offence. In a majority of cases this was no more than a hypocritical farce – enquiry agent gives evidence of how one fine morning, out of all the hotel bedrooms in England and Wales, he happened to go into one containing the respondent and another and how he observed an unmade bed with items of sleeping apparel thereon etc. Judge asks a few laconic questions. Divorce granted. Hearing lasts approximately ten minutes. However, the fact that a matrimonial offence was a prerequisite to a divorce enabled lawyers to claim that they were needed to prove that offence. But now the Divorce Reform Act 1969 has swept away the various matrimonial offences, and in their place it has given us a wonderful new ground for divorce: irretrievable breakdown of the marriage – which is deemed to have occurred if the parties have lived apart for two years (if the respondent consents to a divorce), or five years (if the respondent does not consent). Therefore, as a matrimonial offence no longer has to be proved, there is no need for divorce work to remain in the hands of the lawyers.

Nevertheless, because divorce has a legal penumbra, lawyers are just as heavily involved in it as they were before 1969. And as in other areas in which they operate, they often *prevent*, rather than assist, the parties achieving what they want to achieve – that is, an acceptable and (as far as the circumstances permit) amicable settlement. Time and again one hears of a couple splitting up, having agreed between themselves the terms of a reasonable division of the property, and access to and custody of the children. They then consult separate lawyers to make it all 'legal' – and gradually find themselves sucked into a quagmire of anger and bitterness against each other, prompted by their ex-partner's lawyer's unrealistic demands. With their adversarial outlook and their impatience with anything that smacks of common sense, lawyers are probably the very worst people for the job.

Litigation

But despite strong competition, the prize for that branch of the law which is the least efficient, the most out of touch with the needs of the community, the most riddled with restrictive practices, and which causes the most misery, must be awarded to litigation. Litigation is the process whereby someone goes to Court in order to get compensation ('damages') from another party; and when someone goes to Court to get compensation, it will generally be in respect of an accident – on the roads, at work, in hospital or wherever.

Someone who is injured in an accident is not automatically entitled to compensation, however horrendous his injuries – he first has to prove in Court that his injuries were caused by someone else's negligence (fault). So he consults a solicitor. And then his troubles begin.

First of all, the learned solicitor apparently isn't competent to advise him, but has to go to *another* lawyer, a barrister (or Counsel, to give him his professional name). Counsel are the gentlemen who wear wigs and gowns and argue the case if it ever gets to Court; and they also draw up the Court documents. However, their main function is advising the solicitor all along the line as the action proceeds. The client cannot consult Counsel *direct*, but only through a solicitor. Yet the solicitor will act only as he is advised by Counsel. It's a beautiful system from the lawyers' point of view. By taking Counsel's opinion at every turn, and doing only as he advises, the solicitor unloads all the responsibility and risk, yet gets paid just as much; while Counsel remains insulated from any direct contact with the client, and cannot be criticised (or sued for his performance in Court, however incompetent).

As a solicitor is not *allowed* to present a case in the High Court (i.e. a case involving more than £5,000), he can never be more than Counsel's assistant – in fact his role is Counsel's *enquiry agent*. Due to the subservient nature of this role, litigation (like house conveyancing) tends not to attract the keenest intellects in the profession. Neither will the solicitor who does this work usually be a specialist, but will more likely be a jack of all trades – deriving most of his income from conveyancing, probate and divorce, but taking on litigation matters as and when occasion demands. Consequently the litigation solicitor (or clerk to whom he delegates the matter), unless he makes a brave effort to withstand the various pressures on him to do so, will find that he is acting merely as a go-between between his client and Counsel, and as a post office between Counsel and the other side's solicitor. In fact often the plaintiff's solicitor sees his job merely as a go-between between his client and the defendant's insurance company* or its solicitor – with whom he will correspond in the hope that the insurance company will make a reasonable offer to settle out of Court, without the need for any further legal action.

Unfortunately, insurance companies are not charities but are in the business to make money. And the money they make is the amount by which the premiums they collect exceed the claims they pay out. Moreover, their legal advisers will be adept at stringing along their more innocent adversaries. Adjusting his tactics to the particular degree of ineptitude of the plaintiff's solicitor, or solicitor's clerk, the insurance company's solicitor will know when simply to ignore his letters; when to dangle the offer of a meeting in front of him (which somehow always gets postponed); when to indicate he is waiting for a doctor's report or whatever 'on receipt of which we will be in touch with you' (which somehow always gets delayed). This is borne out by the fact that the average time it takes for the plaintiff's solicitor actually to get round to taking the first step in a legal action, which is issuing the writ, is *17 months from the date of the accident* (as found by the Royal Commission on Legal Services, para. 10.15).

Not surprisingly, most claims never get beyond the correspondence stage. Either they are abandoned; or else the plaintiff accepts whatever derisory sum the defendant's insurance company may offer. In the latter case the plaintiff is generally subjected to considerable pressure from his solicitor to accept the offer. This is because when a case is settled, the defendant's insurance company always pays the *plaintiff's solicitor's costs*; and having been let off the hook with regard to the plaintiff's claim, the insurance company is unlikely to quibble over his solicitor's bill of a few hundred pounds or more. So on being settled 'out of Court' a potentially bothersome and unprofitable case is magically transformed into a straightforward and extremely profitable one.

---

* The injured person claiming compensation is called the *plaintiff*; and the person from whom he is claiming compensation – who he is alleging caused his injuries – is called the *defendant*. This person, however, is only the nominal defendant, the real defendant being his *insurance company* – which takes over the case on the defendant's behalf, and which has to pay any compensation awarded if the case goes to Court.

What happens to those accident victims who are not minded to give up so easily? Suppose one sunny morning someone is run down by a motor car and suffers severe injuries. Remember he is entitled to compensation only if he can prove in Court that his accident was the other driver's fault. So he will go to a solicitor, who will take *Counsel's opinion* on whether – in the light of any witnesses' statements and other available evidence – he, the plaintiff, has a reasonable chance of winning his case. If Counsel's opinion is favourable the solicitor will send Counsel 'Instructions to draft Writ and Statement of Claim' – which is the document which initiates a legal action and which sets out, in legal language, the facts whereby the plaintiff is alleging his injuries were caused by the defendant's fault. When drafted, the plaintiff's solicitor will send it to the defendant's solicitor (i.e. the defendant's *insurance company's* solicitor) who will send it to *his* Counsel, with instructions to draft 'Defence' – a document which, in legal language, *denies* that the plaintiff's injuries were caused by the defendant's fault. Over the ensuing months and years, there will gradually grow a mound of further Court documents – request for 'further and better particulars' of Statement of Claim, request for 'further and better particulars' of Defence etc., each of which will be drafted by the respective parties' Counsel on written instructions from their respective 'instructing solicitors'; and each of which will be couched in tortuous and scarcely intelligible language, in much the same way as the local search and preliminary enquiry forms we have examined.

Somewhere along the line there will be one or more Master's summonses. These are mini trials at which the parties' lawyers argue disputed procedural points – e.g. whether the plaintiff should be allowed to amend his Statement of Claim, whether the defendant should be ordered to supply fuller 'further and better particulars' of his Defence. Then when all the 'pleadings' have been settled there is 'discovery of documents', where the parties' solicitors exchange lists of documents in their clients' possession, stating which they are prepared to disclose, which they claim are privileged. Then the parties' solicitors instruct their respective Counsel to 'Advise on Evidence'. Then there is a 'Summons for

Directions', at which the Master gives directions on any procedural points still outstanding, and decides on the number of expert witnesses which each party shall be allowed to call at the trial. Finally, when there are no further documents to be exchanged, and no further procedural points outstanding, the case is 'set down for hearing' – that is, put in the queue of cases awaiting trial. Then a date will be given by the 'Clerk of the lists'.

That little lot takes on average four years from the date of the accident; and in over a third of all cases the period from accident to trial is *between four and eight years* (ibid. para 22.25). This bizarre time scale is not so much because the procedures themselves are particularly complicated but because

(a) The plaintiff's solicitor will not act except as advised by Counsel, to whom he will send 'Instructions to Advise' at every turn, with weeks and months between each communication.

(b) Litigation which does not settle is the least profitable of solicitors' work (because payment is so long delayed), so the litigation files tend to remain at the bottom of the solicitor's pile. Alternatively he delegates them to some incompetent clerk – who then leaves the firm, passing them on to his equally incompetent successor (the turnover of solicitors' clerks is brisk). It is quite common for these files to lie around the office like great stranded whales, with no effective steps being taken on them from one year to another.

(c) The defendant's solicitor (unlike his opponent) will be expert at his job, and will know how to exploit the various procedures to the full, in the happy knowledge that each half year's delay he can achieve increases the plaintiff's psychological strain and so makes him more likely to settle out of Court; and also makes his case more difficult to prove if it ever does get to Court. For instance, *the average time it takes the defendant's solicitor to supply 'further and better particulars' of Defence is six months* (ibid. para 10.15).

Thus it is not so much a legal battle as a war of attrition; and 97% of plaintiffs who initiate legal actions do not stay the course, but either accept whatever offer the defendant's insurance company may make, or else abandon their claim. Some of those claims will be properly settled out of Court or abandoned – because the plaintiff's injuries are trivial, or there is insufficient evidence to prove the defendant's negligence in Court. But equally, a large proportion of them will be in respect of serious injuries caused by the defendant's palpable negligence. Yet the vast majority of these plaintiffs give up, because they are unable to continue the war of attrition which, in the aftermath of a serious accident or a tragedy, they are psychologically in the worst position to wage – or else because they just can't get their solicitors to bring their case to Court.

The tiny minority who have the stamina to fight on – which more often than not necessitates changing solicitors several times – will have their day (or three or four days) in Court. The plaintiff's solicitor will send Instructions to Counsel to argue the case in Court. And when the day of the trial finally arrives (usually about nine months after the case is 'set down for hearing'), the parties and their solicitors and their Counsel and their witnesses and their expert witnesses will arrive at the Court; and the plaintiff's Counsel will try to show that the accident which happened four years previously was the defendant's fault, and the defendant's Counsel will try to show that it wasn't.

If the plaintiff's claim is in respect of a serious injury, he will probably be advised to have a Queen's Counsel (one of an elite body of successful Counsel who usually conduct substantial cases) – in which case it will be Queen's Counsel who presents the case in Court. Behind him will sit ordinary Counsel, who will have advised throughout and drafted the procedural documents. Behind him will sit the solicitor, who will have fed the facts to Counsel. Behind him will sit the plaintiff, who will have fed the facts to the solicitor. At the other end of the same benches will sit the equivalent legal team representing the defendant. In due course the witnesses, in answer to questions from Counsel, will relate what they remember seeing of the accident. And depending on how they, and the parties themselves, give their evidence and stand up to cross-examination by the opposing Counsel, and any other evidence produced by the parties' Counsel, the judge will decide either that the plaintiff's Counsel *has* shown that the plaintiff's injuries were caused by the defendant's fault (in which case he will order the defendant to pay the plaintiff an appropriate sum in compensation); or that he *hasn't* (in which case the plaintiff gets nothing).

If all goes well for the plaintiff – if he has a good Counsel, a good solicitor, good witnesses who are still available, a good judge, and assuming he also has a good case – he will win his case.

On the other hand if he has an incompetent solicitor who, for example, failed to get some crucial bit of evidence or failed to relay some crucial fact; or an incompetent Counsel; or a Counsel who was substituted at the last minute; or if the key witnesses were no longer available; or else became hopelessly confused when cross-examined by the defendant's Counsel as to what they remembered seeing of the accident (possibly in a split second) four years previously – then the plaintiff will probably lose his case. Moreover, even if the facts are not disputed, there can be no precise criteria for determining such a broad question as: whose fault was the accident? Judge X might think it was the driver's fault; he should have been prepared for someone crossing the road in a crowded shopping area. Judge Y, on the other hand, might think it was the plaintiff's fault for not crossing at the traffic lights. Whether the plaintiff wins or loses his case will therefore depend on whether it happens to be Judge X or Judge Y who is assigned to his case (or even whether it is Judge X who is the trial judge and Judge Y who sits in the Court of Appeal, or vice versa).

Now if the plaintiff loses his case, not only does he get no compensation for his injuries. Unless he gets 'legal aid' he will also have to pay all the legal costs of the case – that is, not only his own costs but those of the defendant; and not only the costs of the trial but all the pre-trial costs as well.

As to how much these costs are likely to be, it is impossible to be precise. Everyone knows that High Court cases are expensive. No-one knows exactly *how* expensive. Surprisingly, there have been no surveys on the subject.

An ordinary Counsel might charge £600 a day for the Court hearing. His instructing solicitor might charge half that sum. And for good measure, Counsel's clerk (his manager) gets a further 10% of Counsel's fees. So for a four day trial – usual for a case where liability and amount are disputed, bearing in mind that a Court day is only *five* hours – the plaintiff's costs would be in the region of £4,000. (If the plaintiff employed a Queen's Counsel, add on another £3,000.) This sum is just for the trial itself. The solicitor's and Counsel's costs for the *pre*-trial work, spanning the previous four years, might be double that figure. So for an average High Court case, the plaintiff's legal costs would be in the region of £10,000 – £15,000, multiplied by two to include the defendant's legal costs.

What sort of justice is this which gives an accident victim compensation only after a four year war of attrition, if he wins his case; or else makes him pay £20,000/£30,000 for the Court's decision that he is *not* entitled to any compensation, if he loses?

Most accident victims, of course, do not have these sums at their disposal, and therefore *cannot* bring their cases to Court unless they get 'legal aid'.

Legal aid is a scheme whereby a plaintiff who has a reasonable case, and whose income and capital are below a certain (not very generous) limit, can bring his case to Court in the usual way; and the State will pay his legal costs. It would seem that a plaintiff of humble means, who gets legal aid, is in a happier position than his middle-class counterpart. Unfortunately this is not necessarily so; and often a legally-aided case is even more problematical, for a number of reasons.

First, the plaintiff's solicitor will not usually take any steps towards getting the necessary evidence until the legal aid certificate has been granted (because it does not operate retrospectively). As the certificate will normally be granted six to nine months *after* the accident, by the time the solicitor gets round to interviewing the witnesses, inspecting the scene of the accident etc., the necessary evidence to prove his client's case may easily have disappeared. Secondly, the plaintiff's case is often hampered by the bureaucratic procedures and rules of the Legal Aid Committee – which may require Counsel's opinion to be taken at any stage before it allows the action to proceed; also the Committee has to give its consent before the plaintiff can change his solicitor.

But the chief drawback is that the Legal Aid Committee (comprising solicitors and Counsel) has to agree that the plaintiff has a reasonable case (i.e. a reasonable chance of *winning* his case) before it will grant legal aid; and it will be guided by Counsel's opinion which the plaintiff's solicitor will obtain and submit with the legal aid application. Thereafter at any time up to the trial, the Committee will withdraw the legal aid certificate *if the defendant's insurers make an offer to settle out of Court, which the plaintiff's legal adviser considers is reasonable in the circumstances.* A case, which recently made the headlines, shows what obviously goes on all the while. A father, whose son was paralysed by a medical mishap, brought a case against the Health Authority, whose insurers offered to settle for £2,000. The father's solicitor considered that as there was insufficient evidence to prove negligence, this offer was 'reasonable in the circumstances'. The father's legal aid was consequently withdrawn. Nevertheless he fought on, financed the case himself, eventually got it to Court – and was awarded £491,000. He was obviously a man of exceptional stamina. For 99.9% of plaintiffs, their solicitor's opinion that the defendant's offer is 'reasonable in the circumstances' – and the consequent withdrawal of their legal aid – means that that offer *has* to be accepted and their case abandoned. We wouldn't let a car mechanic or a taxi-driver decide that a plaintiff – whose claim might cost the defendant's insurance company half a million pounds if it came to Court – has to settle for an out of Court payment of £2,000. But apparently it's quite safe to let the plaintiff's *solicitor* decide this. Solicitors are, after all, *professional* men, and of course there can never be any question of collusion.

The accident victim, however badly injured, has to surmount two giant hurdles before he is entitled to any compensation. First, the rules which dictate that he gets compensation only if his accident was someone else's fault *and* there is sufficient evidence to prove it; second, the judicial machine which takes four or five years to decide whether he *has* surmounted the first hurdle. The hardship and strain caused by these rules, and the judicial machine which administers them, is incalculable. Were it not for the fact that so many people make so much money out of them, both machine and rules would have been consigned to the refuse heap a century ago.

Just as we could have a rational and efficient conveyancing system, so we could have a system whereby accident victims receive compensation automatically, without having to prove their injuries were caused by anyone else's fault, and therefore without having to go anywhere near a lawyer. Indeed they have such a system in New Zealand and Sweden.

Neither need it impose any greater burden on the taxpayer. By dismantling so much of the existing legal system, and releasing so much of the legal aid funds and insurance premiums, as currently go to provide lawyers to argue (and judges to decide) whether Mr. X's accident was or was not Mr. Y's fault, we would release ample funds from which Mr. X could be compensated *irrespective* of whether his accident was Mr. Y's fault. In other words, the average accident case which comes to Court, where the plaintiff has got legal aid, costs the taxpayer something in the region of £50,000: £15,000 for the plaintiff's lawyers' costs – payable by the legal aid fund; £15,000 for the defendant's lawyers' costs – payable by the defendant's insurance company and recovered in premiums paid by the public; and perhaps £20,000 for the judge's salary, and the army of Court and legal aid officials and staff, and notional rent of the Court buildings. Instead of £50,000 paying for this archaic and unwieldy procedure – whereby at the end of the day (or four or five years) the accident victim may recover nothing – it could go into a central compensation fund from which he would be automatically and *immediately* compensated.

In 1978 the Pearson Commission recommended a first step along these lines – i.e. taking *road accident victims* out of the legal system, and compensating them automatically from funds raised by a levy on petrol. A bold suggestion. But of course nothing was done about it. Nothing ever *is* done about the legal system. From time to time a particularly horrendous case makes the headlines, or a Royal Commission makes proposals for sweeping reforms, or some dignitary thunders some well-phrased denunciation, or the Lord Chancellor announces plans for a major shake-up – but nothing ever changes, and lawyers continue on their merry moneyed way. If the law is an ass, the legal profession is an elephant. It can be beaten over the head with a cudgel, but all it apparently feels is a slight and not unpleasing tickling. But you, my gentle reader, have in your hands a more effective weapon. The elephant may be impregnable, but it relies on *you* for its staple diet – that is, your conveyance. The animal is harmful. I urge you not to feed it.

*

My other book *Lawyers Can Seriously Damage Your Health* explores the themes of this litigation section. In particular it chronicles the case histories of three accident victims, who between them employed a total of eleven solicitors and eleven Counsel; and proves – by referring to, and in some cases reproducing, the original documents – that all the lawyers involved were incompetent, and most of them were corrupt. One of the plaintiffs was the father of an eight year old girl who was disastrously brain-damaged in a road accident. After a ten year struggle her father won substantial compensation, but by then it was too late for his much planned rehabilitation to achieve any significant improvement in his daughter's condition – and he himself died of a stroke shortly after the case was finally concluded.

Lawyers Can Seriously Damage Your Health is available from me (address on rear cover), price £3.95, post free.
'It has the ring of truth' – The Times.

Appendices

Appendix 1 – Land Registry Offices and Registration Districts

Opposite is a list of all counties in England and Wales, of which approximately 85% are now registration districts. The letter in brackets after the county denotes which land registry office deals with that county. When a county is simply listed, the *whole* of that county is a registration district. Where underneath a county there are inset certain towns or areas in italics, it means that the whole of that county is a registration district *except* those towns or areas. Conversely, where a county appears in *CAPITALS* it means that county is *not* a registration district *except* for those towns/areas inset thereunder. Thus the whole of Berkshire is a registration district (dealt with by Gloucester Land Registry); the whole of Essex is a registration district except Castle Point, Maldon etc; Norfolk is not a registration district except for Great Yarmouth and Norwich (which are dealt with by Kingston Land Registry).

An asterisk * after the county denotes that the whole of that county was a registration district on or before 1975.

When a registration district is declared, the houses therein are registered only on a *subsequent sale* – so the list won't necessarily tell you whether the house you are buying (or selling) is registered or not. If you are in any doubt ring up the appropriate land registry office, or send form 96.

Land Registry Offices

B Old Market House, Hamilton St. *Birkenhead* L41 5FL (051 6472377)

CO Greyfriars Business Centre, 2 Eaton Rd. *Coventry* CV1 2SD (0203 632

CR Sunley House, Bedford Park *Croydon* Surrey CR9 3LE (01-686 883

D Southfield House, Southfield Way *Durham* DH1 5TR (091 3866151

G Bruton Way *Gloucester* GL1 1DQ (0452 28666)

H Lyon House, Lyon Rd. *Harrow* Middlesex HA1 2EU (01-427 8811)

K Earle House, Portland St. *Kingston-upon-Hull* HU2 8JN (0482 22324

L Birkenhead House, East Beach *Lytham St.Annes* Lancs FY8 5AB (0253 736

N Chalfont Drive *Nottingham* NG8 3RN (0602 291166)

PE Touthill Close, City Road *Peterborough* PE1 1XN (0733 555666)

PL Plumer House, Tailyour Rd., Crownhill *Plymouth* PL6 5HY (0752 791

ST Brickdale House, Swingate *Stevenage* Herts SG1 1XG (0438 315464

SW Ty Bryn Glas, High Street *Swansea* SA1 1PW (0792 458877)

TE Units A1–A3 Stafford Park 15 *Telford* TF3 3AL (0952 290355)

TW *Tunbridge Wells* Kent TN2 5AQ (0892 510015)

W 1 Cumberland Drive *Weymouth* Dorset DT4 9TT (0305 776161)

N.B. Prefix the address with 'XY District Land Registry'.

Avon (PL)
Bedfordshire (PE)
Berkshire* (G)
Buckinghamshire (ST)
Cambridgeshire (PE)
Cheshire (B)
Cleveland* (D)
Clwyd (SW)
Cornwall (PL)
Cumbria (D)
Derbyshire (N)
Devon (PL)
Dorset (W)
  North Dorset
  Purbeck
  West Dorset
Durham (D)
Dyfed (SW)
East Sussex (TW)
Essex (PE)
  Castle Point
  Maldon
  Rochford
  Tendring
Gloucestershire (G)
Greater London*
Greater Manchester* (L)
Gwent (SW)
Gwynedd (SW)
Hampshire (W)
Hereford and Worcester (SW)
  Leominster
  Malvern Hills
  South Herefordshire
  Wychavon
  Wyre Forest
Hertfordshire (ST)
Humberside (D)
Isle of Wight (W)
Kent* (TW)

Lancashire (L)
Leicestershire (N)
LINCOLNSHIRE (K)
  Lincoln
Merseyside* (B)
Mid Glamorgan (SW)
NORFOLK (K)
  Great Yarmouth
  Norwich
Northamptonshire (PE)
NORTHUMBERLAND (D)
  Blyth Valley
  Castle Morpeth
  Wansbeck
North Yorkshire (D)
Nottinghamshire (N)
Oxfordshire (G)
Powys (SW)
SHROPSHIRE (TE)
  Bridgnorth
  The Wrekin
SOMERSET (PL)
  Taunton Deane
  West Somerset
South Glamorgan* (SW)
South Yorkshire* (N)
Staffordshire (B)
SUFFOLK (K)
  Ipswich
  Waveney
Surrey* (TW)
Tyne and Wear* (D)
Warwickshire (G)
West Glamorgan* (SW)
West Midlands* (CO)
West Sussex (W)
West Yorkshire* (N)
WILTSHIRE (G)
  Thamesdown
  West Wiltshire

OFFICE COPY

H.M. LAND REGISTRY

TITLE NUMBER LN197923

This register consists of   2   pages

A. PROPERTY REGISTER

containing the description of the registered land and the estate comprised in the Title

COUNTY OR COUNTY BOROUGH

KENT

PARISH OR PLACE

GRAVESEND

THE FREEHOLD land shown and edged with red on the plan
of the above title filed at the Registry registered on
1 March 1921 known as 9 Brook Street.

NOTE:- The transfer dated 14 June 1963 referred to in
entry No. 3 of the Charges Register contains a
declaration relating to party walls.

B. PROPRIETORSHIP REGISTER

nature of the Title, name, address and description of the proprietor of the land and any entries

TITLE ABSOLUTE

	PROPRIETOR, etc.	
1.	~~FREDERICK NURKINS of 9 Brook Street, Gravesend, Kent registered on 1 July 1963~~	~~Price £3,800~~
2.	HENRY D'ASCOYNE and EDITH D'ASCOYNE of 9 Brook Street, Gravesend, Kent registered on 13 April 1972	Price £8,400

ISSUED BY THE TUNBRIDGE WELLS DISTRICT LAND REGISTRY
SHOWING THE SUBSISTING ENTRIES ON THE REGISTER ON

21 AUG 1974

C. CHARGES REGISTER

taining charges, incumbrances, etc., adversely affecting the land and registered dealings therewith

RY BER	
..	1 March 1921 – The land is subject to the following covenants contained in a conveyance dated 7 June 1912:

The purchaser for the benefit of the remainder of the vendor's land hereby covenants with the vendor and his successors in title to observe the restrictions set out in the schedule hereto:

THE SCHEDULE before referred to

No buildings shall be erected on the said land except private dwellinghouses and outbuildings thereof and no buildings erected on the said land shall be used for the sale of intoxicating liquors whether for consumption on or off the premises and no buildings erected on the said land shall be used except as private dwellinghouses.

2. 1 March 1921 – The passageway included in this title is subject to rights of way.

3. 8 July 1963 – A transfer dated 14 June 1963 by Dolphin Developments Co. Ltd. to Frederick Nurkins contains restrictive covenants. (Copy in Certificate)

4. 13 April 1972 – CHARGE dated 6 March 1972 registered on 13 April 1972 to secure the monies therein mentioned.

5. PROPRIETOR – ABBEY NATIONAL BUILDING SOCIETY of Abbey House, Baker Street, London N.W.1 registered on 13 April 1972.

ISSUED BY THE TUNBRIDGE WELLS DISTRICT LAND REGISTRY
SHOWING THE SUBSISTING ENTRIES ON THE REGISTER ON | 2 1 AUG 1974 |

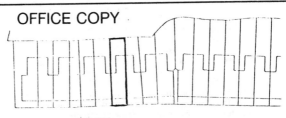

OFFICE COPY

LE NUMBER LN197923

BROOK STREET

ISSUED BY THE TUNBRIDGE WELLS DISTRICT LAND REGISTRY | 2 1 AUG 1974 |

Appendix 3

PRELIMINARY ENQUIRIES
(Form Con 29 Long)

GENERAL ENQUIRIES

REPLIES

These replies are given on behalf of the proposed Vendor and without responsibility on the part of his solicitors. They are believed to be correct but the accuracy is not guaranteed and they do not obviate the need to make appropriate searches, enquiries and inspections.

1. Boundaries
(A) To whom do all the boundary walls, fences, hedges and ditches belong?
(B) If no definite indications exist, which has the Vendor maintained or regarded as his responsibility?

1.
The deeds are silent but inspection may reveal.

2. Disputes
(A) Is the Vendor aware of any past or current disputes regarding boundaries, easements, covenants or other matters relating to the property or its use?
(B) During the last three years, has the Vendor complained or had cause to complain about the state and condition, or the manner of use, of any adjoining or neighbouring property? If so, please give particulars.

2.
None to vendor's knowledge.

3. Notices
Please give particulars of all notices relating to the property, or to matters likely to affect its use or enjoyment, that the Vendor (or to his knowledge, any predecessor in title) has given or received.

3.
None to vendor's knowledge.

4. Guarantees etc.
(A) Please supply a copy of any of the following of which the Purchaser is to have the benefit:
    agreement, covenant, guarantee, warranty, bond, certificate, indemnity and insurance policy,
relating to any of the following matters:
    the construction of the property, or any part of it, or of any building of which it forms part;
    any repair or replacement of, or treatment or improvement to the fabric of the property;
    the maintenance of any accessway;
    the construction costs of any road (including lighting, drainage and crossovers) to which the property fronts, and the charges for adopting any such road as maintainable at the public expense;
    a defective title;
    breach of any restrictive covenant.
(B) (i) What defects or other matters have become apparent, or adverse claims have been made by third parties, which might give rise to a claim under any document mentioned in (A)?
    (ii) Has notice of such defect, matter or adverse claim been given? If so, please give particulars.
    (iii) Please give particulars of all such claims already made, whether or not already settled.

4.
There are none with the deeds.

246

5. Services

(A) Does the property have drainage, water, electricity and gas services? Which of them are connected to the mains?

(B) Is the water supply metered?

(C) Do any of the services (except where part of the mains) pass through or over property not included in the sale?

(D) If so, please give details of route and particulars of any easement, grant, exception, reservation, wayleave, licence or consent authorising this.

(E) Please supply a copy of any licence to abstract water and of any consent or licence relating to drainage, issued in respect of the property or the activities carried on there.

5.
The property is connected to the usual services but please rely on inspection for the route of the pipes etc.

6. Facilities

(A) Except in the case of public rights or where particulars have already been given, what rights are there for the use of the following facilities, whether enjoyed by the owner or occupier of the property, or over the property for the benefit of other property:
— Access for light and air;
— Access for pedestrians and vehicles;
— Emergency escape routes;
— Pipes and wires for services not dealt with in Enquiry 5;
— Access and facilities for repair, maintainance and replacement.
Please supply copies of any relevant documents.

(B) Has any person taken any action to stop (whether immediately or at some future time) the use of any facility? If so, please give particulars.

(C) In respect of maintenance, repair or replacement work on any land or fixtures affording any facility:
(i) What work has been done by the Vendor (or, to his knowledge, any predecessor in title), and when?
(ii) What work has the Vendor been called upon to do which has not yet been done?
(iii) What sums has the Vendor contributed to work done by others, and when? Is any demand for such sums still outstanding?
(iv) What sums has the Vendor called upon others to contribute, and when? Is any demand still outstanding?

6.
None to vendor's knowledge.

7. Adverse Rights

(A) Is the Vendor aware of any rights or informal arrangements specifically affecting the property, other than any disclosed in the draft contract or immediately apparent on inspection, which are exercisable by virtue of an easement, grant, wayleave, licence, consent, agreement relating to an ancient monument or land near it, or otherwise or which are in the nature of public or common rights?

(B) (i) Please give the full names, and ages if under 18, of all persons in actual occupation of the property.
(ii) What legal or equitable interest in the property has each of those persons?

(C) Is the Vendor aware of any other overriding interests as defined by the Land Registration Act 1925, s.70(1)?

7.
This question is too wide to permit a specific reply, but the property is sold subject to any there may be.

8. Restrictions

(A) Have all restrictions affecting the property or its use been observed up to the date hereof? If not, please give details.

(B) Where such restrictions have in the past required any person's consent or approval of plans, does the Vendor have written evidence of that consent or approval?

8.
No notice of any breach has been received by the vendor.

9. Planning etc.

(A) (i) When did the present use of the property commence?

(ii) Has this use been continuous since it commenced?

(B) During the four years immediately prior to receipt of these enquiries:

(i) Were any of the buildings on the property erected, or have any been altered or added to?

(ii) Have any other building, engineering, mining or other operations been carried out in, on, over or under the property?

(iii) Has any condition or limitation on any planning permission not been complied with?

If so, please give details.

(C) Please supply a copy of:

(i) Any planning permission authorising or imposing conditions upon the present use of the property, or the erection or retention of the buildings on it.

(ii) Any bye-law approval or building regulation consent relating to those buildings.

(iii) Any current fire certificate.

9.
We presume continuous since it was built.

No.

Please enquire of local authority.

10. Fixtures Fittings, etc.

(A) Does the sale include all of the following items now on the property, and attached to or growing in it?

Trees, shrubs, plants, flowers, and garden produce. Greenhouses, garden sheds and garden ornaments. Aerials. Fitted furniture and shelves. Electric switches, points and wall and ceiling fittings.

(B) What fixtures and fittings affixed to the property are not included in the sale?

(C) If the property has any fixed oil burning appliance, what arrangements are proposed for the sale to the purchaser on completion of any stock of oil?

10.
We are enquiring.

11. Outgoings

(A) (i) What is the rateable value of the property?

(ii) Have any works been carried out at the property which might result in a revision of this?

(B) Does the hereditament, in which the property to be sold is included for rating purposes, also include any other property?

(C) What annual or periodic charges, other than general and water rates, affect the property or its occupier?

11.
Please enquire of local authority.

12. Completion

(A) How long after exchange of contracts will the Vendor be able to give vacant possession of the whole of the property?

(B) The Purchaser's solicitors wish to complete by adopting the Law Society's Code for Completion by Post (1984 edition). Do the Vendor's solicitors agree?

12.
The usual month.

Yes.

Appendix 4 – Local Search Questionnaire

1. (A) Are all the roadways, footpaths and footways referred to in the Description of the Property maintainable at the public expense within the meaning of the Highways Act 1980?

    1. (A) YES

  (B) If not, please state whether the Council have passed any resolution either to:—
(i) make up any of such roadways, footpaths or footways at the cost of the frontagers, or
(ii) adopt any of them without cost to the frontagers.

    (B) —

  (C) (i) Have the Council entered into any outstanding agreement relating to the adoption of any such roadway, footpath or footway?
(ii) If so, is such an agreement supported by a bond?

    (C) —

2. (A) Have the Council been notified by the appropriate Secretary of State of:—
(i) any order, draft order or scheme for the construction of a new trunk or special road, or
(ii) any proposals for the alteration or improvement of an existing road, involving the construction, whether or not within existing highway limits, of a subway, underpass, flyover, footbridge, elevated road or dual carriageway
the centre line of which in either case is within 200 metres of the property?

    2. (A)

    (i) NO

    (ii) NO

  (B) Have the Council approved any proposals by themselves for:—
(i) the construction of a new road, or
(ii) the alteration or improvement of an existing road, involving the construction, whether or not within existing highway limits, of a subway, underpass, flyover, footbridge, elevated road, dual carriageway
the limits of construction of which in either case are within 200 metres of the property?

    (B)

    (i) NO
    (ii) NO

  (C) Have the Council approved, or have they been notified by the appropriate Secretary of State of, any proposals for highway construction or improvement that involve the acquisition of the property?

    (C) NO

  (D) Has either the Secretary of State or the Council published for the purposes of public consultation any proposals for the construction of a new road indicating a possible route the centre line of which would be likely to be within 200 metres of the property?

    (D) NO

3. Are there any outstanding statutory or informal notices (other than notices shown in the Official Certificate of Search and notices served consequent on an order made or a resolution passed to acquire the property recorded in reply to Enquiry 14), which have been issued by the Council under the Public Health Acts, Housing Acts or Highways Acts?

    3. NO

4. Have the Council authorised any proceedings in respect of an infringement of the Building Regulations?

    4. NO

5. (A) (i) (a) Does foul drainage from the property drain to a public sewer?
(b) If the Reply to (a) above is 'Yes', please indicate whether connection to the public sewer is effected by:
(1) drain and private sewer;
(2) drain alone.
(ii) (a) Does surface water from the property drain to a public sewer?

    5. (A) (i) (a) YES

    (b)

    (1) NO
    (2) YES
    (ii) (a) YES

(b) Does surface water from the property drain to a highway drain or sewer the subject of an agreement under s.21 (1) (a) of the Public Health Act 1936?

(b) NO

(c) If the Reply to either (a) or (b) above is 'Yes', please indicate whether the connection to the appropriate sewer or highway drain is effected by:

(c)

(1) drain and private sewer;

(1) NO

(2) drain alone.

(2) YES

(iii) Is there in force in relation to any part of the drainage of the property an agreement under s.22 of the Building Act 1984?

(iii) NO

(B) (i) To the Council's knowledge is any sewer serving, or which is proposed to serve, the property the subject of an agreement under s.18 Public Health Act 1936?

(B) (i) NO

(ii) If the Reply to (i) above is 'Yes', is the agreement supported by a bond?

(ii) —

(C) Is any public sewer to which the property drains a sewer of a kind described in s.24(4) of the Public Health Act 1936?

(C) YES

(D) If the Reply to either Enquiry (A) (i) (a) or (ii) (a) above is 'No', do the Council know whether there is a foul or surface water sewer (as appropriate) within 100 feet of the property and at a level which makes it reasonably practicable to construct a drain from the property to that sewer?

(D) —

(E) Are the Council aware of any resolution affecting the property:

(E)

(i) under s.12 or s.13 of the Public Health Act 1961, or

(i) NO

(ii) under any local Act as to the recovery from frontagers of the expense of sewering highways?

(ii) NO

6. (A) Except as shown in the Official Certificate of Search, or in the Register kept pursuant to s.92A of the T&CP Act 1971, has any enforcement or stop notice under s.87 or s.90 of the T&CP Act 1971 been authorised by the Council for issue or service (other than notices which have been withdrawn or quashed)?

6. (A) NO

(B) Are there any entries in the Register kept pursuant to s.92A of the T&CP Act 1971?

(B) NO

(C) Where can that Register be inspected?

(C) Planning dept.

(D) If an enforcement notice has been served or issued, has it been complied with to the satisfaction of the Council?

(D) —

7. (A) (i) What stage has been reached in the preparation of a structure plan for the area which includes the property?

7. (A) (i) Plan approved

(ii) Have the Council made public any proposals for the alteration of an approved structure plan?

(ii) NO

(B) (i) What stage has been reached in the preparation of local plans for the area which includes the property?

(B) (i) Borough plan on deposit

(ii) Have the Council made public any proposals for the alteration of an adopted local plan?

(ii) NO

(iii) Do any of the proposals made public by the Council in relation to local plans:

(iii)

(a) indicate the primary use for the area which includes the property?

(a) YES, Residential

(b) include any provisions for the property?

(b) NO

(C) (i) Is an old style development plan in force in the area which includes the property?

(C) (i) NO

(ii) If so, does the plan:

(a) indicate the primary use for the area?

(b) include any provisions for the property?

(D) (i) Have the Council made public any proposals for the preparation or modification of a non-statutory plan for the area which includes the property?
(ii) If so:
(a) what stage has been reached?
(b) do any proposals indicate the primary use of the area or include any provisions for the property?
(E) Is the property included in any of the categories of land specified in s.71 Land Compensation Act 1973?

(D) (i) NO

—

(E) NO

8. Except as shown in the Official Certificate of Search, have the Council resolved to make a direction under Article 4 of the T&CP General Development Order 1977 relating to the restriction of permitted development?

8. NO

9. Except as shown in the Official Certificate of Search, have the Council resolved to make any order under s.45, s.51 or s.60 of the T&CP Act 1971?

9. NO

10. Has compensation been paid by the Council under s.169 of the T&CP Act 1971?

10. NO

11. (A) Are there any entries relating to the property in Part I or Part II of the Register kept pursuant to s.34 of the T&CP Act 1971?
(B) Where can that Register be inspected?

11. (A) Planning permission for 3 bedroomed house
(B) Planning dept.

12. Is the property within a conservation area designated under s.277, T&CP Act 1971 prior to 31 August 1974?

12. NO

13. Have the Council authorised the service of a building preservation notice under s.58 of the T&PC Act 1971?

13. NO

14. Except as shown in the Official Certificate of Search, have the Council made any order (whether of not confirmed by the appropriate Secretary of State) or passed any resolution which is still capable of being implemented for the compulsory acquisition of the property?

14. NO

15. (A) Is the property included in a programme of slum clearance which has been submitted, or been the subject of a resolution to submit, to the Department of the Environment, or has otherwise been adopted by resolution of the Council?
(B) Except as shown in the Official Certificate of Search, have the Council resolved to define the area in which the property is situated as a General Improvement Area.

15. (A) NO

(B) NO

16. Except as shown in the Official Certificate of Search, is the property included in an area for which the Council have passed a resolution to make or vary a smoke control order under s.11 of the Clean Air Act 1956?

16. NO

17. Is a resolution in force bringing into operation Schedule 1 to the General Rate Act 1967, as to rating of unoccupied property? If so, please specify:
(i) the categories of properties affected;
(ii) the effective date of the resolution;
(iii) the proportion of the rate due.

17. YES

(i) All
(ii) April 1981
(iii) 100% (domestic)

18. Is the property situated in an area where registration of title under the Land Registration Acts is compulsory on sale? If so, please specify the District Registry and the date of compulsory registration.

18. YES
Croydon Land Registry

Appendix 5
Copy Probate

In the High Court of Justice

The District Probate Registry at NEWCASTLE UPON TYNE

BE IT KNOWN that   GEOFFREY GEORGE MIDDLETON of 17 New Road
Radlett Herts

died on the   19th day of   September   1969

domiciled in England and Wales

AND BE IT FURTHER KNOWN that at the date hereunder written the last Will and Testament

(a copy whereof is hereunto annexed) of the said deceased was proved and registered in the District Probate Registry of the High Court of Justice at NEWCASTLE UPON TYNE
and Administration of all the estate which by law devolves to and vests in the personal representative of the said deceased was granted by the aforesaid Court to AUBREY HERBERT FOWLER of Carmelite Priory Boars Hill Oxford

and HARRY GEORGE FOWLER of 62 Blockley Road North Wembley Middlesex

the Executors named in the said Will

And it is hereby certified that an Inland Revenue affidavit has been delivered wherein it is shown that the gross value of the said estate in the United Kingdom
(exclusive of what the said deceased may have been possessed of or entitled to as a trustee and not beneficially) amounts to £6666.05
and that the net value of the estate amounts to £6602.79

Dated the 26th day of   June   19 75

District Registrar.

252

Appendix 6 – Sale of a lease (house or flat)

The instructions in this appendix should be followed in conjunction with those in Chapter 11.

Leases are registered at the Land Registry in the same way as freeholds, so your lease will be either registered or unregistered depending (broadly) on whether or not the house or flat was in a registration district when you bought the lease. If your lease is registered you therefore obtain an office copy of the register in the same way as you would in the sale of a freehold. In addition, you also need a copy of the actual lease, which unfortunately you cannot get from the Land Registry; so you will have to write to the Head Office of your building society and ask for the deeds (i.e. land certificate and lease) to be sent to a local branch from where you can then get a copy. Alternatively, there may be a copy in the file kept by the solicitor who acted for you on your purchase (which is *your* property).

If the lease is unregistered, instead of a land certificate, the deeds will consist of the lease and a series of 'assignments' tracing ownership from the original lessee to yourself. (Of course if *you* were the original lessee there would just be the lease.)

To the contract on p.150 make the following variations:

First paragraph (beginning 'This contract is made . . . ') – no variation.

WHEREBY IT IS AGREED the vendors will sell to the purchasers and the purchasers will buy from the vendors: the leasehold interest in the dwellinghouse/flat known as 15 Muggleton Mansions, Muggleton Close, Thong, Wiltshire, being the residue of the term of [99] years from — as the same was created by a lease dated —, for the sum of £— and subject to the following conditions:

Paragraphs 1, 2 & 3 – no variation.

4. The property is sold subject to the terms, rent reserved, and lessee's covenants contained in the lease, a copy of which having been given to the purchaser's solicitor, no objections shall be made or questions asked in respect thereof.

5. The vendors' title shall commence with the lease, and shall continue [by supplying office copy of title number AB12456 under which the lease is registered at H.M. Land Registry] [with an assignment between AB and CD dated . . .]

6. No variation.

N.B. Insert the first only of the square brackets in clause 5 if the lease is registered; the second only, if it is unregistered. If the lease is unregistered, the assignment specified in clause 5 should be at least 15 years old, unless the first assignment after the lease was granted took place *less* than fifteen years ago, in which case clause 5 should read simply: 'the vendors' title shall commence with the lease.'

Send the contract, copy lease, and office copy if registered, to the purchaser's solicitor and wait for the preliminary enquiries. These will largely be the same as on the sale of a freehold, except that there may be some extra ones relating to the lease (e.g. 'Please mark on the plan the dustbin area referred to in clause — of the lease'; 'Have any additional regulations been made pursuant to clause — of the lease?'), which should not cause you any difficulty.

One question which you may be asked – if your lease is not registered with Title Absolute – is 'Can the freehold title be produced?' This means that while you have shown or agreed to show how you came to own the lease, the purchaser's solicitor is asking if there are any documents with the deeds which show that the person who originally granted the lease (the lessor) owned the freehold – i.e. that he had the right to grant the lease in the first place. The sort of document there might be is an *office copy of the freehold title* if it is registered, or else a copy conveyance or two, if unregistered. Therefore inspect the deeds at the building society's local branch, and if there are any documents which look as if they relate to the freehold, ask the building society's clerk to copy them (at your expense). If there aren't any freehold documents, but the lessor's freehold is registered (as it probably will be), you could ask the lessor to give your purchaser's solicitor an authority to inspect the register, so he can get an office copy direct from the Land Registry. If the lessor is unco-operative and you can't get any documents relating to the freehold, the purchaser's solicitor will normally accept the position. Incidentally, if there are documents relating to the freehold title, do not let the purchaser's solicitor alter the contract on account of them: your attitude should be that he is welcome to whatever documents there may be on completion, but this is an optional extra on your part.

Normally, you will not need the lessor's consent to the sale, but some of the more expensive leases do require his consent, in which case there will be a lessee's covenant: 'Not to assign the lease without the lessor's written consent, such consent not to be unreasonably witheld.' If there is such a covenant you will have to ask the purchaser for references, and submit them to the lessor.

254

After exchange of contracts, two points only:

(1) You should add to the assignment or transfer (the document which the purchaser's solicitor prepares which transfers the lease to the purchaser – assignment if unregistered, transfer if registered) the following clause at the end: 'Provided that there shall be no implied covenant that the covenants in the lease relating to the repair and decoration of the property have been complied with.' Without these words, by selling as 'beneficial owner' you would impliedly covenant that all the covenants in the lease have been observed, including those relating to repair and decoration – which might be a dangerous thing to do. The National Conditions of Sale, to which your contract is subject, allow you to insert these words.

(2) The 'ground rent' reserved by the lease is usually payable in arrear. If it is, a proportion should be *deducted* from the purchase price in respect of the period from the date to which it is paid, to the date of completion. If paid in advance, an appropriate proportion should be added to the purchase price. In the same way, deduct or add any periodical *maintenance charge* paid in arrear or advance. You should keep the last rent receipt as you will be asked to produce it on completion.

Appendix 7 – Purchase of a lease (house or flat)

The instructions in this appendix should be followed in conjunction with those in Chapters 12 and 13. Where a particular point applies to a house or a flat, this is stated. Otherwise there is no distinction between the two, but either is referred to as 'the property'. (Flat includes maisonette.)

Whereas a freeholder owns the property for ever, a leaseholder owns it only for a certain period. Most houses are freehold, but some houses and all flats are leasehold. The person who grants the lease is called the lessor; the person who owns the lease is called the lessee.

A lease is a document whereby the lessor – who owns the freehold – grants to the lessee the right to have the property for a certain period, usually 99 years, in consideration of a lump sum, with the lessee paying a nominal rent throughout the term.* Once the original lease has been granted it can be sold and sold again, in the same way as a freehold. Therefore you will be buying either a *new* lease from the lessor, or an *existing* lease from the current lessee. In the latter case you will get only the *remainder* of the original term, as will *your* purchaser when you come to sell.

The first step is for the solicitor for the lessor or vendor (depending on whether you are buying a new or an existing lease) to send you the draft contract with a copy of the lease.

The lease itself

1. The most important part of the lease is the clause, usually near the beginning, which states that the lessor *demises* the property (plus garage if one is included) to the lessee for a certain term of years – usually 99 – from a certain date (usually the quarter day before the date the lease was originally granted), at a certain yearly rent. Usually this rent is nominal, although in the more expensive flat leases it can be significant, and it sometimes increases throughout the term.

The property, particularly if it is a house, should be defined by reference to a *plan* attached to the lease.

---

* There is another type of lease (with which we are not concerned) whereby the lessee *rents* the property, usually for a few years, at the market rent.

The term of years is fixed at the outset, and when it eventually expires the lease comes to an end and the property reverts back to the lessor (subject to the Leasehold Reform Act 1967 in the case of a house). A building society may be unwilling to lend money on a lease with only thirty or forty years left to run.

2. In addition to being granted the right to have the property, the lessee should also be granted appropriate ancillary rights – e.g. a right of way for vehicles over the road leading to the property (and garage), if it is not a public highway; a right of way over any common parts; the right to use any communal garden; the right to use the drains and pipes etc. connected to the property.

3. The bulk of the lease will consist of a list of obligations (covenants) on the part of the lessee. These will include a covenant to use the property only as a private dwelling, and not to make any structural alterations or additions. Normally there will not be any requirement to obtain the lessor's prior consent to a sale; but if, unusually, there is a covenant by the lessee not to *assign* (sell), this must be qualified by the words: 'without the lessor's consent not to be unreasonably witheld.' *Otherwise the lease would be unsaleable.*

There will be other numerous lessee's covenants – some leases are reasonably concise, others drool on for page after page (particularly in the case of a flat) – but hopefully they will be self-explanatory, e.g. not to do anything which causes a nuisance to the other lessees, not to obstruct any common parts, and so on. These lessee's covenants are made with the lessor, and sometimes with the management company if there is one.

4. Near the end of the document there will be a provision that if (a) the rent is unpaid for 21 days, or (b) the lessee's covenants are not observed, the lessor may re-enter the property and put an end to the lease – which threat is more theoretical than real, as the Courts make sure that such a right is not exercised except in extreme cases. However, there should NOT be any provision that the lessor may end the lease if the lessee becomes *bankrupt*. If there is, the lease will be virtually unsaleable as no-one would grant a mortgage on it.

5. If under the terms of the lease the lessor or management company is responsible for insuring the block, there should be a covenant by that body to insure the block for its full rebuilding cost, and to lay out all insurance monies received in rebuilding/ reinstating the building.

6. One of the lessee's covenants will be to keep the property in good repair. If the property is a *house* this will be straightforward – to keep the house and structure in good repair and properly painted.

If the property is a *flat* it will be more complicated. In the case of a

257

small block or a single house which has been converted into two or three flats, there may be a simple ad hoc arrangement whereby each lessee covenants to keep his flat – inside and outside – in good repair, with the upstairs lessee(s) being responsible for the roof, and the downstairs lessee(s) being responsible for the drains. However, the more usual arrangement is for each lessee to covenant to keep the inside of his flat in good repair; and for a separate body – either the lessor or a management company – to covenant with the lessee to keep the structure and common parts in good repair and properly painted, and recover the cost from the individual lessees in the block.

Either arrangement can lead to difficulties. Firstly, the actual wording of the lease: if a legal draftsman can use fifty words to describe a house without defining it any more precisely than if he had simply used its postal address, think what he will be able to do with the lease of a flat – where there actually *are* some complicated provisions to be imposed (see p. 115/116). Secondly, it is one thing to impose elaborate repairing obligations on a lessor or a management company, or on the individual lessees; it is another thing to compel their observance. In fact one anti-social lessee (e.g. who is out of the country for long stretches and whose cistern periodically overflows) can make life pretty impossible for the other lessees in the block; and the law being what it is, there are no speedy sanctions. Thirdly, the individual lessees have to pay their proportion of the costs incurred by the management company, or the lessor's managing agent, in repairing the structure of the building etc; yet they usually have no control over that management company or managing agent – a situation which can make for incompetence or even corruption.

The lessee of a house has the whole house within his control and ownership; and subject to the standard lessee's covenant to keep it in good repair (which the lessor normally will not be interested in enforcing anyway), and the restrictions in the lease (which are more theoretical than real), he is in much the same position as a freeholder.

Unfortunately, a flat lease is much more complicated and problematical – basically because the lessee owns only *part* of a building, but is nevertheless concerned with how the remainder of the building is maintained; because he has to rely on people (the lessor, the management company, his co-lessees) over whom he has no control; and because the rights and obligations of the parties involved are usually laid down in an atrociously worded lease. If you are buying a flat you will just have to hope that your block will not be a problematical one; and by making some common-sense enquiries, you have a chance of getting some warning before committing yourself to the purchase.

Enquiries and checks before Exchange of Contracts
In the case of a house, you should make the same checks, enquiries and 'searches' as set out in Chapter 12 for the purchase of a freehold house. You are, after all, buying a house and should be just as concerned to check that it has no quasi-legal defects.

In the case of a flat, in general you should also make these checks and enquiries. You are, in effect, buying *part* of a building – and equally you need to check that the block had planning permission, that you have a right of way to the garage, that there are no proposals for road widening in the offing, and so on. However, some of the points in Chapter 12 will not be relevant, while others will be *more* relevant. For instance, you obviously don't need to bother about the position of boundary fences if there is no right to use the garden. On the other hand, if the flat is part of a recently converted house, you should be more careful to check with the local Council that planning permission for the conversion was granted, and the building regulations have been complied with. You will have to use your common sense in deciding which points to pursue, which to leave alone.

In addition check the following points:

1. Ascertain as far as possible what the yearly running and repairing expenses are likely to be, and whether there is any annual maintenance charge payable in advance or arrear. See the accounts for, say, the previous three years, and ask the managing agents or lessor (i.e. whoever is responsible for maintaining the building) if there is any major repair or exceptional expenditure in the offing. Also ask when the next outside painting is due and how much it is likely to cost.

It is difficult to advise whether or not to employ a surveyor (see p. 191), but remember you are directly concerned with the state of repair of the structure of the whole building.

2. Flat-owners are more prone to neighbour problems than house owners, because the neighbours are nearer and there are more of them. Ask the neighbours – vertical and horizontal – how they get on with your vendor (if you are buying an existing lease), and also ask them for their comments on how the block is run. That way you are more likely to learn of any problems than if you asked your vendor (or his solicitor). Also spend as much time as possible in the *evening* in the flat. A prudent precaution is to ask the neighbours

to turn on their television, hi-fi, or whatever to its normal volume
and see how it sounds in the flat you are buying.

3. Sometimes the individual lessees will each own a share in the
management company, and a small number of them will form a
management committee responsible for decisions concerning the
running and upkeep of the block. In such cases it would be useful to
put your questions to the Chairman or Secretary.

4. If (unusually) the lessee/vendor needs the lessor's *consent* to the
sale, it is up to you to supply references to the vendor's solicitor; and
you should not exchange contracts without some written indication
from the lessor that such consent will be forthcoming.

The checks and enquiries you make will (as far as possible) be the
same whether you are buying an existing or a new lease. However,
the legal procedures vary, so they are dealt with separately, as
follows:

THE PROCEDURE FOR BUYING AN *EXISTING* LEASE

As stated, the solicitor for the vendor will send you the draft
contract and a copy of the lease.

The contract will be basically in the same form as for the purchase
of a freehold, with some minor variations – see appendix 6 for the
variations you may expect.

If the lease is registered* it will have its own separate register and
filed plan, as in the case of a registered freehold, and the vendor's
solicitor will also send you an office copy. The proprietorship
register sets out the name of the current lessee (your vendor), and the
charges register sets out the current mortgages. The property
register, as well as containing the address of the property, sets out
brief details of the lease.

If the lease is not registered you won't get any copy register, of
course; only the copy lease with plan attached.

Either way, you read and try to understand the lease, and check
the property, the plan (particularly in the case of a house), the term
of years, the rent (and that they tally with the office copy, if
registered). As for the rest of the lease, there isn't very much you can
do about it, as it has already been granted and the wording is
therefore fixed. However, if it contains a serious error – e.g. if there
was an unqualified covenant not to assign (sell) or a provision for
forfeiture in the event of the lessee's bankruptcy – you should not

---

* The lease will be registered if the property was in a registration district either (a)
when the lease was first granted; or (b) when it was sold thereafter, having 21 years
or more still to run *if the freehold was registered*; or (c) when it was sold thereafter,
having 40 years or more still to run *if the freehold was unregistered*.

proceed unless the vendor can get it rectified (by getting the *lessor* to alter the offending item). Apart from those obvious errors, the most likely defect of a *flat* lease is that it omits any provision for repairing the *structure* of the building.

Send a copy of the lease to your building society's solicitor. This is a useful safeguard as he may pick up something you had overlooked; and in any case you should get his written approval *before* you exchange contracts so he cannot raise any objections afterwards. In particular, he has to approve the *insurance* provisions in the lease.

If the lease is registered, under the words 'Proprietorship Register' (on the office copy) you will see the words 'Title Absolute' or 'Good Leasehold Title'. The former signify that the Land Registry has checked the lessor's freehold title and guarantees that he had the right to grant the lease; the latter signify that the Land Registry has *not* checked the lessor's freehold title and does *not* give such a guarantee.

If the lease is not registered with 'Title Absolute', or if it is not registered at all, the usual procedure is for the purchaser to ask the vendor's solicitor whether the *lessor's freehold title* can be obtained – i.e. an office copy if registered, or previous conveyances going back 15 years if unregistered – in order to check that the lessor had the right to *grant* the lease. If you can get the lessor's freehold title, check it in the same way as if you were buying the freehold; in particular, check that the property as shown on the lease plan falls *within* the lessor's property as shown on his land registry or conveyance plan. If the lessor is not co-operative, and is not prepared to show his freehold title (although if registered, he would only have to give the vendor's solicitor an *authority* to get an office copy), the purchaser's solicitor generally accepts the position. In theory this is a dangerous practice – to pay over your life's savings to someone who can prove that he owns the lease, but cannot prove that the lessor had the right to grant that lease in the first place. In practice, as far as I know, it seems not to cause difficulty. This is one of the many grey areas in the conveyancing system, and the procedure for checking freehold title to unregistered property is itself a grey area, as already explained. Again, make sure that your building society's solicitor is advised of, and accepts, the position.

Having carried out the checks, enquiries and 'searches', as previously mentioned, follow the procedure under the heading 'Exchange of Contracts' in Chapter 12.

After Exchange of Contracts

If, under the terms of the lease, the lessor or management

company arranges the insurance, ensure that a note of your interest as purchaser is put on the insurance policy immediately contracts have been exchanged. If it is up to the individual lessee to insure the property, you or your building society should at once arrange insurance.

If the lease is registered

The name of the current lessee (your vendor) will be on the proprietorship register, and the transfer form is the same as for a transfer of a freehold. You go through the same procedures as set out in Part I of Chapter 13, and obtain the same documents on completion (land certificate, transfer, form 53 or undertaking to discharge the vendor's mortgage etc.), and carry out the same formalities after completion, as for the purchase of a registered freehold. In addition, there will be the original lease (executed by the lessor) to be handed over on completion.

If the lease is unregistered

You go through the same procedures as are set out in Part II of Chapter 13, except that whereas in the case of a freehold the title deeds consist of a series of conveyances, in the case of a lease the title deeds consist of the original lease (executed by the lessor) and a series of 'assignments' tracing the ownership from the first lessee to the vendor.

The wording of an 'assignment' is slightly different from a conveyance, since the vendor is not conveying the freehold but assigning the residue of his term of years. Follow the wording of the conveyance on p. 217 but with the following alterations:

Line 1. Substitute ASSIGNMENT for CONVEYANCE.

Lines 7-9. Substitute the following for the existing paragraph: WHEREAS a lease (hereinafter called 'the lease') dated — between —and — created a term of [99 years from 25th March 1973] in 12 Mustard Street etc., the residue of which term is now vested in the vendors, who have agreed to sell the same to the purchasers for £—.

Line 13. Substitute 'hereby assign' for 'hereby convey'.

Line 15. Insert after the address: . . . as the same is comprised in and demised by the lease TO HOLD the same unto the purchasers for all the residue of the said term now unexpired [as joint tenants etc.], subject to the payment of rent and the lessee's covenants therein contained.

(If your vendor was not the original lessee, you will be able to use the assignment to him as your model.)

Purchase of a lease (house or flat)

For the rest, you follow the instructions from the conveyance on p. 217 to the end of the chapter (with 'assignment' substituted for 'conveyance'). In particular, the same procedures for the pre-completion search and making sure the vendor's mortgage has been discharged, apply.

If the property is in a registration district, and the lease has at least forty years left to run (or at least twenty-one years if the *freehold* is registered), the lease has to be registered after completion. The documents must therefore be sent to the Land Registry, either by your building society's solicitor, or by you (with form 2B in the former case, form 2A in the latter). If the lessor's title is registered, or you managed to obtain 'examined' copies of the freehold title deeds (see (3) p. 269), you/your building society's solicitor should apply for your lease to be registered with 'Title Absolute'.

Whether the lease is registered or unregistered

On completion, check the last rent receipt and that it contains no reference to any breach of the lessee's covenants; and get a letter from the lessor stating that he is not aware of any breach of the lessee's covenants.

Deduct from the purchase price any proportion of the rent *and annual maintenance charges* payable in arrear, from the date to which such rent or maintenance charges were paid to the date of completion, as you will be responsible for subsequent demands even if they are in respect of a period before you took possession. Whether there are any annual maintenance charges payable in arrear is something you will have ascertained from your pre-contract enquiries. Conversely, if there are annual maintenance charges payable *in advance* your vendor will seek to add a proportion, from completion to the date to which they have been paid, onto the purchase price.

If each lessee owns a share in the management company (or lessor company), the appropriate share transfer signed by your vendor should be handed over.

It is customary to assume that on the grant of the original lease the lessee's solicitor duly obtained the consent of the mortgagee of the lessor's *freehold* to the grant of the lease. In view of the consequences of his not having done so (see below), it would be a wise precaution to insist on evidence of such consent.

THE PROCEDURE FOR BUYING
A *NEW* LEASE FROM THE LESSOR

The lessor's solicitor will send you the draft (proposed) lease with the draft contract. The contract will provide, basically, that the lessor will grant you a lease of the property for the term of years and for the price stated, in the form attached.

The contract should also provide for the lessor to show his freehold title – i.e. proof that he has the right to grant the lease. You should therefore get an office copy of his register or photo-copies of his conveyances (going back at least fifteen years), which you check in the same way as if you were buying the freehold. In particular, you check that the property (house or flat) as shown on the lease plan falls *within* the lessor's property as shown on his land registry plan or conveyance plan.

In theory you have the right to suggest amendments to the draft lease, although the lessor's solicitor will generally present it on a 'take it or leave it' basis. However, if there is a significant omission or error – e.g. the lease did not include a right to use the estate roads, or inadvertently contained a provision for forfeiture in the event of the lessee's bankruptcy – the lessor's solicitor would obviously have to agree to amending it.

Anyway, check the property, the plan (particularly in the case of a house), the term of years, the rent; and that the lease contains the standard provisions (particularly for the repair of the structure by the lessor or management company, in the case of a flat) which we have discussed.

Then send a copy of the draft lease to your building society's solicitor and get his written approval – so he can't subsequently raise objections.

Having carried out the checks, enquiries and 'searches', as previously mentioned, follow the procedure under the heading 'Exchange of Contracts' in Chapter 12.

After Exchange of Contracts

The contract will have the 'agreed' form of lease attached to it, and the lessor's solicitor will have two fair copies typed out for you and the lessor respectively to execute, and exchange on completion. This lease takes the place of a transfer or conveyance.

The legal formalities relating to the grant of a new lease are akin to a transfer or conveyance of *part*. If the lessor's title is *registered* you should do a land registry search on form 94B. If the lessor's title is *unregistered* you should do a land charges search and, if the lessor is a limited company, a Company search (p. 270).

264

Completion

Hand over your executed part of the lease and get the lessor's executed part (with the plan attached also executed).

If you were buying a freehold house, you would have to make sure that the vendor's mortgage(s) were paid off on completion; otherwise your house would be subject to them. When you are buying a new lease the lessor is, in effect, selling you a chunk out of his property, although his mortgage(s) will *not* be paid off. Therefore you must obtain a *consent to the lease* signed by the mortgagee of the lessor's freehold title – or, if there is more than one mortgagee, a separate consent signed by each. Otherwise the lease will not bind the mortgagee if he has to realise his security.

If the property is in a registration district, the lease will have to be registered after completion – preferably with 'Title Absolute'.* To this end, on completion:

If the lessor's title is registered

The lessor's solicitor should hand over an undertaking to lodge the lessor's land certificate at the Land Registry, and notify you or your building society's solicitor of the reference number (see paragraph 6, p. 208).

If the lessor's title is unregistered

Follow the procedures in para (3) on p. 269, substituting *lessor* for *builder*, and – where appropriate – *lease* for *conveyance*.

(Incidentally, you should still do this even if the property is not in a registration district.)

*

N.B. 1. Remember the instructions in this appendix should be followed *in conjunction* with those in Chapters 12 and 13 – unless the latter have been specifically superseded by the former.

N.B. 2. Although in some cases buying a lease is only marginally more complicated than buying a freehold – e.g. buying a straightforward existing lease (with seventy years still to run) of a house, registered with title absolute – other cases are considerably *more* complicated. If you are in any doubt anywhere along the line, I suggest you avail yourself of the 'Consultation Pack' as detailed on the inside cover.

---

* The land registry form to accompany the documents is 3B if lodged by your building society's solicitor, 3A if lodged by you.

Appendix 8 – Purchase of a new house from a builder

The instructions in this appendix should be followed in conjunction with those in Chapters 12 and 13. I call the developer – who has built the house which he is selling to you – the *builder*.

The contract which you receive from the builder's solicitor when you are buying a new house will be more elaborate than in the case of a purchase of a secondhand house (see p. 106); and should include the following additional provisions:

(1) The road leading to the house will probably *not* be maintained by the Council, in which case: (a) you should be given a right of way for vehicles over it, and (b) the builder should covenant with you to make the road up to the Council's standards, and indemnify you in respect of any road charges. In the case of most sizeable developments, the Council requires the builder to enter into a road-making agreement with the Council, supported by a 'bond' in case the builder defaults. Under such an agreement, the individual purchaser is protected. In the absence of such an agreement or covenant by the builder, the individual purchaser would be liable for whatever road charges were payable when and if the Council takes the road over. Your local search (Q.1) will show whether or not the road is maintained by the Council; and if not, whether there is a road-making agreement between the builder and the Council. Remember, your friendly Council clerk will answer any queries.

(2) You should be given the right to use the drains, pipes and cables under the builder's adjoining land, connecting your house to the respective mains; and you should check from the builder's land registry plan, or plan attached to his conveyance, that the drains and pipes go direct from his land to the mains – and that the estate road goes to the public highway – without going under or across anyone else's land.

The above rights and covenant should be incorporated in the transfer or conveyance which will ultimately transfer the house to you. In fact a draft transfer or conveyance is usually attached to the contract (so that when you agree the contract, you also agree the contents of the transfer document).

(3) There should be a provision in the contract whereby the builder undertakes to remedy building defects which appear within

266

a certain time after completion. Also, if the house will not be finished by the time you are expected to exchange contracts, there should be a provision whereby the builder agrees to complete it to some sort of standard.

Both these provisions are usually covered by the contract providing for the National House-Building Council's warranty to be given to you on completion. This warranty (now called a 'Ten Year Notice') (a) signifies that the house was periodically inspected by NHBC's inspectors while it was being built, and has been completed in accordance with the NHBC's standards; and (b) provides for general defects appearing up to two years, and major structural defects appearing up to ten years, to be remedied by the builder or (if he defaults) by the NHBC itself.

Practically all houses are now built in accordance with these NHBC provisions, and building societies will not generally lend money on a new house unless it is. However, whether the NHBC's warranty *does* afford the purchaser any safeguards, or whether it is just a public relations exercise, is a matter of some doubt. Many moons ago a *Which?* report concluded that there were just as many defects in houses which had been inspected by NHBC inspectors as in those which hadn't. And I have been in a house, duly inspected and passed by the NHBC, which flooded every time it rained when the wind was in a certain direction. The NHBC took no interest in the matter, and the builder remedied the defect only when the purchaser finally resorted to legal proceedings.

Whether the NHBC has improved its performance – as opposed to its paperwork – since those days I do not know.

In any case, if the house will not be finished by the time you are expected to exchange contracts, add a provision (if not already included) that the house will be completed in accordance with the building regulations, and to your building society's reasonable satisfaction.

(4) Sometimes the purchaser is expected to exchange contracts when there are substantial works still to be done, or when the house has not even been started. In these cases there should be a provision in the contract that the house will be completed either in accordance with a certain set of plans (which you have inspected and approved), or else in accordance with an existing specified show house – and *try* adding a provision that it will be completed to your surveyor's reasonable satisfaction.

(5) A common cause of frustration – perhaps the most common – is that builders rarely seem able to complete a house by the estimated date. Ideally there should be a date for completion in the contract, but if there are substantial works outstanding at the time

267

contracts are exchanged, the most you will probably get is a provision whereby the builder undertakes to 'use his best endeavours to complete the house with all due expedition', or some such not very meaningful formula.

(6) It may not only be your own house that concerns you. How quickly will the other unfinished houses in the vicinity be completed, and how is the builder going to leave the surrounding land? The foreman may be reassuring, but builders are reluctant to give any promise in a written agreement. You should be alive to this risk, even if you cannot do anything about it. I know someone who bought a house on a new estate, and who was driven to distraction during the subsequent two years by the continual traffic of dumpers and lorries to and from the builder's yard which was opposite her house. This is the sort of thing you don't think of until it happens.

(7) If the contract does not expressly state that the deposit is held (whether by estate agents or the builder's solicitor) as *stakeholders*, then the builder can use it to reduce his overdraft. In effect, you will have paid the builder part of the purchase price before he gives you anything in return. In view of the high rate of bankruptcies in this particular industry, you would be unwise to part with your deposit on such terms *unless* the builder can offer you the NHBC agreement simultaneously with the exchange of contracts – which does afford some protection against the loss of your deposit consequent on the builder's bankruptcy or fraud.

In general, if when you exchange contracts, the house, road and neighbouring houses are more or less completed, then your position will be much the same as the purchaser of a secondhand house, subject to (7) above. The less of a finished article there is when you exchange contracts, the more precarious is your position, in that the more you have to rely on the builder. You will also find that you are in a weak bargaining position if you try to make any amendments to the contract, which is usually presented on a 'take it or leave it' basis – whether you are acting for yourself or whether you have a solicitor acting for you. To get the house you have to take the risks.

Where the line between an acceptable risk and an unacceptable risk should be drawn depends on the individual drawing it; but if you are presented with a contract which requires you to make *stage payments* as the building progresses, or which requires you to pay more than the 10% deposit *before* the house is completed and transferred to you, then my advice is to take advice before signing – and the notes in this appendix do not apply to such a contract.

When it comes to making your local search, the Council may need a plan of the plot to be attached to the forms. Alternatively, the builder's solicitor may have lodged a layout plan with the Council, in which case you need quote only the plot number.

Your attitude to any restrictive covenants which purport to preclude building, or stipulate what sort of houses may or may not be built on the land, should be *less* cavalier than if you were buying a secondhand house. If the development infringes or might infringe any such covenants – e.g. there is a covenant that no buildings shall be erected on the land except with the written consent of X or his successors, and no consent has been obtained – then the builder should have insured against the possible consequences. If he has not, then you should consider taking out an insurance policy yourself. The risk is not great; but whereas in the case of a secondhand house any restrictive covenants precluding or restricting building would normally be held to have been waived, this is not so with a new house.

After Exchange of Contracts

Before completion, write to the Council's *Building Control* department for confirmation that the house has been completed in accordance with the building regulations. Building regulations cover only a limited range of matters, principally concerning the structure, and do not cover planning permission conditions. However, this confirmation is the nearest a purchaser of a new house can get to an official certificate that the house has been properly completed.

Unless your house is a 'one-off', the builder will own adjoining land (land means land and any building on it, remember); and this necessitates some variation of the conveyancing procedure. In the case of *registered* property, these variations are explained in paragraph 6, p. 208. In the case of *unregistered* property there are four points as follows:

(1) There should be an accurate plan (preferably with measurements) showing your plot (usually by red edging) attached to the contract and the conveyance to you; and in the latter case the builder should *execute* this plan, as well as the conveyance itself.

(2) Check that your plot, as shown on this plan, falls *within* the builder's land, as shown on the plan attached to the conveyance to him.

(3) You will not get any of the builder's previous original title deeds on completion, but will merely inspect them. On completion you, or preferably your building society's solicitor, should write on

269

the *copy* deeds in your possession: 'Examined with originals at office of Messrs. Blink & Co.' On completion you should also ensure that a note of your particular purchase is written on the original conveyance to the builder: 'By a conveyance dated ... No. 21 Mustard Street etc. was conveyed to Mr. & Mrs. Gentle Reader.' Also inspect any similar notes written on this conveyance to ensure that your plot (or any part of it) has not been previously sold to anyone else. I have already given my opinion on the efficacy of these measures, but this is all that can be done. (On the *credit* side, the conveyance will probably have been drawn up by the builder's solicitor, and a copy is usually attached to the contract – so you will be saved a job.)

(4) As the builder's mortgage(s) will not be to a building society, there is no question of accepting any *undertakings* to discharge them: the actual mortgage deed in respect of each mortgage, with the receipt endorsed thereon executed by the mortgagee, must be handed over on completion. However, if the mortgage includes *other* property as well as your plot – as it often will – an alternative is to get a written release signed on behalf of the mortgagee (usually a bank) releasing your plot from its mortgage.

Also, in the case of *unregistered property* only, in addition to the land charges search, a Company search is necessary just before completion if the builder is a *limited company* – as he (it) almost invariably will be. This is done by inspecting the builder/company's file at Companies House, 55/71 City Road, London EC1, where you can still inspect the microfilm file despite the move to Cardiff. (It may be that your building society's solicitor will do this company search and so save you the job; or you can instruct a firm of 'law agents' – address in Yellow Pages – to do it.)

The reason for doing this search is twofold. Firstly, to find out what mortgages there are affecting your plot. At the end of the file you will find a list setting out all the builder's current mortgages; and any mortgages which include your plot must be dealt with as explained in (4) above. However, if on the list of mortgages you see something called a 'floating charge', the lender under that 'floating charge' does not need to sign a specific release as long as nothing has occurred to convert the 'floating charge' into a 'fixed charge'. In such a case it is customary for the builder's solicitor to hand over a letter on completion stating that nothing has occurred to convert the floating charge into a fixed charge – or, to use the technical term, that the floating charge has not 'crystallized'.

The other reason for inspecting the builder/company's file (only in the case of unregistered property, remember) is to make sure that the builder is not in the process of being wound up – in which event it could not sell any of its property except through its liquidator. This book is a chronicle of the absurdities of the conveyancing system, and I may as well end with a choice example: any purported sale by a company after winding up proceedings have been *commenced* is void. Yet a purchaser will not necessarily *know* from inspecting the company's file whether winding up proceedings have been commenced, because there is a delay of one to three months between when a winding up petition is presented (which marks the commencement of winding up proceedings), and when a note thereof is put on the company's file.

Appendix 9 – Building society's solicitor's fees
Land Registry fees

Mortgage not exceeding	Building Society's solicitor's fee
£10,000	£79
£15,000	£94
£20,000	£101
£25,000	£109
£30,000	£113
£35,000	£114
exceeding £35,000	£114 + 75p. for each £5,000

N.B. These 'guidelines' have been agreed between the Building Societies Association and the Law Society; and the figures given are for when the Building Society's solicitor is *not* acting for the purchaser as well. They have no statutory force; but if your Building Society's solicitor tries to charge you significantly more, complain to him, and (if your complaint is unheeded) to the *Building Society Head Office*. Building Societies are in competition with each other, and presumably want a good relationship with the public.

Price of house not exceeding	Land Registry fee
£20,000	£25
£25,000	£30
£30,000	£35
£35,000	£40
£40,000	£50
£45,000	£60
£50,000	£70
£60,000	£80
£70,000	£100
£80,000	£120
£90,000	£140
£100,000	£160
£150,000	£180
£200,000	£200

Glossary

Abstract of title – Typed summary of vendor's title deeds.

Administrator/Executor – Someone who administers the property of a deceased person, by virtue of *Letters of Administration* or *Probate*; and who can deal with it as if he were the owner.

Assignment – The deed which conveys unregistered leasehold property from vendor to purchaser.

Bank draft – A cheque drawn by a bank and which cannot be stopped.

Certificate of value – A clause inserted at the end of a conveyance or transfer, certifying the purchase price is not over £30,000, and the document is therefore exempt from stamp duty.

Charge – synonymous with mortgage.

Charge Certificate – A land certificate where the property is mortgaged.

Company – A legal entity, denoted by 'Ltd.' 'Limited' or 'Plc' after its name, which can own and dispose of property (and carry on business etc.) in the same way as an individual. A developer or builder will almost invariably be a company.

Deed/title deed – A document, usually a *conveyance*, which is executed by the vendor, and which conveys unregistered property to the purchaser. (Also describes Land Certificate.)

Easement – A right enjoyed by the owner of property over *adjacent* property, e.g. a right of way, a right of drainage etc.

Engrossment – Fair copy of conveyance/transfer (drawn by purchaser).

Execute – in the case of an *individual*, to sign a document (or plan) in the presence of a witness, who also signs and adds his address. In the case of a *company*, to affix the company seal in the presence of a director and secretary, who also sign. A *deed* has to be *executed*.

Fee simple – denotes property is *freehold*.

Filed plan – plan of the property which is part of the register.

Form 53 – the form which discharges a mortgage on registered property.

Freehold – where property is held for ever; as opposed to *leasehold*, where it is held only for a stated number of years.

Joint tenants/tenants in common – Two people owning property jointly can be either *joint tenants*, which means that on the death of one, the survivor gets the whole automatically; or *tenants in common* which means that the deceased's share is added to his/her estate.

Land – Land and *any building* on it.

Land Certificate – A copy of the register between stiff covers, issued by the Land Registry, which counts as a title deed.

Land Charges Registry – A register of miscellaneous interests in unregistered property (e.g. second mortgage, wife's interest in the matrimonial home), which are registered against the *name* of a property owner, and which bind any purchaser of that property.

Land Registry – Central Government department which maintains a separate *register* for each registered house, and which guarantees that the 'proprietor' whose name is on the register *is* the owner. The register takes the place of previous title deeds.

Lease – A document which grants someone the right to have the property for a stated number of years. A *leaseholder* owns the property for a stated number of years, as opposed to a *freeholder*, who owns it for ever.

Mortgagee – Someone who lends money secured by a mortgage (e.g. building society).

Office Copy – An official copy of the register made by the Land Registry, which can be obtained (free of charge) by the owner, or anyone else with his written authority.

PD or LA or Inland Revenue Stamp – A stamp impressed on the transfer or conveyance by the Stamp Duty office (even if no stamp duty is payable), on presentation of form LA 451 after completion.

Personal representative – An administrator or executor.

Registration District – Area in which land registration is compulsory on sale.

Requisitions on title – Written questions asked by the purchaser's solicitor on the vendor's title deeds.

Root of title – The conveyance from which a vendor agrees to trace his title, usually at least fifteen years old.

Stakeholder – Someone who holds the deposit after exchange of contracts, and who may not part with it except by agreement of both parties.

Statutory receipt – A receipt discharging a mortgage on unregistered property, endorsed on the mortgage itself.

Subject to contract – A phrase which, if incorporated in a document, means that document shall not be a contract, or evidence thereof.

Title number – The Land Registry reference number allotted to each register.

Trustees for sale – Joint owners technically hold the property as 'trustees for sale' – a throwback to ancient land law (which can be ignored for the purpose of domestic conveyancing).

Index